The series *Greece Beyond the Guidebooks* takes the reader behind the bare facts and descriptions in the guides to the stories which lie behind the sites and monuments of a unique people and culture, particularly those which the guidebooks overlook.

Many places have interesting stories associated with them, but this can be as true of few parts of the world as it is of Greece. Because of its eventful history, and the fertile imagination of its people, every town and village, every mountain and island, hill and valley, cave and spring, has come to be associated with a rich variety of memories and tales.

In each volume the author has made his own selection from the history, myths, legends, folk-tales, customs, controversies, curiosities and mysteries which make each region of this fascinating country both unique and memorable.

Other books in this series:

2. Athens: the Suburbs
3. Attica

Now in preparation:

4. The Saronic Gulf
5. The Isthmus: Corinth and Megara
6. The Northern Cyclades

For more details, see pages 158-159

ATHENS

THE CITY

John L. Tomkinson

Anagnosis

Athens, Greece

Anagnosis
Harilaou Trikoupi 130
145 63 Kifissia
Athens, Greece
www.anagnosis.gr

ISBN 960-87186-0-0

PREFACE

Athens is probably the oldest continuously inhabited city in Europe. The earliest traces of settlement, which are found on the Acropolis, date back to 3,000 BC. Since that time, apart from temporary evacuations of the population during wartime, the city has been inhabited without a break until the present day.

To visit Athens and its acropolis is to visit the cradle of the European spirit, the birthplace of democracy and freedom. This much is so well known as to be a clicht. For this reason the very familiarity of its chief sights may surprise the visitor, as Sigmund Freud discovered: "When, finally, on the afternoon of our arrival, I stood on the Acropolis and cast my eyes upon the landscape, a surprising thought suddenly entered my mind: 'So all this really does exist, just as we learnt at school!'"

Yet there is much more to this city, and its history and culture, than its justly world-famous classical heritage. Athens did not cease to exist when it had lost its pre-eminence as a city state. The life of its people went on under Macedonian, Roman, Byzantine, Crusader and Turkish rule; and this continuity has left traces which may still be detected, despite strenuous attempts to eradicate them, (sometimes by archaeologists, who ought to have known better).

Although today almost one third of the population of Greece lives in the Greater Athens area, it was by no means certain that Athens would become the capital of the modern Greek state. During the War of Independence both Aigina and Nauplia served as provisional capitals. When independence was achieved, Athens was a small town and largely in ruins. Christopher Wordsworth reported: "The streets are almost deserted; nearly all the houses are without roofs. The churches are reduced to bare walls and heaps of stones and mortar. There is but one church in which the service is performed. A few new wooden houses, one or two of more solid structure, and the two lines of planked sheds which form the bazaar, are all the inhabited dwellings that Athens can now boast." There was a debate over whether Corinth, Argos, Megara or Athens should be selected as the capital. Even when Athens was chosen, in 1834, many Greeks believed that this was but a temporary expedient, awaiting the liberation of Constantinople.

The disasters of the early and mid twentieth century led to successive influxes of political and economic refugees. Then there followed by a long period of hasty, opportunistic and badly-regulated development, during which the establishment of an adequate urban infrastructure seems to have been almost entirely neglected, leaving at the end of the century a horrendous legacy of environmental problems. Yet today there are signs that Athens is awakening. Attempts are being made both to recover, and to exhibit to best advantage, its historic sites and treasures; while at the same time some long-awaited improvements in infrastructure and in the regulation of urban life, essential if Athens is to take its rightful place as one of the leading cities of the European Union, are at last coming to fruition.

This volume covers the area of the modern city of Athens proper, excluding the many satellite cities of the suburbs which have sprung up all around it. [For these, see volume two in this series, *Athens: The Suburbs*].

ACKNOWLEDGEMENTS

My thanks are due, among others, to Aris Karey, Vicky Aggeli, Panayis Marketos, Katianna Micha, Constantine Aœvalis, the management of the *Hotel Grande Bretagne, Sheraton* (for illustrations pp.136-138); together with the staff of the libraries of the British School of Archaeology, the Gennadeion, and Athens College. Responsibility for the text and illustrations in this volume lies with the author.

John L. Tomkinson

PLACE-NAMES

Since there is no one-to-one correspondence between the Greek and Latin alphabets, there is sometimes no single way of representing a Greek place-name in English. In addition, a long-accepted rendering of a famous name into English may reproduce neither the verbal nor the written forms used in Greece.

Many settlements have an ancient name quite distinct from its modern designation. Many have two modern names, one in *kathaverousa,* an artificially created language which harks back to ancient forms, and one in *demotiki,* the language of contemporary popular speech. The *katharevousa* name of a settlement *may* be a recognisable form of the ancient name. However this is occasionally based upon a very approximate identification of a modern site with an ancient settlement, or even an identification now known to be incorrect. *Demotiki* is now the official language of the state, but the older forms are frequently retained for place-names; and in any case the *katharevousa* form may still appear in books, and on maps and road signs.

For the sake of clarity, in this series any universally accepted English version of a name will be used in preference to all others. In addition, in order to help readers more easily identify the places mentioned, the most common alternative forms of place-names are provided as page headers. Even so, spelling has a certain fluidity in Greece, and the visitor should be aware that he/she may come across several different spellings of the same version of a place-name in both Latin and Greek script on maps and road signs.

VISITING THE SITES

The avoidance of disappointment is the key to a pleasant and rewarding trip. The visitor should be aware of the need to confirm in advance the accessibility of places mentioned in the text before attempting a visit, although in the case of many of the lesser-known sites this will, in practice, be impossible. The opening hours of major archaeological sites are well-published and routinely observed. Minor sites may be fenced off, padlocked and permanently unmanned, or they may be entirely unprotected and deserted. Experience teaches that museums may choose to close during the tourist season, sometimes with no more notice than a message scribbled on a sheet of paper attached to the door. In general, churches are usually accessible only in the mornings, and small chapels may be permanently locked up, except perhaps for the one day in the year when their name day is observed.

All the sites covered in this volume lie on or near routes served by the Athens Metro, the yellow trolley buses or the blue and green suburban buses.

Contents

The Great Mistress of the Sacred Rock

"The Athenian"

The city of Athens and its patron goddess emerge into the light of history as inseparably coupled. In Mycenean times each Greek city was built around a central palace, and each palace was under the protection of its own patron goddess. Athena was the goddess of the palace on the Acropolis. In Greek, the name of the city and that of its goddess are essentially the same: She was "The Athenian". Athena was Athens, and Athens was Athena. Remarkably, the ancient Athenians seem to have exhibited, during much of their history, precisely those virtues and skills which the citizens traditionally attributed to their goddess. When the Athenians imagined their goddess, they did so in their own image.

An Unusual Birth

According to the ancient myths, Zeus, the father of the gods, fell in love with a beautiful titaness, Metis (or "Cunning Intelligence"). She repeatedly changed her shape to avoid Zeus' unwelcome attentions, but, as was his way, he persisted. In the end he caught up with her, and she became pregnant.

An oracle then announced that Metis' would bear Zeus two children: first a daughter then, a son, and the son would be mightier than his father. Just as Zeus had once overthrown and dispossessed his own father, Chronos, so he would in his turn be overthrown by his own son. In a desperate attempt to avoid sharing his father's fate, Zeus gave Metis drugged ambrosia, and then swallowed her whole.

Some time afterwards a terrible headache came upon him. In great pain, he sought the advice of Hermes, whose only suggestion was that Hephaestos, the smith of the gods, should open his head in order to allow whatever it was that was the cause of his pain to escape. Zeus was so desperate that even this drastic remedy was preferable to doing nothing, and Hephaestos was duly summoned to cleave open Zeus' head with his mighty axe. When he did so, to the astonishment of all the immortals, the goddess Athena sprang out with a great war-cry, fully-formed, wearing armour, and bearing arms.

Zeus' strange daughter not only became the patron of many arts at that time normally considered masculine preserves, such as ceramics, she was also credited with a distinctly unfeminine warlike nature. When the Olympian gods were faced with a titanic struggle against the giants, Athena played a major role in the war, defeating the giant Enkelados in single combat. She came to be depicted not merely as a virgin goddess, but, as one ancient Roman writer put it, as a *virago*: as a female who was capable of playing a leading role in a world dominated by men.

11

There is considerable evidence of the development, at the beginning of the classical period in ancient Athens, of a strong climate of male chauvinism. This is very evident in myth and legend, and several other instances of it will be mentioned subsequently. It came to be said that the reason for the birth of this goddess lay in a wager between Zeus and his consort, Hera, as to which of them could generate the better progeny entirely alone and unaided. By herself, Hera managed to produce only the crippled god, Hephaestos, and a monster; while Zeus was able to bring forth, in Athena, one of the greatest of the immortals. This story seems to have been a picturesque way of saying something which the philosopher Aristotle was later to teach more openly and directly: that the father alone is responsible for generating his children, and for providing them with their inherited characteristics, and that their mother affords them nothing more than a temporary shelter and sustenance in her womb during her pregnancy. This strange idea came to be generally accepted throughout much of the ancient world.

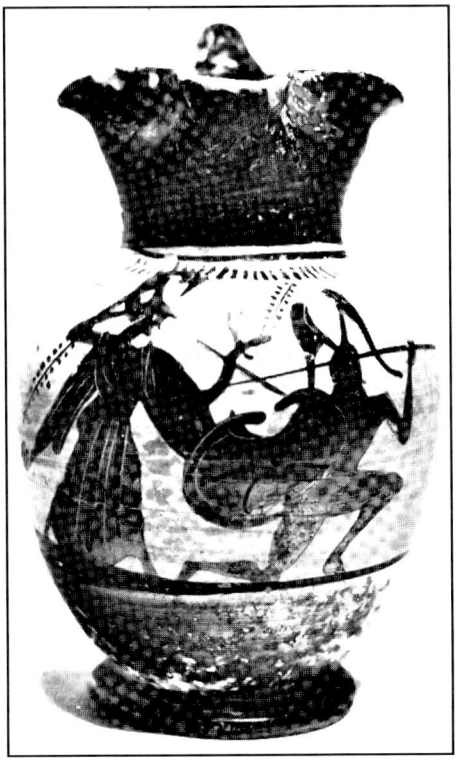

The victory of Athena over the giant, Enkelados (Bari)

The Contest between Athena and Poseidon

Despite the close connection between the goddess and the city, the Athenians believed that Athena had once been forced to compete to win her pre-eminent position in the city. It was said that in the time of the first king, Kekrops, the god Poseidon, discontented with his own dominion over the seas, and jealous of the authority his brother Zeus exercised over the land, was determined to gain a foothold there. One day he appeared on the Acropolis of Athens, to demonstrate his power to the citizens, and, in so doing, his usefulness to them. In the presence of the king and all the people, he struck a great blow with his trident on the rock, causing a saltwater spring suddenly to gush out. At that point, the goddess Athena put in an appearance, and, using her own powers, caused an olive tree to emerge out of the ground, and grow to maturity and fruitfulness in front of their eyes. She then explained to the citizens some of the many ways in which the fruit of this tree could be useful to them. Kekrops and his people were so impressed that they pledged their loyalty to Athena. Poseidon, angry and humiliated, promptly challenged Athena to single combat, but Zeus intervened to keep the peace, appointing the Olympian gods as arbiters. All the gods supported Poseidon and all the goddesses Athena. As the president of the divine council, Zeus was obliged to remain neutral, leaving the goddesses with a majority of one, and so the city was awarded to Athena.

The resentful sea-god caused a disastrous flood on the plain, and in order to conciliate him, the men of Athens decided no longer to be known by their mothers' names, as had been the custom in the past, but to use their fathers' names instead. They also deprived the women of Athens of all their civic rights; even of the right to call themselves Athenians.

The print of Poseidon's trident on the rock was shown to visitors down to Roman times. The well or "sea" which the god had created lay within the strange temple known as the Erechtheion. The traveller Pausanias described it as a deep well of sea water, and claimed that when the south wind blew, the sound of the waves of the sea could be heard from inside. The olive-tree planted by Athena was exhibited in the Pandrosion, an enclosure just to the west of the Erechtheion, down to the second century AD. Although it had been destroyed when the buildings on the Acropolis were burned by the Persians in 480 BC, on the return of the Athenians it immediately put out new shoots.

Behind this ancient story of a contest between the gods seems to lie the memory of a deliberate choice, made at some date, to give precedence to the cultivation of the olive over sea-faring activities.

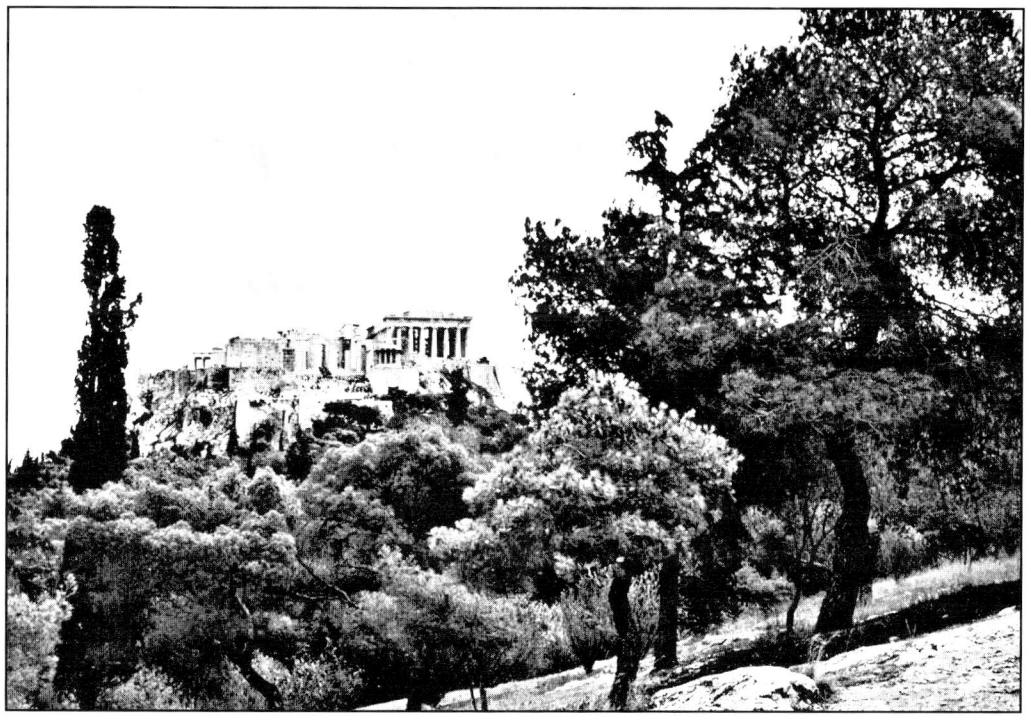

The Acropolis from the Museion Hill

An Earth-Born People

The Athenians asserted that their first king, Kekrops, had no parents but had sprung directly from the earth. He was said to have been a perfectly formed human being from the waist up, and a writhing serpent from the waist down. Ancient myths frequently justified political and social arrangements and attitudes, and it is likely that in this odd manner the Athenians were buttressing their own claim to be the rightful owners of the land, contrasting themselves with other Greeks who were more recent immigrants from the north.

The Baby in the Box

The second king of Athens was also earth-born, but he was a fully-formed human being. His birth came about in the following strange manner:

One day, Athena asked the god Hephaestos to manufacture some weapons for her. She offered to pay him but, ominously, he insisted on doing it "for love." While she was watching him fashion the weapons, he attempted to rape her. She managed to break away, and the god's seed fell upon the ground.

The child which grew out of the earth, Erechtheos, was rescued by Athena and placed for safety in a chest, together with a guardian serpent. The chest was entrusted to the care of Aglauros, the eldest of the daughters of King Kekrops, who was strictly instructed that on no account was she to open it and look inside. Inevitably, after some time, she was overcome by curiosity, and she and her sister, Herse, decided to peek, and opened the box. Pursued by the serpent which lurked inside, in their terror they leapt from the walls of the Acropolis, and were dashed against the rocks below.

Under the protection of the goddess, the boy in the box grew up to become the second king of Athens, and the strange small temple on the Acropolis known as the Erechtheion was later raised in his honour. A sacred serpent was always kept there, fed with honey cakes.

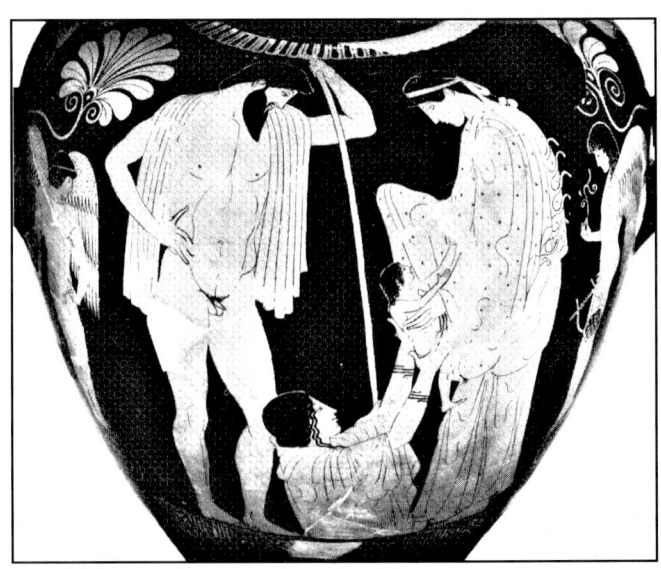

The birth of Erechtheios/Erechthonios (Munich)

The Call of Duty

Ancient myths have been told and retold over many centuries, and during that time they have frequently been adapted to serve fresh purposes. This leads to considerable inconsistency in the stories which have come down to us. Another story has the daughters of King Kekrops die in a very different way.

In the days of King Erechthios, nearby Eleusis was an independent kingdom, and its ruler, Eumolpos, was a son of Poseidon and a Thracian

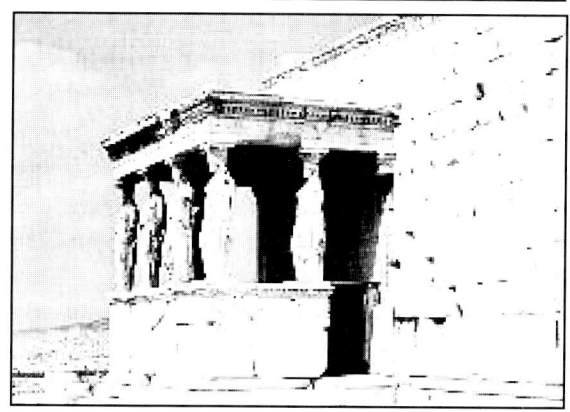

The Erechtheion

princess. Wishing to establish the sovereignty of Poseidon on the Acropolis, Eumolpos waged war against the city with the aid of a force of Thracians.

With a crucial battle impending, Erechtheos consulted the oracle of Apollo at Delphi, and was told that he could win the war only if he sacrificed one of his daughters. With the consent of his wife, he asked Aglauros to do the patriotic thing and kill herself. Obediently, she hurled herself from the walls of the acropolis. Impressed by her example, two of her sisters followed suit. Erechthonios was successful in that the battle was won, although in the very moment of victory, he was killed by the still vengeful Poseidon.

In later years, Aglauros was honoured by the *ephebes*, the young Athenian males doing their two-year military service, who swore their oath of allegiance to the state at her shrine. Clearly, the purpose of *this* story was to impress upon the young men that they were expected not to flinch from sacrificing their lives for their city during battle, when a "mere girl" had given them such a striking example.

An Unsavoury Meal

The fortunes of the daughters of King Pandion, show that the family lives of the early, semi-legendary kings of Athens were somewhat lacking in refinement.

Pandion once called upon King Tereus, from Thrace to help him win a war. Having brought it to a successful conclusion, he awarded Tereus with the hand of his daughter, Procne, in marriage as a sign of his gratitude. She had a son by him, whom they named Itys.

In time Tereus fell in love with Pandion's other daughter, Philomela, and lured her to Thrace for a visit. When she arrived, he raped her. Then he cut her tongue out and imprisoned her, so that she would not be able to tell anyone what had happened. However, during her captivity Philomela wove a tapestry in which she illustrated the story of what had happened to her, and had it sent to her sister.

Procne was outraged, both at the crime committed against her sister, and at her husband's infidelity, and she determined upon a dreadful revenge. She first killed their son, Itys; then she boiled his body and prepared the meat with herbs as for a meal. Then when her husband returned she promised him a special treat, and offered his son's body to him at table without mentioning what it was. In this way Tereus ate his own son.

When he discovered what the two women had done to him, he was outraged, and pursued them with an axe. Just as he was about to catch them, they prayed to the gods to be turned into birds, and their wish was granted. Procne became a swallow, and Philomela a nightingale, while Tereus was turned into a hoopoe.

The Hero of Athens

Greece is a land of legends, and many of the ancient city states had stories about great heroes in their past. Surprisingly, in view of its importance over many centuries, Athens could boast only one famous hero, Theseus.

The Young Hero

Theseus was the son of King Aegeos of Athens and Aethra, daughter of the king of Troizen, in the Peloponnese. Aegeos had two wives but no son by them. But when he stayed one night in Troizen, he made the king's daughter, Aethra, pregnant. When he returned home, he left a sword and a pair of sandals under a rock near the town, with instructions that if she bore a son, when he came of age he was to collect them and take them to Athens. Aegeos also asked her to tell their son to travel in secret, as he feared that the fifty sons of his brother, Pallas, were plotting against him, and would kill his heir to secure the throne of Athens for one of themselves.

Aethra did bear a son, Theseus, and when he arrived at manhood he travelled to Athens to present himself to his father, first collecting the sword and shoes from under the rock. As the roads at that time were infested with robbers, his grandfather tried to persuade him to take the shorter and safer sea route, but Theseus insisted on journeying by land. On the way he had many adventures, which were later collected to form a cycle of legends.

Even in Athens, perils awaited the young prince. A sorceress named Medea had insinuated herself into Aegeos' affections and replaced his wives. Instantly recognising Theseus on his arrival by means of her secret powers, and afraid of losing her influence over her husband if he should be recognised and accepted by his father, she filled Aegeos' mind with the suspicion that the young stranger was his enemy and sought his throne. She persuaded him to send their young guest to certain death by having him attempt to capture the savage bull of Marathon. She thought that he would be killed, but Theseus unexpectedly succeeded in the mission. Then she prepared a poisoned potion and persuaded Aegeos to give it to his son; but as the youth raised the cup to his lips, Aegeos recognised the sword he was wearing, realised that he was about to poison his own son, and dashed the drink to the floor. He drove Medea from the city, acknowledging Theseus as his son and heir. The sons of Pallas went to war to prevent Theseus displacing them, but he soon defeated them.

The Athenians were at that time forced to pay an onerous tribute to Minos, king of Crete. This was because Androgeos, Minos' son, had been killed in Attica. In consequence, this powerful king had declared war on Athens, while the gods had sent a drought and an outbreak of the plague. The Athenians consulted the oracle of Apollo, and were advised to sue for peace. This was granted, but only at the price of a tribute of seven youths and seven maidens to be sent to Knossos every nine years. These were said to be devoured by the Minotaur, a monster with a bull's body and a human head, which was kept in a labyrinth under the royal palace. This labyrinth was so complex that whoever went inside could not find his way out unassisted.

Theseus resolved to deliver his city from this burden. When the time came for sending the tribute and the victims were chosen, he volunteeed himself. The ship left for Crete under black sails, as was customary, but Theseus promised to change these for white sails as a sign to his father, should he return alive.

When they arrived in Crete, and the youths and maidens were exhibited before Minos, Ariadne, the king's daughter, instantly fell in love with Theseus. She secretly provided him with a sword, with which to face the Minotaur, and with a ball of thread with which he could find his way out of the labyrinth after he had killed it. As a result, he slew the Minotaur and escaped, taking Ariadne with him, and sailed for Athens.

On their way back they put in at Naxos, where Theseus abandoned Ariadne while she was sleeping on the beach. Later he claimed that Athena had appeared to him in a dream and commanded him to abandon her.

Theseus also forgot the signal he had promised his father, failing to raise white sails when they drew near the shore of Attica. When the old king saw the ship returning with black sails he thought his son had perished, and in his grief threw himself from the rock, from the spot where the small temple of Athena of Victories was later erected. In this way, Theseus became king of Athens.

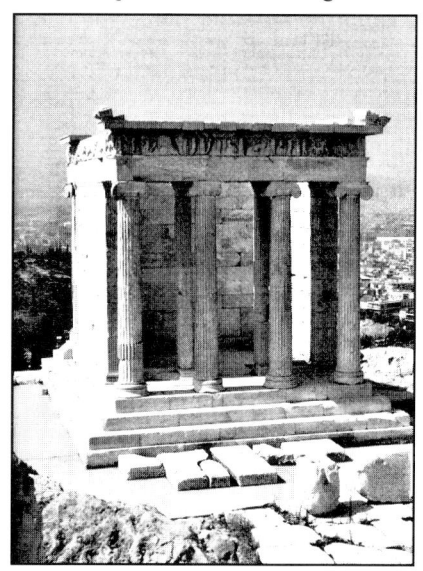

The small temple of Athena Nike on the Acropolis, According to some ancient authorities, it is the place where King Aegeos threw himself from the rock in despair, when he saw his son's ship returning with black sails

Many ancient writers tried to explain why Theseus appeared to be so selfish and thoughtless. Some conjectured that when they reached Naxos, the god Dionysos carried Ariadne off. They said that by that time Theseus had fallen in love with her, and because of his grief at losing her, he forgot to change the sails. Catullus thought that Theseus just forgot about Ariadne. When she woke up and realised that she had been abandoned, she called upon the Furies to punish Theseus, and it was as a result of this curse that he forgot to change the sails, and so inadvertently caused his father's death.

Warrior Women

One of the most celebrated of Theseus' adventures was his expedition against the Amazons. Their queen, Antiope, brought gifts to his ship to present to him. He invited her aboard and then immediately set sail and carried her away.

There were in the same ship three young brothers from Athens. One of these fell desperately in love with Antiope and, revealing the secret only to one of his intimate acquaintances, used him to communicate his passion to the Amazon queen. When she rejected him contemptuously, the distraught young man drowned himself. His death caused Theseus considerable distress. But then he recalled an oracle he had once received, which had commanded him that wherever, in a strange land, he was most sorrowful, he should build a city, and leave some of his followers to be its governors. For that reason he founded a colony and entrusted the dead man's two surviving brothers with its rule.

When Theseus returned to Athens, he married Antiope, and she bore him a son, Hippolytus. But soon afterwards, the Amazons invaded Attica in revenge for the kidnapping of their queen, setting up their camp outside the city. Both armies were uncertain whether to launch an attack. Then Theseus decided to give battle. At first the Athenians were routed on their right wing, and retreated as far as the Areopagos Hill. But when fresh forces arrived the Athenians forced the Amazons back, killing a great number and chasing the others to their ships.

When Theseus, who seems to have been rather inconstant in his affections, later married Phaedra, Antiope turned up at the wedding with some of her comrades, all armed for battle, and threatened the guests. They hastily killed her, Theseus himself striking the fatal blow.

Did the Amazons Really Exist?

The Amazons appear in the earliest Greek sagas. They were familiar to Homer as "those who go to war like men," and to Herodotus as "killers of males"; a tribe of women descended from the god of war governed by two queens, one for defence and one for domestic affairs. Only women bore arms, fighting on foot and on horseback, wielding spears, bows and battle-axes. The girls had their right breasts removed in order to draw a bow and throw javelins. Some said that it was removed by slicing or cutting, others that it was burnt off while the girls were young. One ancient authority claims that each girl was required to remove her own breast.

The survival of their society was ensured by mating, for a short period each year, with men from neighbouring tribes. The resulting male children were either given away to foreigners, killed, or reared as slaves for mating. Their arms and legs were mutilated to prevent them ever challenging the women's supremacy, and they were used for tasks traditionally reserved for women in other societies.

Although historians have usually considered the Amazons to be legendary, the ancient Athenians never entertained the slightest doubt that they really existed. The graves of those slain in the fighting at Athens were pointed out to visitors for centuries after the battle. In the fifth century BC, the historian Herodotus reported about warrior women who rode the steppes of southern Russia, and lived in a unique matriarchal society.

Today, new discoveries in Russia suggest that a steppe tribe around the time of Herodotus buried female warriors with their weapons, while their men stayed home and did "women's work". Archaeologist J. Davis-Kimball writes:

"Fifty ancient burial mounds near the town of Pokrovka, Russia, near the Kazakhstan border, have yielded skeletons of women buried with weapons, suggesting the Greek tales may have had some basis in fact. Nomads known as the Sauromatians buried their dead here beginning *circa.* 600 BC..."

The skeletons of several women were found with their legs angled into a bow-legged position as if astride a horse. Davis-Kimball thought that they may have been symbolically riding into the next world. One girl of fourteen or so was buried with forty bronze arrow-heads in a quiver on her left side, an iron dagger on her right, with a bronze arrowhead in a leather pouch around her neck, and a boar's tusk at her feet. Another had a bent arrowhead lodged in a body cavity, suggesting death in battle.

The women were buried with a wider variety and a larger quantity of artefacts than the men, indicating a more influential role in society, although in addition to the significant minority that held weapons, many other female graves contained mirrors, and stone and glass beads.

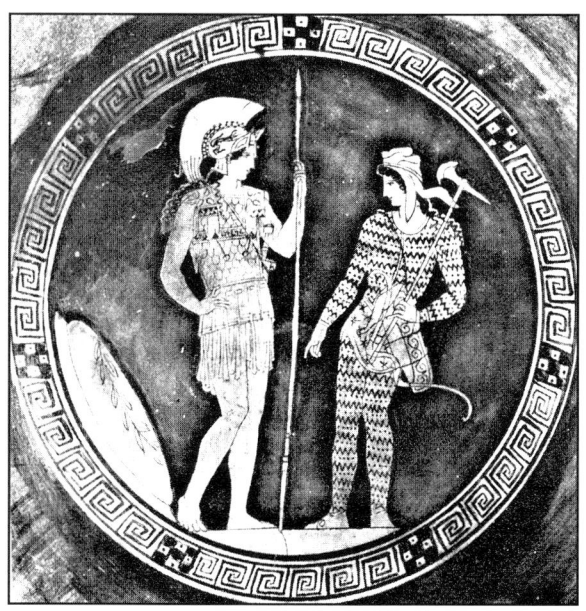

Amazons (Naples)

Davis-Kimball shows that they began grazing their sheep, horses, and camels, on the steppes around 600 BC. She argues that they could not have been the Amazons of Greek myth, who were said to have lived further to the west, but they may have been one of many similar nomadic tribes which occupied the Eurasian steppes in the Early Iron Age.

Although it is clear that the Pokrovka nomads were not the Amazons of myth, they could have provided the inspiration for them.

A Hero Rejected

In later life, together with Pirithous, a friend, Theseus is said to have abducted the young Helen of Sparta taken her to Aphidnai, in Attica, and then got themselves imprisoned in the Underworld. While they were there, Helen's brothers, Castor and Pollux, arrived in Athens demanding their sister's return; and when the Athenians

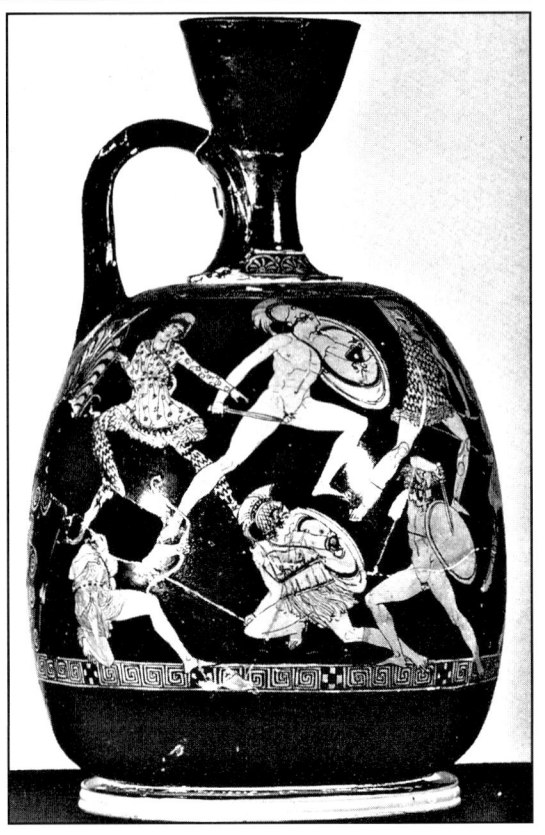

Battle with the Amazons (Naples)

said that they did not know where she was hidden, the twins prepared to assault the city. War was averted only when Akademos, having found out where Helen was being held, told her brothers, and they left with her. When Theseus had been set at liberty, returned to Athens, and resumed the leadership of the state, he found that he had lost his former popularity.

Despite the legends narrated about him, Theseus is a semi-historical figure. To him was attributed the unification of the various townships of Attica into a single state. In commemoration of this he instituted the Panathenaic festival in honour of Athena. A man named Menestheus put himself at the head of those who regretted that the union of the townships of Attica had robbed them of their tiny kingdoms, and felt that Theseus was treating them as his subjects. Despairing of ever receiving the full support of the Athenians, Theseus left the city. Having cursed the Athenians from the village of Gargettos, on his way out, he took ship for Skyros. There he had lands left him by his father, and enjoyed the friendship, or so he thought, of king Lycomedes. But he, jealous of Theseus' fame, led him up to the top of a high cliff on the pretext of showing him the extent and condition of his estates, and then pushed him from the rock.

The Murder of the Ox

As the chief religious centre of the life of the city, the Acropolis was the scene of ancient state rituals. The altar of Zeus was the scene of a curious annual sacrifice known "the murder of the ox", which took place each year at the end of June or beginning of July, when threshing was nearly over. According to an ancient tradition, it was originally instituted to bring an end to a drought which had once afflicted the region, but the manner in which it was carried out strongly suggests that the early Athenians may have entertained some nagging doubts about the morality of the practice of animal sacrifice.

At the beginning of the ritual, cakes of barley mixed with wheat were laid on the bronze altar, and then several oxen were then repeatedly driven around it. That beast which first ventured up to the altar to eat the offering was chosen for the sacrifice.

A double-headed axe and a knife, with which the beast was to be slain, were first wetted with water by girls especially chosen for the purpose, then sharpened, and finally handed to the butchers. One of the butchers felled the ox with the axe, while another cut its throat with the knife. As soon as the ox was dead, those who had killed it would flee the scene. The carcass was skinned and its flesh was eaten. The the ox's hide was filled with straw and sewn up. Then the stuffed animal was set on its feet and attached to a plough as if it were ploughing.

After this, a solemn trial was held, presided over by a very important state official, the king-archon, to determine who had murdered the ox. First, the maidens who had brought the water to wet the axe and the knife would be accused of the crime. They would accuse the men who had sharpened the instruments. These in their turn would accuse those who had handed the implements to the butchers. They would accuse the butchers themselves. Finally, the butchers would lay the blame on the axe and the knife themselves. These objects would then be found guilty of the crime of the murder of the ox, formally condemned, sentenced, and cast out to sea.

It has been suggested by some experts in the history of religions that the rationale behind this ritual is a very ancient one indeed, and may even go back to the customs and attitudes of prehistoric hunting tribes. There is some evidence that early hunters treated their game in some ways as equals with the men who hunted them, and tried to placate the spirits of the animals they killed. Sometimes they formally, and very courteously, apologised to their victims following the kill. In this ceremony at Athens, the community which offered the sacrifice laid the ultimate blame for the death of the animal upon the instruments of sacrifice themselves. In this way it seems that they hoped to divert the ill-will of the potentially dangerous spirit of the dead ox away from themselves and the city towards the inanimate objects cast into the sea.

The Wonder of the World

During 480 and 479 BC the Persians, under King Xerxes attempted the subjugation of Greece, and burned Athens before being forced to retreat. When the citizens returned, they found that all the fine buildings on the Acropolis had been laid waste. At first they determined not to rebuild any of the temples, to allow the wrath of the gods to work itself out against the Persians. But their resolution soon wavered. Themistocles, Aristides and Kimon successively vied with each other in rebuilding, but Pericles surpassed them all. He put the considerable prosperity that accrued to Athens in the middle of the fifth century to beautifying the city with monuments that would do credit to its new fame. He wanted to make Athens an artistic and cultural pan-Hellenic centre.

Plutarch wrote: "Then works grew up, no less stately in size than exquisite in form ... yet the most wonderful thing of all was the rapidity of their execution... For which reason Pericles' works are especially admired, as having been made quickly to last long. For every particular piece of his work was immediately unique even at that time for its beauty and elegance; and yet in its vigour and freshness looks to this day as if it were just executed."

The general artistic supervision of the buildings was assigned to Pheidias, who designed works that were unique in magnificence, harmony and grace, while Iktinos and Kallikrates were in charge of their actual construction.

Illusions to Counter Illusions

The centre-piece and most celebrated of the new projects was the temple to Athena the Virgin, known as the Parthenon. A deliberate attempt was made in the design of this building to achieve perfection, using a very sophisticated knowledge of optics. It seems to be constructed according to a plan based entirely upon straight lines, yet there is hardly a single straight line in it, although the tolerance for error is a fiftieth of an inch. Its perceived aesthetic perfection is a deliberately contrived optical illusion of a high level of sophistication only fully revealed by the work of Roger Penrose during the mid-nineteenth century. It had been realised that our eyes play tricks upon us, and that in order to produce in observers the visual impression of a perfectly designed and constructed building, it would be necessary to take these distortions of perception into account by compensating for them in the construction.

The ancient architect realised that if the temple was constructed on a perfectly flat surface, our eyes, being deceived by the bright sunlight, would falsely perceive the floor to sag in the middle. He saw that if the columns were constructed perfectly perpendicular to the base platform on which they were erected, they would appear to lean slightly outwards. Similarly, he realised that if all the columns were made with the same diameter, the outer columns would appear slightly thinner than the others due to the effect of the bright Attic sunlight; for the more well-lighted an object is, the less voluminous it appears. Moreover, if each of the columns were to be erected with exactly the same diameter from top to bottom, they would each appear to be narrower in the middle than they really are.

The architects thus employed all their insight and skill to compensate for these and other distortions

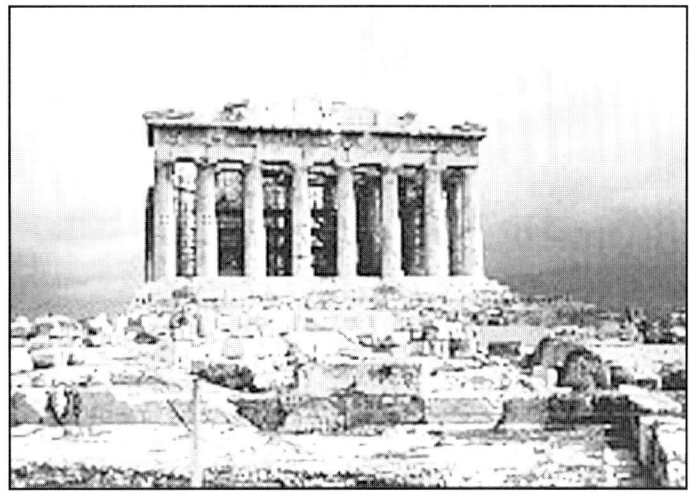

Wonder of the World

of visual perception in their design. Thus the surface of the platform on which the columns stand has been made slightly convex, so that it appears to be flat. The outer columns have been made to lean slightly inwards, so that if each were to be extended upwards they would meet in the centre about one thousand metres above the roof. This exactly eliminates the illusion that perfectly perpendicular columns would create, of leaning slightly outwards. The forty-six outer columns were deliberately made slightly thicker in their middle drums, where most of the light falls, so as to appear perfectly straight. The corner columns, being lighted from both sides, have been made slightly larger in diameter than the others.

These "special effects" are by no means limited to the major features of the construction. The frieze decorations were also systematically distorted to allow both for the effects of being seen from a distance and also for being viewed from the vantage point of the observer below. Thus the figures on the frieze stoop slightly downwards. The lower parts of the decorations have a depth of three centimetres, while the upper have a depth of five and a half.

The ancient architects understood not merely those illusions which viewing a large building in a glaring light might generate, they knew how to compensate for them. But most surprising is that they also knew exactly *by how much* to compensate for them.

One much-praised aspect of the appearance of the Parthenon, however, was not the result of ancient knowledge and skill. Travellers of the eighteenth and nineteenth centuries praised its beautiful golden patina. This had developed over the centuries, and could not have been foreseen by the ancient builders. It was due to the oxidisation of tiny particles of iron in the marble. Much of the building would, in any case, originally have been hidden, for much of it was painted in gaudy colours, the reliefs being picked out in bright blue, red and gold.

The Chryselephantine Idol

The statue of Athena in the Parthenon stood on a base two metres in height and was some ten metres tall. The goddess wore a long dress and a Medusa-head breastplate. On her helmet was a sphinx flanked by griffins. She held the goddess of victory in her left hand, and a gold-tipped spear in her right. Her sandals were adorned with the battle between the lapiths and centaurs, while her shield depicted the struggle between the Athenians and the Amazons on the outside, and that of the gods and the giants on the inside.

Pheidias first built a wooden framework, and then covered it with gold plate and thin leaves of ivory. According to Thucydides, over 1,000 kg of pure gold was used, while the unplated parts of the body (face, hands and feet) were made of ivory. Jewels were inserted for the pupils of the goddess' eyes. It was, in itself, a civic treasury, since the plates of gold and ivory and the jewels could be removed if required in an emergency.

It seems certain that this statue was never intended to inspire religious piety. It was consciously executed as a work of art, and as a demonstration of the economic wealth, and military and political power of the city.

Its creation was not unaccompanied by scandal. Pheidias was accused of using less gold on the statue than he had been allocated, and of appropriating some of it for himself. The

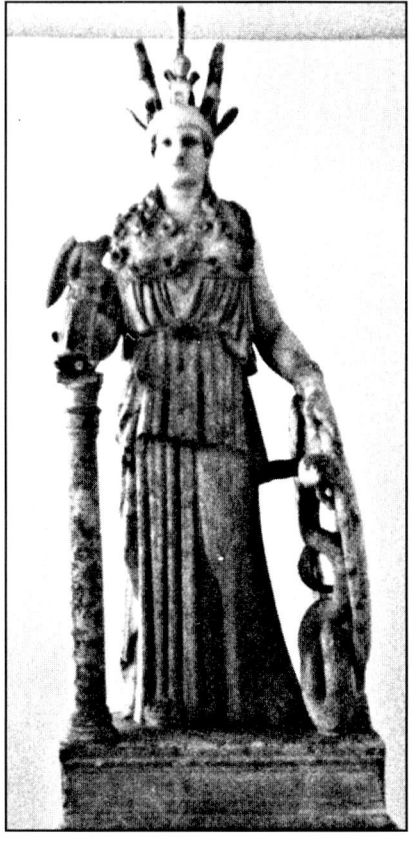

A small copy of Pheidias' statue, discovered on the site of the Varvakeion School, now the Central Market. (Nat. Arch. Mus., Athens)

indignant artist promptly had all the gold plating removed and then weighed to establish his innocence. But then it was discovered that he had unobtrusively included portraits of himself and his patron, Pericles, on Athena's shield, an act considered by many to be sacrilege. According to tradition, he languished in jail for this offence until he died.

The Roof of Light

The Roman writer Vitruvius tells us that a peculiar, dreamlike light pervaded the interior of the Parthenon, so that the statue of the goddess appeared as though suspended in air. Scholars have often wondered how this effect could have been achieved, and how the temple was illuminated.

The eastern walls were made of the whitest and purest marble, so as to reflect sun's rays into the interior, but that by itself would have been insufficient to have created the special effect Vitruvius described.

The mystery was only cleared up by Evliya Chelepi, a Turkish traveller, who visited Athens in 1667. He described the roof, supported on beams of gilded cypress wood, as consisting of sheets of marble so thin and smooth as to be almost diaphanous. The sunlight passed through them, casting a diffuse light throughout the interior. He tells us that these were joined together by cement, rather than by using the more normal method of strips of lead, so that nothing might hinder the penetration of the light or cast a shadow.

The New Mistress of the Sacred Rock

The political eminence of Athens was short-lived. The Parthenon was completed in 431 BC. Thirty years later Athenian power already lay in the past, and would never be recovered. Yet for many centuries the cultural hegemony of the city continued to ensure a succession of respectful visitors. But history was not kind to the Parthenon. In 305 King Dimitrios used it for wild parties, and quartered his harem there. In 298 the gold plate on the statue of Athena was stolen; while in a bizarre ceremony in 39 BC, the Roman general Mark Anthony "married" the goddess in her temple.

The ancient world was brought to an end not by barbarian incursions, but by the triumph of Christianity and a new way of thinking. In 435 AD the Emperor Thodosius II issued a decree closing all pagan temples. At that time the great Neo-Platonic philosopher, Proclus, had a house on the southern slopes of the Acropolis. One night he dreamed that a beautiful woman appeared to him dressed in the likeness of Athena, and told him to prepare a room in his house for the Queen of Athens, who was being ejected from her ancient home.

With the end of paganism, worship did not cease in the Parthenon. It was first transferred from the goddess of wisdom to the Christian God, under the title Holy Wisdom (*Ayia Sophia*). Afterwards it was known as the cathedral of the Virgin of Athens (*Panayia Atheniotissa* - literally, "the All-Holy Lady of Athens"). The virgin daughter of Zeus had been replaced by the Virgin Mother of God, each in turn being acknowledged as the "Mistress of Athens".

With the end of the old respect for philosophy, scholars no longer visited the city, which became a provincial backwater. Yet there were still moments of glory when Athens once again took the centre of the stage; although, in accordance with the new spirit of the times, it was a barbaric splendour.

During the latter part of the tenth century, a threat to the Byzantine Empire came from the north. From 978 to 996 Bulgarian tribes, under Czar Samuel, devastated Attica and the Peloponnese. The Bulgar threat was finally neutralised only when their forces were defeated by the emperor Basil II, and fifteen thousand prisoners were

25

taken. The emperor ordered them to be divided into groups of one hundred. Then every member of each group except one was blinded, and the one remaining was blinded in one eye only, so that he could lead the others back to their commander. Unable to endure the sight of so many maimed men, Czar Samuel died of apoplexy within a few days. In 1018, emperor Basil "the Bulgar-Slayer" arrived in Athens to celebrate his military successes. In the Parthenon-church, he solemnly offered thanks to God for his victories, leaving behind when he left, it was said, many splendid offerings.

Later the Western Crusaders were to convert the Parthenon into a Catholic church; and later still the Turks would employ it as a mosque, and then as a gunpowder store.

Modern Barbarians: The Soldiers

During the perid of Turkish occupation, the Acropolis was used as a garrison and stronghold. Gunpowder was stored there, and a chance lightning strike in 1645 caused considerable damage to the ancient structures.

In 1685 the Venetians attempted to take recapture Greece for Christendom, beginning with a highly successful campaign in the Peloponnese under admiral Morosini. He wished to follow up his victories there with the capture of Negropont (modern Halkida) but as it was well guarded, and the summer campaigning season was almost over, he decided to take Athens instead.

On 11th September 1687, a force ten thousand strong landed at Piraeus and moved on the city. When a siege failed to reduce the citadel, Morosini decided to bombard it into submission. When he was informed that the Turks stored their supplies of ammunition in the Parthenon, and that their women and children were also taking shelter there, he ordered cannon fire to be directed at the ancient edifice. When it was hit, there followed a huge explosion which almost cut the building into two ruinous halves. The victorious Venetians then debated whether or not to destroy the citadel entirely, but decided that they did not have time. Instead, they settled for taking some of the sculptures back with them to Venice as they evacuated the city at the conclusion of the campaign.

"... I conceived the project of taking some of the beautiful ornaments, especially those which could add to the splendour of the Republic. With this intention, I instigated the first steps for detaching from the facade of the Temple of Minerva [Athena], where the most beautiful sculptures are, a statue of Jupiter [Zeus] and the reliefs of two magnificent horses. But hardly had the workers started to remove the large cornice than it fell from this extraordinary height, and it is a miracle that no harm came to the workers. The blame for this accident lies in the construction of the temple, built with stones placed on top of one another, without mortar and with marvellous skill, but which were all displaced by the shock of the explosion."

The modern reader may beg leave to differ from Morosini in his attribution of blame for the results of his clumsy act of vandalism.

Modern Barbarians: The Collectors

The Destruction of the Parthenon

Worse was to follow. Wealthy western aristocrats were beginning to arrive in Greece, and they all wanted to take home souvenirs of their "adventures" abroad.

In 1799, Lord Elgin went to Constantinople as British Ambassador. There he initiated a scheme to remove the best pieces of classical architecture and sculpture in order "to benefit the progress of the fine arts in Great Britain," putting together a team of craftsmen under Giovanni Lusieri, a Neapolitan artist.

His agents arrived in Athens in 1800. The Turkish governor allowed them to begin work only after six months negotiations, and then only upon payment of five guineas a day. But as soon as they began to erect scaffolding, he abruptly ordered them to stop, fearing that they might be able to peer inside his harem.

After that, a frustrated Elgin resolved to go straight to the top. According to his own account, he obtained a *firman* from Sultan Selim III to "remove some blocks of stone with inscriptions and figures." Armed with this, his agents returned to Athens in 1801, when the governor was unable to obstruct him any longer.

When the Parthenon had been erected, three sets of sculptures had adorned it: the metopes, the frieze and the pediments. The pediments at either end had already been

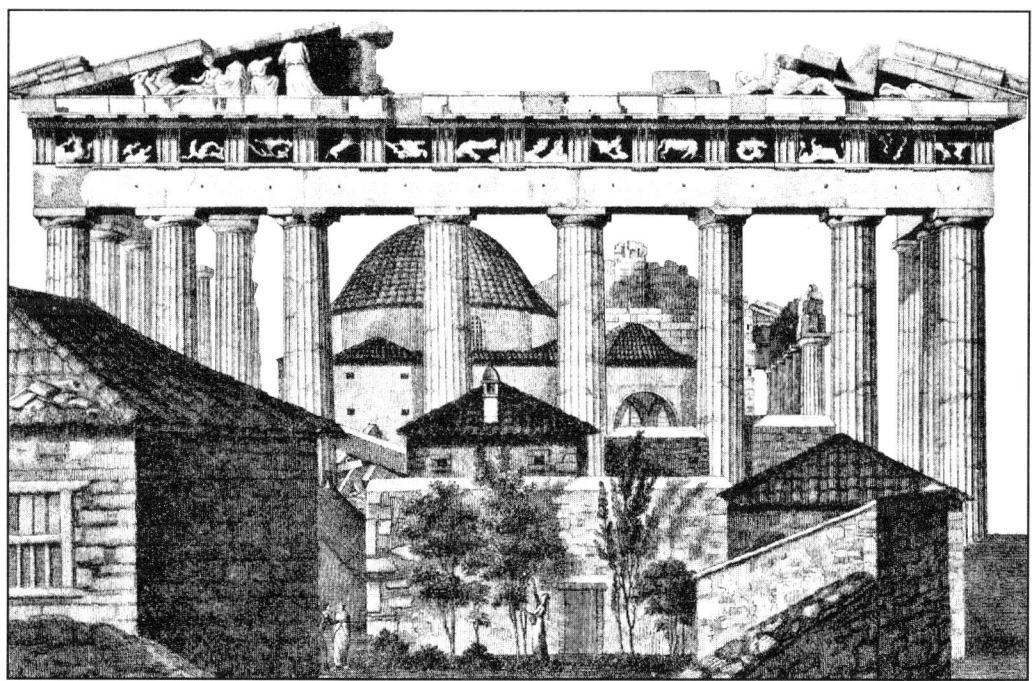

The ruined Parthenon (Stuart & Revett, 1793)

so badly damaged that it is only from Pausanias' descriptions of them that we know what they represented. The metopes and the frieze were integral parts of the structure of the building, carved onto its sides after construction. There were ninety-two metopes, which illustrate battle scenes: the Trojan War on the north side; a battle between the Greeks and the Centaurs on the south; the war of the gods and giants on the east; and that of the Greeks and Amazons on the west. The frieze, a single which was a single continuous sculpture one hundred and sixty metres long, shows the procession at the Panathenaic festival.

On December 26, 1801, Elgin asked Lusieri to obtain "samples of each cornice, each frieze, each column capital, of the roof decorations of the grooved pillars, of the various architectural orders of the metopes and in general, of anything, as much as possible." Elgin's agents sawed off the backs of some of the frieze slabs to reduce their weight and make the task of transportation easier.

Cotemporary visitor to Athens Edward Clarke described Lusieri and his team removing one of the metopes:

"... while the workers were trying to adjust the direction of the movement of the load ... part of the marble structure subsided under the pressure of the machines and voluminous Pentelic marble pieces collapsed noisily, scattering their white fragments among the ruins. The Turkish Sirdar, seeing the profanation, removed from his mouth the pipe he was smoking and with his eyes full of tears, he stated resolutely: 'Finished!' and nothing would persuade him to permit the continuation of ruining the building."

Despite his distress, this Turkish official seems subsequently to have proved quite susceptible to persuausion.

Outrage

Elgin's actions were also deplored at the time by the painter, Edward Dodwell:

"During my first tour of Greece I had the inexpressible mortification of being present when the Parthenon was despoiled of its finest sculpture, and when some of its architectural members were thrown to the ground. I saw several metopes ... taken down ... and in order to lift them up, it was necessary to throw to the ground the magnificent cornice by which they were covered. The south-east pediment shared the same fate; and instead of the picturesque beauty and high preservation in which I first saw it, it is now comparatively reduced to a state of shattered desolation."

When Byron and Hobhouse visited in 1909, Elgin's agent was boxing up the last of the sculptures. Byron expressed his feelings in his *Curse of Minerva*:

"... loath'd in life, nor pardon'd in the dust,
May hate pursue his sacrilegious lust!"

Byron and Hobhouse left Athens on the same ship as boxes containing the last of the marbles. At one point, the Greek porters carrying the statues put them down and refused to move them, claiming that they could hear cries coming from the figures in the crates. As they watched them being loaded, an old man approached Hobhouse: "You are carrying off the works of our fore-fathers. Guard them well, for one day we shall ask for them back again." Dodwell adds: "Nor have I any hesitation in saying that the Athenians in general, nay, even the Turks themselves, did lament the ruin that was committed; and loudly and openly blamed their sovereign for the permission he has granted!"

One consequence of Elgin's actions, pointed out by Edward Dodwell, is that it excused the havoc the Turks were themselves wreaking:

"During my stay in Athens, since the Christians had started the work of extermination, the Turks imitated these acts still more basely. On order of the Sirdar, the Erechtheion epistilium towards the Pandrossion side was lowered and placed at the fortress gates. As I thought he, the Sidar, planned to lower still other parts of the beautiful building, I had the courage to protest against the indecency of the deed. The Sirdar then, showing me with his finger the Parthenon, the Caryatids and the Erechtheion, shouted at me angrily: 'What right do you have to complain? Where are now the marbles which your own countrymen have taken away from these temples?'"

Elgin, aware of the criticism, even among his own countrymen, protested: "Every traveller coming added to the general defacement of the statuary in his reach; there are now in London pieces broken off within our day. And the Turks have been continually defacing the head; and in some instances they have actually acknowledged to me that they have pounded down the statues to make them into mortar: it was ... with these feelings, that I proceeded to remove as much of the sculptures as I could; it was no part of my original plan to bring anything away but my models." The British Museum *Guide* asserts that the Marbles were in danger from "the vandalism of stone robbers, lime-burners, curio-hunters and religious iconoclasts." Certainly, like other statuary not removed, they would have been in some danger from bombardment during the Greek War of Independence; and certainly they would have been eaten away by motor vehicle pollution during the later twentieth century, a fate that has been allowed to befall the remaining Caryatids .

An Ideal Custodian?

One overloaded ship sent back by Elgin sank in deep water off Kythera, and seventeen cases were lost, although most of these were recovered four years later. The Marbles were probably originally intended to decorate Elgin's country house in Scotland. But for some time they languished in various sheds in London until, in 1816, when Elgin found himself in financial difficulties, he sold them to the Crown for £35,000, at which time ownership was transferred to the Trustees of the British Museum.

In 1992, *The Times* wrote: "The British Museum has proved an ideal custodian of the statues." Unfortunately, this is not entirely true. The marbles appear to have suffered significant damage at the hands of those entrusted by Parliament with the duty of conserving them.

At the time of the sale of the Marbles, Elgin admitted to the House of Commons that the damp London climate had already caused some decay. When Lord Duveen's new gallery was opened to house the sculptures in 1938, it was decided to "improve" their appearance by removing spots of discoloration caused by dirt. Unfortunately, the spots were not dirt; they were due to oxidisation, and formed part of the natural honey-coloured patina of the surface of the marble. On 8 October 1938 the British Museum Standing Committee found that "through unauthorised and improper efforts to improve the colour of the Parthenon sculpture ... some important pieces had been greatly damaged." Originally it was claimed that the cleaning involved only soap and water, and in any case, any damage was invisible to the untrained eye. But the Museum's chief cleaner, in a newspaper interview in 1939, stated that his workers "were given a solution of soap and water and ammonia. First we brushed the dirt off the Marbles with a soft brush. Then we applied the solution ... To get off some of the dirtier spots I rubbed the Marbles with a blunt copper tool." Disciplinary action was taken against two officials.

More recently, the Museum authorities have used the gallery in which the Marbles are exhibited to stage "theme parties". Wealthy guests pay large sums of money to dine in ancient Greek costume, using the Parthenon Marbles as a backdrop to their meal.

Are the Marbles "Stolen Property"?

In 1816, the British government promised to return the Marbles as soon as Greece gained its independence. That promise was not kept. Just before the end of the Second World War the British government again promised to return them as compensation to their wartime allies for losses they had incurred during the fighting. When the war ended the Marbles were not returned; at that time Prime Minister Attlee told Parliament that the moment was "inopportune." Leaders of the British Labour Party, while out of government, have repeatedly promised to return them to Greece. On gaining office, British readers will hardly be surprised to learn, the promise is "forgotten" as a matter of course.

Based upon Elgin's permit to "remove some blocks of stone with inscriptions and figures," the Museum argues that the Marbles were acquired legally, and are held legally. But the *firman* authorising their removal, Elgin's sole claim to legal ownership, has never been seen. It was not presented to Parliament in 1816, nor has any copy of it ever been found in the archives of the Turkish government, which is very surprising indeed. Only a copy of an Italian translation, attributed to Elgin's secretary, is available. Since we do not have the original *firman*, we do not know if it was correctly translated. More to the point, since no one has ever been able to provide independent confirmation of the existence of this document, we do not know whether the alleged"original" ever actually existed.

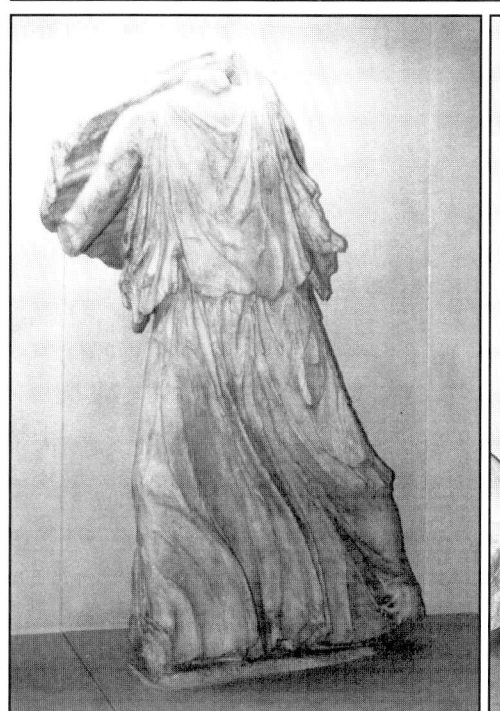

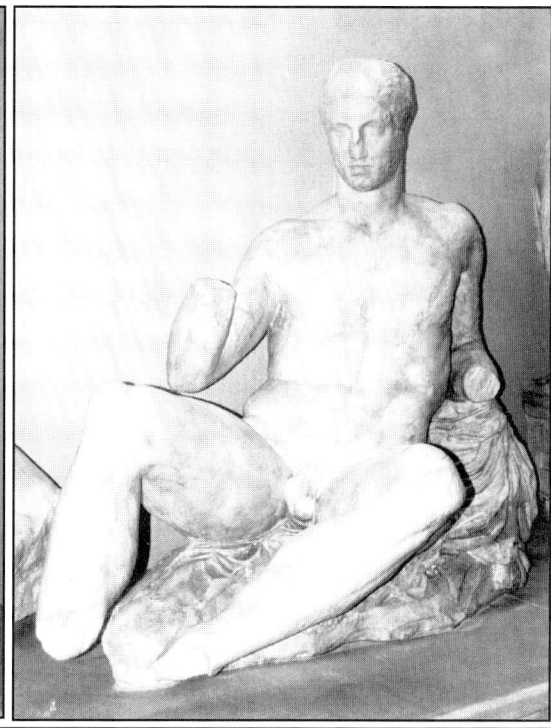

*Casts
in an
Athens
Metro
Station*

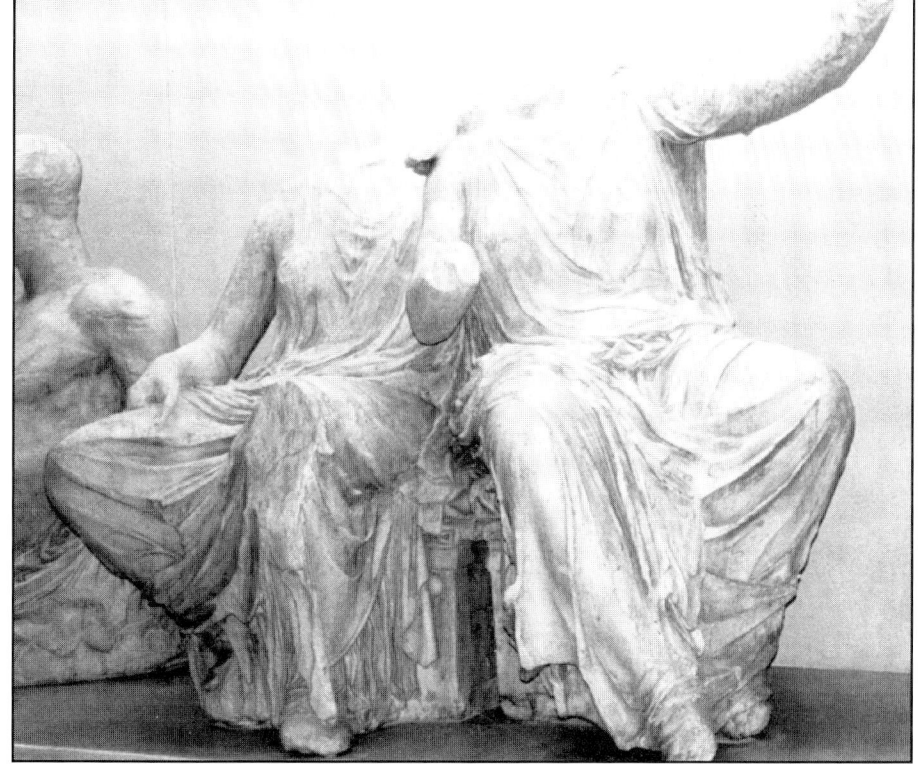

Recently evidence has come to light that Elgin initially did not know that his agents were removing marbles at all. When he found out, he congratulated them on succeeding beyond "our most ardent hopes." Elgin's successor as Ambassador disclosed that the Ottoman government denied that those who had sold them to Elgin had any right to dispose of them. No contract of purchase or shipping permit has ever been found. According to a Report of 1816, Lord Elgin had used his position as ambassador, together with bribery, to obtain them.

Many contemporaries believed the Parthenon Marbles to have been stolen, and that, as integral parts of a unique work of art, from which they were hacked away, they should be returned to their original site. Greek public opinion has strongly favoured restitution.

Modern Barbarians: The Archaeologists?

The Acropolis suffered considerable damage during the long struggle for independence. The Bavarian officer to whom the fortress was finally handed over by the Turks said: "I entered the Acropolis and saw heaps of tumbled marbles. In the midst of the chaotic mess of column capitals, fragments of columns, marbles large and small, were bullets, cannon balls, human skulls and bones...."

The problem following independence, after the failure of a bizarre plan to build a royal palace atop the Acropolis for the new king of Greece, was what to preserve, and what to destroy in order to uncover what lay beneath. The aims of discovering, clearing and exhibiting everything from the classical period and preserving the picturesque character of the rock with the relics of its continuous history are in direct contradiction to each other. The archaeologists have removed and destroyed almost everything which dates from later than the classical period. The most spectacular act of learned Philistinism was the destruction of the Frankish Tower. This famous landmark was a unique relic of the Crusader occupation of Athens, and the last place on the Sacred Rock where the owls of Athena still nested. At the very least, it should have been demolished and re-erected elsewhere. As a result of the work of the archaeologists, the Acropolis is now little more than a barren rock, cleared of all traces of the continuity of history.

The original old quarter of Athens, dating from Turkish times and perhaps earlier, which stood on the site of the ancient *agora*, suffered a similar fate after the Second World War, when American archaeologists were allowed to remove every building in the district except for a single church in order to expose the foundations and drains of the buildings of the classical period.

The result creates the false impression that there is no historical continuity connecting the ancient city to the modern buildings all around, and in a sense serves to disinherit the Greeks of today of their past. Archaeologists and conservationists may not always be the best guardians of our heritage.

A Honeycombed Hill

The hill of the Acropolis is studded with caves. In one Apollo and Creusa were said to have conceived Ion, ancestor of the Athenians and all Ionian Greeks.

After the battle of Marathon, when the runner Pheidippides claimed he had encountered the god Pan on the road to Sparta as he ran there to get help, and after the god was credited with spreading panic among the Persian forces during the battle, the Athenians built a shrine to him in another cave.

The spring of Klepsydra, in its natural cave was well-known in ancient times, but its location was subsequently forgotten, so that when the Turks were besieged on the Acropolis in 1822, they were forced to surrender for lack of water. When the Greeks recovered the sacred rock, they remembered its exitence, searched, and located it. Odysseas Androutsos had it cleared, so that when, in 1827, the Greeks were themselves besieged, they were able to use it to supply the garrison.

Many other caves exist, one being discovered as recently as 1937.

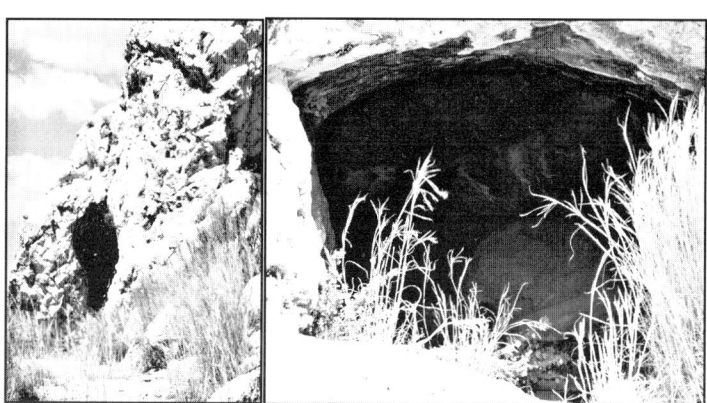
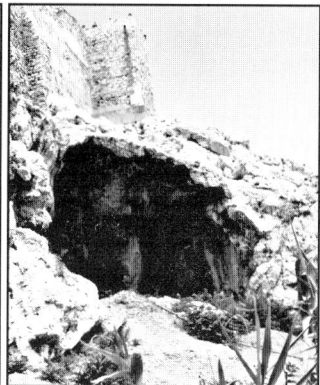

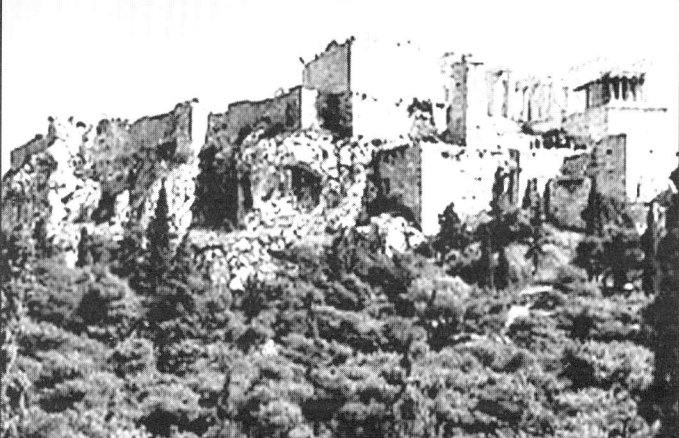

Above: Some of the many caves which stud the sides of the Acropolis

Below left: Entrances to some of the most famous, including the cave of Pan, are best seen from the Aeopagos

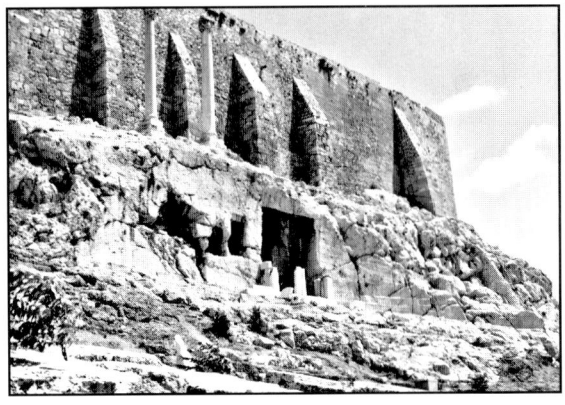

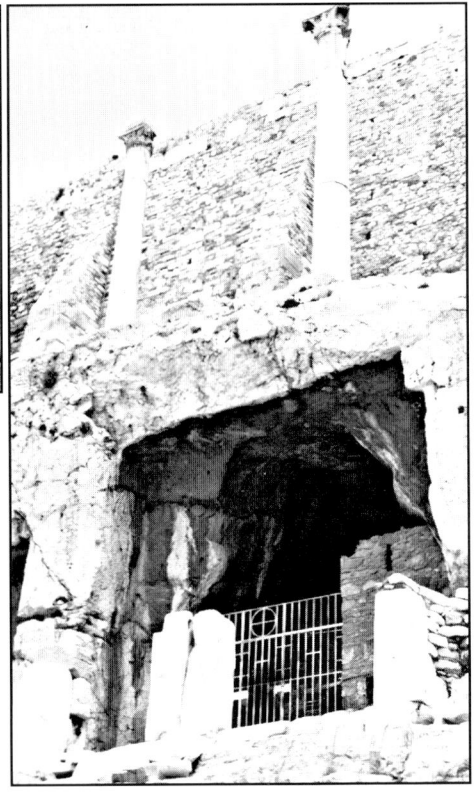

*A cave on the south side once contained
statues of Athena and Dionysos.
The choregic monument of Thrasyllus,
destroyed by Turkish gunfire in 1827,
stood in front of it.
From Byzantine times it became
the chapel of Our Lady of the Cave
(Panayia Spiliotissa).*

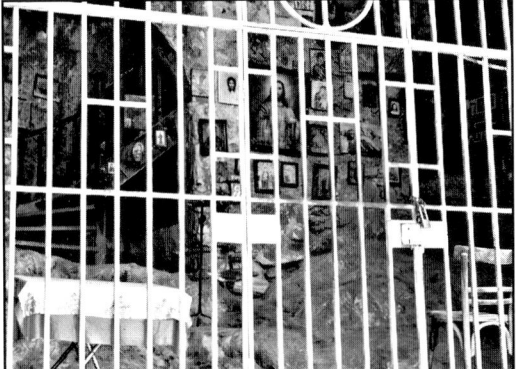

*Mothers would take sick
children there to be cured,
leaving offerings of candles.
Today faded Byzantine wall-paintings
remain, and a solitary lamp is lit
in the cave every night.
Below: Niches carved in
the rock beside the cave
betray its ancient use*

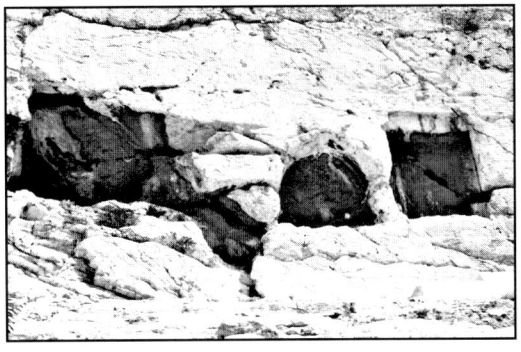

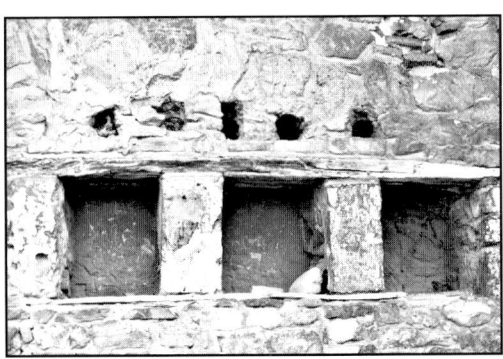

The Theft of the Swastika

On Sunday April 27th 1941, three weeks after launching its attack on the country's northern border, the vanguard of the German army entered Athens. A procession of motor cyclists, made its way through the northern suburb of Kifissia, down Kifissias Avenue and into Queen Sophia Avenue. The streets were deserted and windows firmly shuttered against the unwelcome sight. The grim procession passed the Parliament Building and the Tomb of the Unknown Warrior, crossed the deserted Syntagma Square, and headed straight for the Acropolis, intent upon hoisting there the *Hakenkreutz*, the banner of the Third *Reich*.

The *Evzone* on duty guarding the Greek flag, which always flies over the Sacred Rock, was ordered to haul it down and raise the Nazi banner in its place. He calmly took down the Greek flag, wrapped it around his body, and then plunged to his death from the ramparts of the Acropolis.

When the wife of a staff member at the Swedish Legation complained to the Occupation authorities about the flying of this Nazi symbol over a cultural monument, she was told that it could not be taken down because the German High Command had informed Hitler personally that it had been raised there.

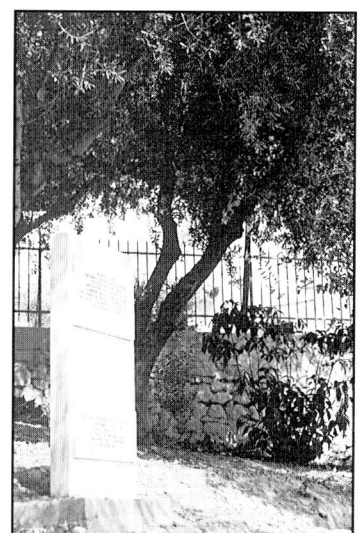

*Monument in the Plaka
to the evzone
who threw himself
from the Acropolis
after taking down
the Greek flag,
at the spot where he fell,
near the small church
of Saint George.*

But at about eleven o'clock on the night of 30th/31st May, two eighteen-year old boys, Manolis Glezos and Apostolos Santas, slipped quietly into a cave on the northern slope of the Acropolis and climbed through an ancient tunnel which led to the summit. They came out near the Erechtheion where, in ancient times, the sacred serpent of Athena was said to emerge in times of trouble.

Moving quietly across the plateau so as not to alert the guards, they hauled down the hated banner, carefully smearing their fingerprints on the pole so that no one else could be blamed for their actions. Then they returned the way they had come. In the Cave of Aglauros they ripped out pieces of the banner with a penknife to take as souvenirs, and abandoned there the remnants of the torn flag, which was very large, before they emerged to make good their escape.

The enraged German authorities threatened the unknown culprits with death, but a Greek writer later wrote: "Do they truly imagine that there is a single Greek, however deeply and incurably Germanophile, who does not feel satisfied and proud at this heroic madness?" It later emerged that the two culprits had actually been stopped and questioned on their way home by a Greek police officer, who had chosen neither to pursue his enquiries any further, nor to report the matter to higher authority. The Germans later dismissed all the police in the first and third districts of Athens "for allowing the theft of the swastika."

When, on June 22nd, the Italians formally took over the Occupation, a large Italian flag was raised beside the Greek and Nazi banners. People commented that seeing the Greek flag between the other two reminded them of "the Crucified One, hanging between the two thieves."

After three and a half years of suffering endured by the people of Athens, on October 12th 1944, the Germans themselves pulled down their banner, before laying a wreath on the Tomb of the Unknown warrior, and pulling out of the city. Two days later, on Saturday October 14[th.] the first British troops arrived, followed three days later by Prime Minister George Papandreu and the Greek government in exile. A few days after that, in a rare show of national unity, Prime Minister George Papandreu, the entire Government and the citizens of Athens went to the Acropolis to ceremonially re-hoist the Greek flag.

This faŋade of national unity did not last, and a bitter civil war was to follow liberation. Ironically, the subsequent fortunes of Manos Glezos reflect those of many patriots who had risked their lives by resisting the Occupation. Having been condemned to death *in absentia* by the Germans for his patriotic act, Glezos was condemned to death by the Greek Government for treason in 1948, his "crime" being sympathies with the Greek Communist Party, which had played a leading role in the resistance. His sentence was later commuted to six years imprisonment; but in 1959 he was again sentenced for treason, this time to five years, being released in 1962. Glezos was later vindicated by being elected to the Greek Parliament as a member for the Panhellenic Socialist Party (PASOK).

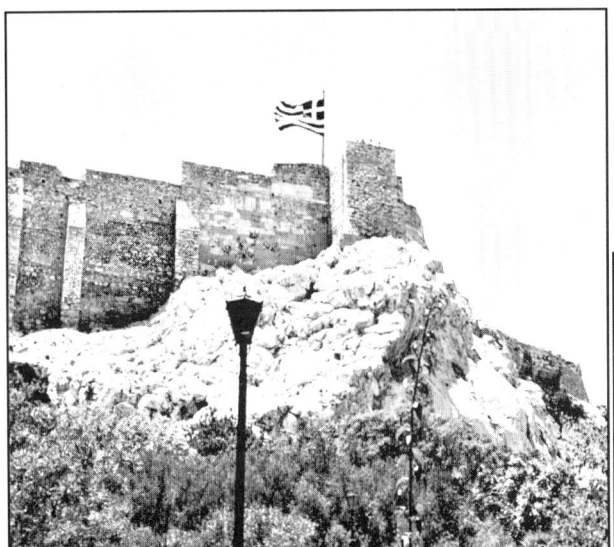

Left: The Greek flag flying over the Acropolis

Below: Plaque recalling the exploit of the two courageous young Greeks

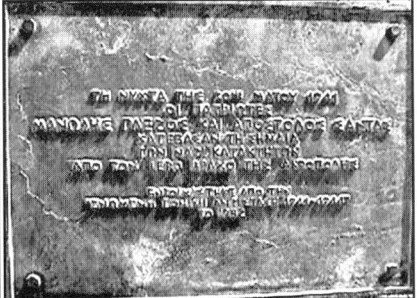

The Hill of Judgement

Trial of Ares

The hill of the Areopagus, below the Acropolis, was used in ancient times as a place of assembly and as a court of law. The name was commonly supposed to mean "the hill of Ares," after the god of war. It was explained by the tradition that Ares was the first to be tried for murder in this place. The case arose because of bad relations between the gods, because of their frequent consorting with humans and fathering of human offspring, but it also reflects the ancient belief in the importance of family honour found Mediterranean peoples, and the function of a system of justice in preventing the bloody clan vendettas which would otherwise result.

One day, the son of Poseidon was caught by Ares in the act of attempting to violate Alkippe, his daughter by Agraulos. Since it was a matter of family honour, he promptly killed the offender. But the god was himself then impeached by Poseidon, the murdered man's father. Ares was said to have been put on trial on the Areopagos before the assembly of the Olympian gods, but acquitted.

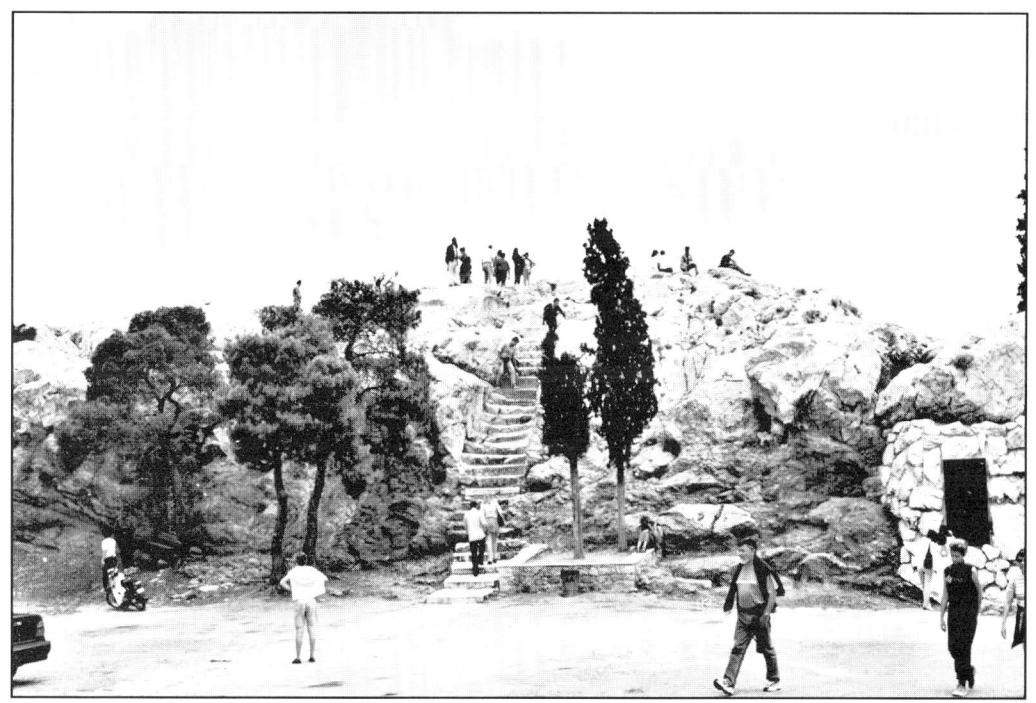

The Areopagos Hill today, busy with tourists trying to negotiate the extremely slippery steps carved into the rock

Flight from the Furies

Agamemnon, commander-in-chief of the Greeks in the War of Troy returned home to Mycenae only to be brutally murdered in his own home. During his absence, his wife Clytemnestra had been unfaithful, and, together with her lover, she plotted to murder him. As he got out of hs bath, she presented him with a new tunic with the cuffs of the sleeves sewn up on the inside. As he struggled with it, she took an axe to him. The conspirators also intended to slay his son Orestes. His sister, Electra, saved his life by sending him away to his uncle, and reminded him in messages of his duty to avenge his father's death. When Orestes came of age he consulted the oracle at Delphi, which confirmed his obligation to avenge his father. He returned to Mycenae in disguise and slew both Clytemnestra and her lover.

The slaughter of a mother by her own son, although justified by the guilt of the victim and the express command of the oracle, still aroused unusual horror. The Furies, who avenged such acts, pursued Orestes from place to place, giving him no rest, until at last, after many adventures, he sought refuge in Athens. The Furies were three goddesses of revenge who tormented the guilty. Artists depicted them with fiery eyes, hair of writhing serpents, and bearing torches and whips. They were attracted by serious crime, and especially by violation of the obligations of filial piety, and would pursue wrongdoers until they were driven mad and died.

In Athens, Athena appointed the court of the Areopagos to decide Orestes' fate. When the judges were equally divided, the goddess herself cast a vote, and Orestes was acquitted. She commanded that henceforward, where the numbers were equally divided, she should always be understood as casting a deciding vote for mercy.

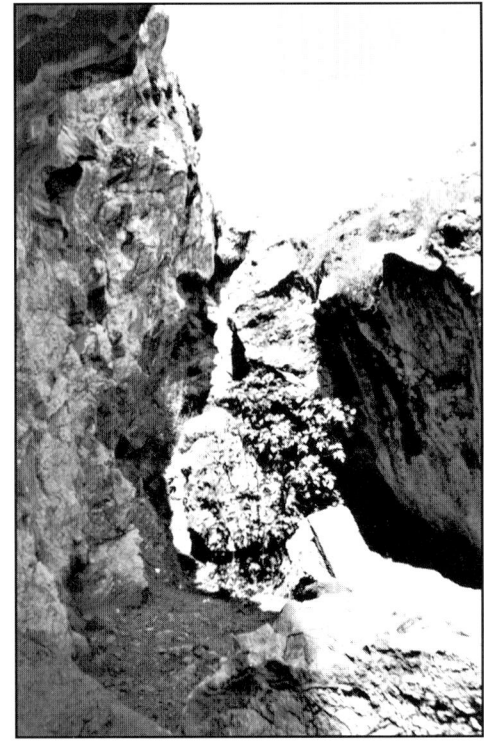

The Furies (Erinyes) came to be known by the Athenians as the Eumenides ("the well-disposed ones"). This apparent reversal of their character was due to the fear which they inspired. It was believed that by referring to them by good names, their hostility might be placated. They were venerated in a cleft in the rock at the foot of the Areopagos. The tomb of Oedipus was supposed to lie nearby, and to be a charm ensuring the safety of the city.

The cleft in the rock
at the foot of the Areopagos Hill,
which was once a shrine to the Furies

Saint Paul on the Areopagos Hill

The *Acts of the Apostles* records that on his way to Rome to stand trial, Saint Paul visited Athens (AD 51). He first argued in the synagogue with the Jews, and then in the agora with some Epicurean and Stoic philosophers. They were curious about his preaching and brought him to the Areopagos in order that he might there give them a more formal account of his doctrines. An intellectually fertile city, its citizens spent much of their time in intellectual discussion and argument.

Paul, standing in the middle of the Areopagus, observed that among the religious objects he had noticed as he arrived in Attica was an altar bearing the inscription, "To an unknown god." He claimed that he could reveal the nature of this mysterious divinity whom the Athenians already worshipped without knowing who exactly he was. He then explained their "unknown god" was the god known to the Jews:

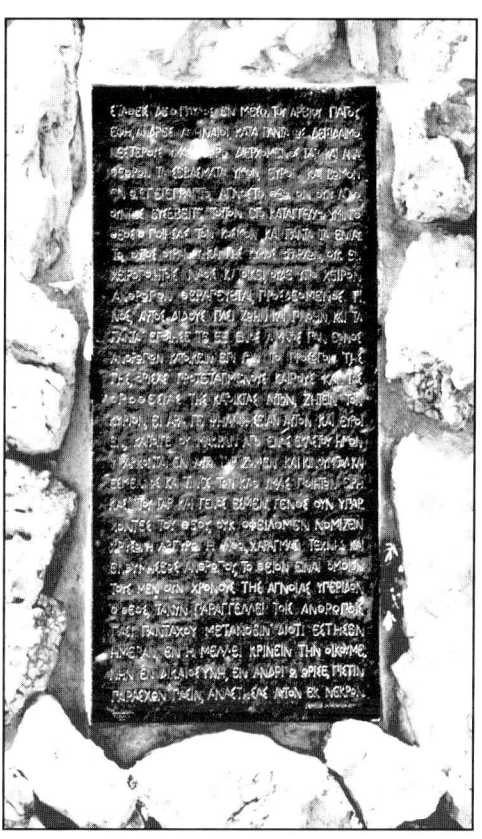

> "The God who made the world and everything in it, being Lord of heaven and earth, does not live in shrines made by man, nor is he served by human hands, as though he needed anything, since he himself gives to all men life and breath and everything."

He went on to point to the gradual development of monotheistic thought in the Greek tradition. Finally, he called upon the Athenians to accept this God, and Jesus, risen from the dead, or face judgement.

It seems to have been his belief in the resurrection which provoked most response. The *Acts* says that some mocked; but others wanted to hear more. Some Athenians were baptised, among whom was Dionysios, an influential member of the Areopagos.

The practice of dedicating an altar and offering sacrifices to "an unknown god" was a common one in the ancient world. It was a way of ensuring that the people were not visited by bad fortune because they had unintentionally offended an obscure or unknown deity by ignoring him.

A large tablet let into the side of the Areopagos Hill records the words of Saint Paul's sermon.
Each year the archbishop of Athens, with government and civic dignitaries, attends a special ceremony here on the eve of the feast of SS Peter and Paul to commemorate his visit.

Thesion Hill

A Misnamed Temple

Because the exploits of Theseus are depicted on the frieze, the temple known as the Thesion was long believed to be dedicated to Theseus, and erected to house his bones brought from Skyros. Archaeologists are now certain that it is really a temple of Hephaistos and Athena, built in 449 BC, in an area where metalworkers had their furnaces. The name *Thesion*, however, has become indelibly associated both with the building and its surrounding area.

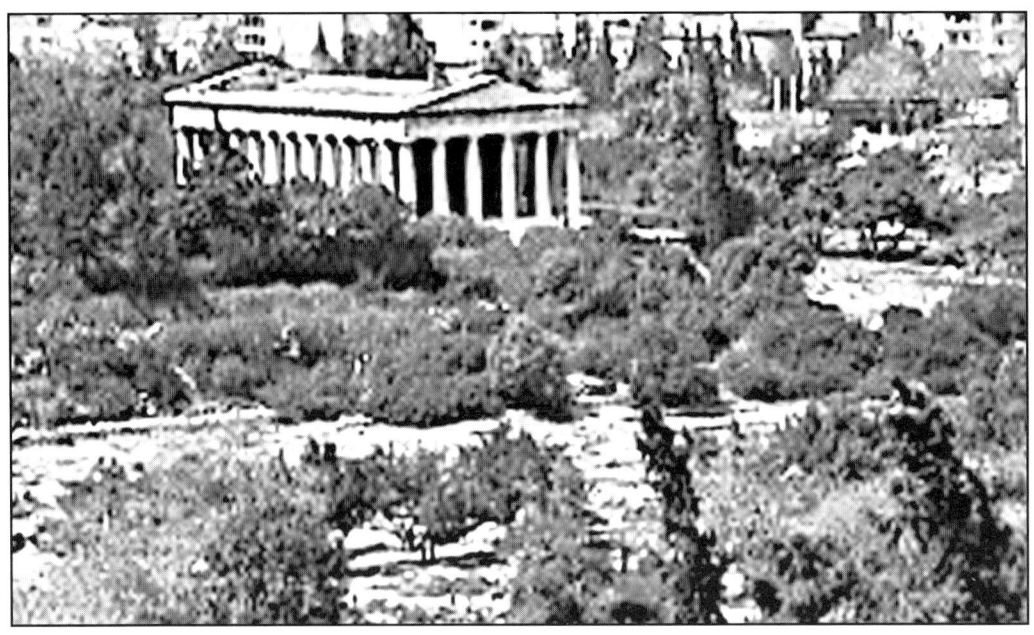

The Thesion, properly the Hephaistion
as seen across the agora, the civic centre of classical Athens

A Bitter God

Hephaistos, the god of fire, was regarded as the patron of all craftsmen, especially of metalworkers, and was particularly worshipped in manufacturing centres such as Athens. Originally he was probably a god who personified the power of of volcanoes, but the fires of volcanic activity came to be associated with the furnaces of the craftsmen who worked in metal.

According to myth, Hephaestos was the son of Hera alone, neither Zeus nor any other god having anything to do with his conception. Born weak, he was rejected by his mother, who threw him from Olympus in disgust, and did so with such force that he landed on the distant island of Lemnos. From that point onwards, he was lame.

Unable to function effectively as a warrior, he became a skilled craftsman, manufacturing marvellous weapons and armour for gods and heroes alike. With the help of the Cyclopes, he fashioned the thunderbolts of Zeus, the shield (or aegis) of Athena, the arrows of Eros, the god of love, the chariot in which the sun god Helios rode across the sky each day, and the invincible armour of Achilles. At the behest of Zeus, he even helped to create the first woman. At a time when the race of mortals included only one sex, Zeus wished to punish Prometheus, and ordered Hephaistos to create the first woman, Pandora, from clay. He did so, and later, from a sealed jar, she released all the evils of the world upon mankind.

Hephaestos never recovered from the way his mother had rejected him at his birth, and nursed a grievance against her. He fashioned a magic throne, which he took to Mount Olympus and presented to her, hurriedly taking his leave immediately afterwards. When she sat down on it, she found herself held securely, and quite unable to escape. The other gods pleaded with Hephaistos to release her, but he adamantly refused. Then Dionysos sought him out, got him drunk, and took him back to Olympus on a mule. Even then, Hephaistos consented to release her only after being given Aphrodite, the goddess of love, as his bride.

The marriage of this, the most desirable of the goddesses to the least handsome of the gods was the occasion for much comedy. Embittered by his lameness, Hephaistos was thought to live in constant suspicion of his beautiful wife, always fearful that she was being unfaithful to him. To catch her in the act he fashioned an extraordinary chain-link net, so fine and strong that no one, mortal or immortal, could escape from it. Then he surprised her with Ares as they lay together, threw the magic net over them, and hauled them, as they were, before the Olympian gods. The indignant Hephaistos demanded that they be punished, but the other gods only roared with laughter at the sight of the naked lovers, and allowed them to go free.

The return of Hephaestos to Olympus (Vienna)

The god's deformed foot is clearly visible

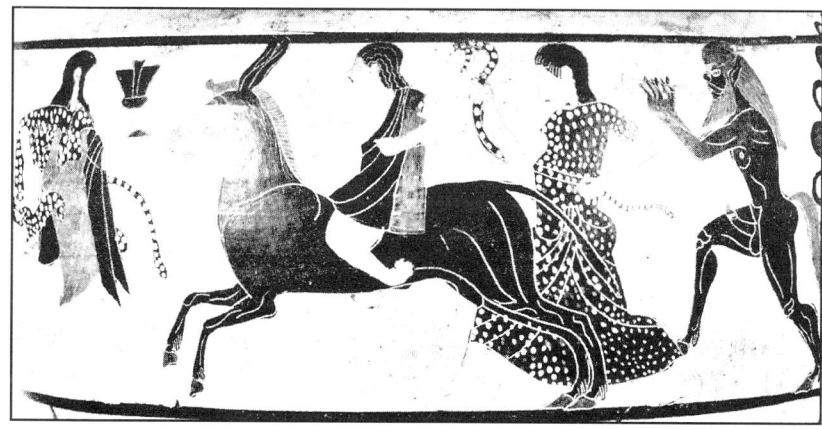

It has been suggested that the reason why the craftsman god was regarded as lame is that in the archaic age a lame man would have best found a living as a craftsman, since he would not have been able to function effectively as a warrior or farmer.

The Festival of Roses

Under Turkish rule, this ancient temple was used as a church, dedicated to Saint George, and known as "Saint George the Lazy," since it was open only once a year on the feast day of the saint. It was the practice of the country people to flood into Athens from the villages around each year on the Tuesday following Easter, and gather in the open space around it. There they would first sing: "Good day to you my lady; and well be with you my children." As they sang, they would lift up their male children three times and pray that they would grow up strong and brave. Afterwards they would make merry with drums and other musical instruments.

The peasants who observed this festival, then known as the *Rousalia*, or feast of roses, many of whom were of Albanian descent, could not account for it to inquisitive visitors. They had simply inherited a custom which they could not explain. However, it was held at the same time of year as the ancient *Anthesteria*, or feast of flowers, in honour of Dionysos, and may represent a genuine survival dating from ancient times. A link exists, in that in the twelfth century, a writer complained that the pagan festival was still being observed in his day, deploring it as "depraved", as though it still retained genuinely Bacchanalian features. It seems likely that this same Dionysic festival was still being observed in the nineteenth century under another name.

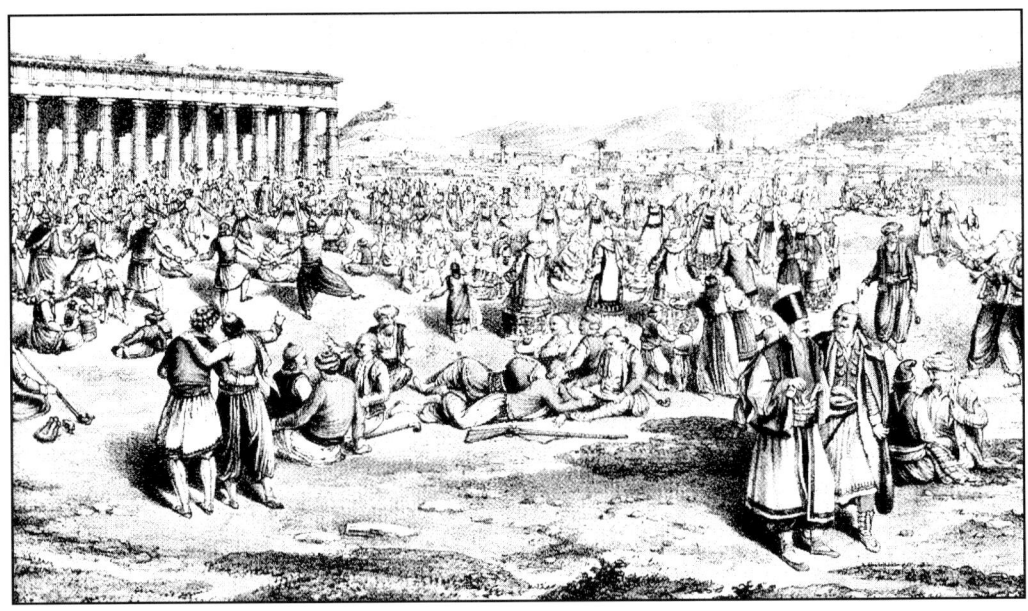

The Rousalia (Dodwell, 1806)

Diva

The Odeion of Herodes Atticus was built by a wealthy benefactor of Athens in memory of his wife, Regilla. [See volume two in this series: *Athens the Suburbs*] Today it is used for summer concerts. In September 1944 the audience in the Odeion, which included the leaders of the German and Italian occupying forces, witnessed a remarkable performance of Beethoven's *Fidelio*. The significance of the message this opera, with its condemnation of tyranny and glorification of freedom, could not have been lost on the high-ranking officers present, who within a month were to evacuate the city. But that night the audience witnessed something else equally remarkable. The message of imminent liberation was delivered by an unknown young stand-in named Maria Kalogeropoulos, or Callas.

Maria was born in New York in 1923 to George Kalogeropoulos a pharmacist from the Peloponessos, who had emigrated earlier in that year. Like many Greeks, when he took US citizenship he simplified his surname, choosing "Callas". Life was not easy during the depression, and Maria did not have a happy childhood. Her mother was single-minded in her ambition that her daughters should have musical careers. As a child Maria acquired an ear for music by listening to gramophone records and to the radio, and she was sent to piano and singing lessons. From an early age, she performed at children's concerts and on radio programmes. By her own account "an ugly duckling, fat clumsy and unpopular," she suffered from chronic lack of self-esteem, and throughout her life she was tortured by self-doubts and fears

When her father's business ran into difficulties, Evangeleia returned with her daughters to Greece. Thus in 1937, Maria found herself in a two-room apartment in Patission Avenue. She applied for admission to the Athens Conservatory, but at the age of fourteen they would not consider her, so she had to enter the less prestigious National Conservatory, there falsely giving her age as sixteen.

In 1939, the world famous soprano of La Scala, Milan and the New York Metropolitan Opera, Elvira de Hidalgo, went to teach at the Athens Conservatory. When Maria presented herself there for another audition, initially she did not make a good impression: "The very idea of that girl wanting to become a singer was laughable! She was tall, fat and wore heavy glasses... Her whole being was awkward, and her dress much too large, buttoned in front and quite formless. .. Not knowing what to do with her hands, she sat there quietly biting her nails while waiting for her turn." But when she launched into song, Elvira later recalled: "I heard violent cascades of sound, not yet fully controlled, but full of drama and emotion. I listened with my eyes closed and imagined what it would be like to work with such material, to mould it into perfection." For five years, Elvira became Maria's teacher.

She was a remarkable pupil, totally absorbed with music, and soon acquainted with a repertoire far beyond the average student. She could frequently memorise an entire page of a score during a single hearing, which was useful for someone too short sighted to see the conductor's baton.

During the years of the Occupation she had to endure the terrible famine, and later, however wealthy she became, she could never tolerate the waste of food. Luckily, her singing appealed to the Italian troops, and she soon learned that short impromptu solo concerts could earn her food. Characteristically, she used the opportunity to learn Italian, and did it in three months.

The national Opera managed to survive during the war with the active support of the German commander, General Spiedel and the Italians. When, in July 1942, Maria took on the title role of Pucini's *Tosca,* because the leading soprano was indisposed, the Athens press discovered her. Her reputation was reinforced by her performance as Leonora in Beethoven's *Fidelio,* when the original lead singer was unable to learn the part on time. Maria had never sung in German before.

Following the Liberation, fellow performers conspired to push her out of the position she had gained. Some argued that she was too young for a leading role, some that she was technically a US citizen, while others resented her tantrums, for, despite her age, she insisted upon the privileges of a star performer, and was beginning to show the arrogance for which she later became so notorious. Mostly, it was jealousy, for in Athens even artistic appointments were made on the basis of connections (*mesa*) rather than merit. So Maria returned to the USA; and the rest, as they say, is history. Initial disappointment was followed by sensational success at La Scala, the Rome and Paris operas, Covent Garden and the Metropolitan Opera. Her recordings became popular all over the world.

Maria returned to the Odeion in 1957 to perform for the August Athens Festival. But when she offered to donate her fees to support it, she was brusquely told that it did not need her charity. She fell ill on the day of the first concert, and her indisposition was announced only one hour before the performance. The Athenian public reacted angrily, but at her next performance, as soon as she began to sing, the audience was enchanted. They say that the applause could be heard for miles around.

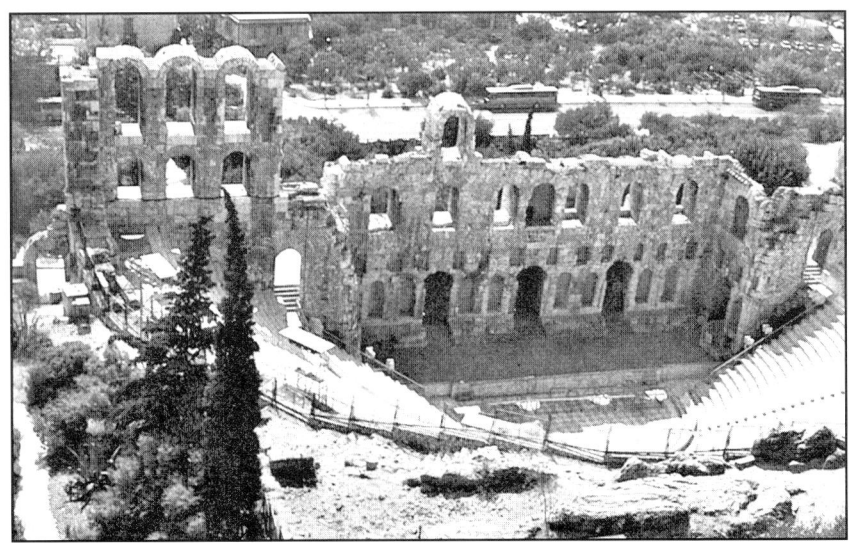

The Odeion of Herodes Atticus

Rock-Sliding for a Good Delivery

Honey was the traditional offering to the nymphs in ancient times, probably the original offering to the indigenous gods of the land before the cultivation of the vine, demonstrating the ancient and persistent nature of their worship. In Athens, neraides, or nymphs, were especially associated with whirlwinds, to which the Hill of the Nymphs was thought to be especially liable. During the nineteenth century whenever uneducated women saw the whirling dust which signified the presence of a whirlwind, they would say "Honey and milk in your path" to appease them.

Situated on the Hill of the Nymphs, the present large church of Saint Marina replaces a small basilica, which still stands beside it. The rocks all around have been levelled for the foundations of ancient buildings, or have holes cut to take votive tablets. Edward Dodwell records that when he was sketching in the area two Turkish women approached a cave there, probably used for burials in ancient times, and left honey, almonds and a small cake inside. Inscriptions found near the summit show that the entire area was dedicated to the nymphs.

The particular nymphs venerated in this place were probably daughters of Hyakinthos, sacrificed to save the city, and the hill was probably the one known in ancient times as the hill of Hyakinthos. These nymphs were the *yenethliai*, who protected women in childbirth. Saint Marina is patron of women in childbirth, and so she is their Christian successor. During the nineteenth century, women would bring sick children and change their clothes in front of the icon of the saint, hoping that their illnesses would vanish with their old clothes. A little further down the hillside, a glassy rock slide was used by barren women who hoped for a child, and by pregnant women, who hoped that their delivery would be as smooth and painless as the slide itself.

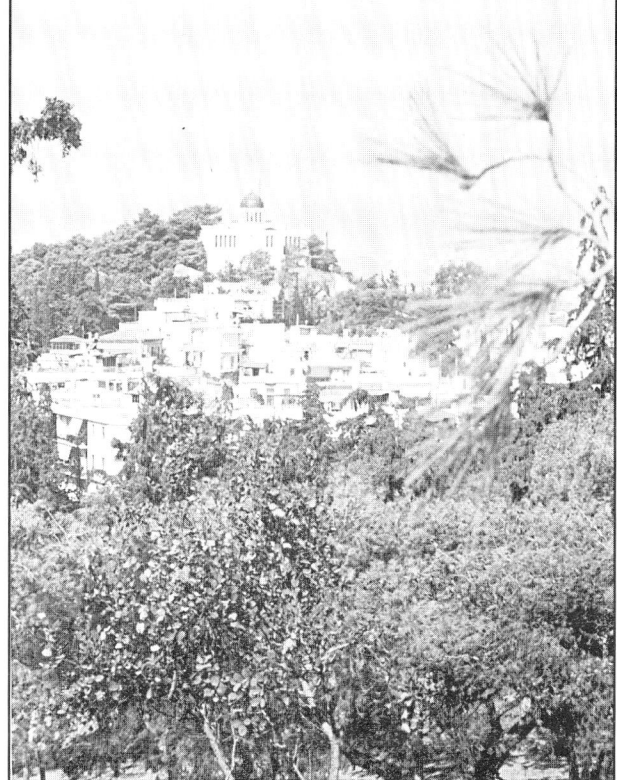

The Hill of the Nymphs, crowned by the Observatory

45

The Hill of Democracy

Was Ancient Democracy Genuine Democracy?

If anywhere can be regarded as the birthplace of democracy, the Pnyx Hill is that place. On this eminence, when Athens was free and democratic, the citizens gathered together to manage the affairs of their state.

The Athenians not only invented democracy, they developed a form of self-government which, in some ways, was closer to the ideal than any achieved since. The individual citizen of the modern state sometimes feels helpless before powerful officials and shadowy pressure groups. One of the founding Fathers of the United States of America declared, with remarkable candour: "The people who own America should govern America." The US constitution was devised on the basis of that principle, and it has been so ever since.

By contrast, Pericles' ideal of Democracy is expressed in his famous "funeral oration", reported by Thucydides:

"... Our administration favours the many instead of the few: this is why it is called a democracy. The laws provide equal justice to all alike in their private disputes, but we do not ignore the claims of excellence. When a citizen distinguishes himself, then he will be called upon to serve the state in preference to others, not as a matter of privilege, but as a reward for merit; and poverty is no impediment...

The freedom we enjoy extends to ordinary life; we are not suspicious of one another, and we do not harass our neighbour if he chooses to go his own way... But this freedom does not make us lawless. We are taught to respect the... laws, and never to forget that we must protect the injured. And we are also taught to observe those unwritten laws whose sanction lies in the universal sense of what is right...

An Athenian citizen does not neglect public affairs when attending to his private business.... We consider a man who takes no interest in the state not as harmless, but as useless; and although only a few may initiate a policy, we are all able to pass judgement on it. We do not look upon discussion as an impediment to political action, but as an indispensable preliminary to acting wisely...."

The "parliament" of Athens was the Council of the Five Hundred (*boule*) which consisted of fifty men chosen each year by lot from each of the ten tribes into which the Athenians were divided. The five hundred never met as a single body; each group of fifty would take one tenth of the year in which to meet to consider urgent business of state, or to prepare measures to place before the full assembly of the citizens. Each day they would choose a different chairman from their number to preside over their meetings.

The Assembly of the Citizens (*ekklesia*) was the supreme authority in the state. It decided upon all important matters, including peace and war and foreign alliances. It determined the forces sent on campaign, appointed generals and heard their reports. It was the ultimate authority in the administration of the empire, supervising state finances, the safeguarding of the food supply, the upkeep of maintenance of public buildings, etc.

All adult male citizens were eligible to attend and take a full part in the proceedings. Early in the fifth century they probably met ten times a year, but later they held forty regular meetings, plus extraordinary sessions as required. Meetings would begin early in the morning and could not continue after dusk. Unfavourable omens, such as thunder, lightning, rain, earthquake or eclipse, would necessitate immediate adjournment.

Order was kept by the fifty members of the Council on duty, who sat on the benches below the speaker's platform (*bema*). Their chairman for the day would preside. The assembly would begin with a sacrifice, and the herald would proclaim a curse against anyone who might deceive the people. Then the secretary would read the agenda provided by the Council, posted up five days beforehand. After each item, the chairman probably called for a show of hands for approval as it stood, or for discussion. For a debate, the herald would say, "Who wishes to speak?" A citizen would advance to the platform, place a myrtle wreath on his head, and address the citizens. Discussion was only limited only by relevance.

Administration was performed by officials who were usually appointed to boards of ten by lot, although a few, requiring special skills or knowledge, were elected to office, e.g. generals. Some boards administered the collection of taxes, others arranged state contracts, such as the right to work state mines. Other boards undertook administrative tasks. Thus market superintendents supervised the cleanliness of the markets and inspected goods for adulteration. They worked on the basis of collegiality. All the members of a board enjoyed equal powers and took turns as chairmen, so that no single person would dominate their proceedings.

When officials left office each year, ten investigators were appointed to receive complaints against their administrative actions and ten auditors examined their accounts. Offending officials could be sent for trial.

The preference for lot over election was to prevent offices being monopolised by citizens wealthy or famous enough to influence the voters. All offices were held for a limited time with limitations on re-election, to ensure that everybody had his chance to hold almost every office at least once in his lifetime.

Ostracism was instituted to preserve the democracy from over-mighty citizens, and to resolve divisive quarrels between would-be leaders. Each year the citizens would vote on whether to hold an ostracism, and if they did, they later voted on whom to exile. The man receiving most votes was expelled for ten years. The term "ostracism" is derived from the *ostraka* or fragments of pottery upon which the citizens would record their votes.

There were limitations to this democracy. Women were not recognised as citizens or enfranchised. To a population of about 45,000 adult males citizens, there were probably 100,000 slaves, acquired during military campaigns and slave raids. They worked for their owners in their homes, on the land, in workshops, trading ships, quarries and mines. They were often bought as an investment, and worked for contractors, hired by the state in mines, for road repairs, street cleaning, in quarries, etc., or worked directly for the state in the civil service or in the police force. Some were set up by their owners as independent craftsmen, and paid their owner a percentage of their profits.

A further limitation of Athenian democracy, one that proved its undoing, was the tendency of the citizens to deny to others the freedoms they enjoyed themselves, by building up economic and political and military hegemony over other Greek states, under the guise of an alliance against an, at that time largely fictitious, Persian danger. In doing so, while at all times they attributed to themselves the best possible motives, they acted arrogantly, diguising self-interest as "justice". The result was almost thirty years war, in which the power of Athens was destroyed and its democracy eclipsed.

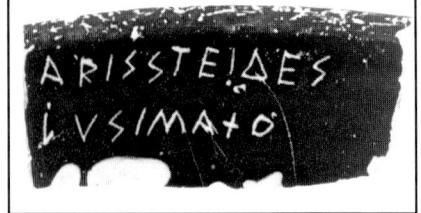

Above: An ostrakon
Large numbers of ostraka from the same workshop, each bearing the same name, show that campaigns were deliberately organised to secure the ostracism of particular persons.
Below: The bema, the public speaking platform

Saint Dimitrios the Bombardier

A small church dedicated to Saint Dimitrios lies on the slopes of the Pnyx Hill across from the Acropolis, in a beautiful copse of cypresses, pines and olive trees. It stands over the remains of the one of the portals of a gate which pierced the ancient city wall at this point. Popular tradition ascribes its foundation to the ninth century, but it has been definitively dated only to the fourteenth. Here, in the middle of the seventeenth century, the Turkish rulers of Athens planned a great massacre of the Christian Greek population, but fate intervened to save them in a truly remarkable manner.

The commander of the Turkish garrison on the Acropolis, Yusuf Aga, planned to massacre the Christians of the city when they were attending the popular celebration of Saint Dimitrios' Day on 26th October 1645. In advance of the festival, he ordered that all the other churches with this dedication were to remain closed for the day, so that the people of Athens would gather at this one spot.

Yusuf Aga planned to bombard it at that point during the celebrations when most people would be present. During the days before the feast, he had all the available cannon, including one of exceptional size, known as *Loumbardiaris,* "the Bombadier", assembled on the Propylaia, the ancient ceremonial entrance to the acropolis.

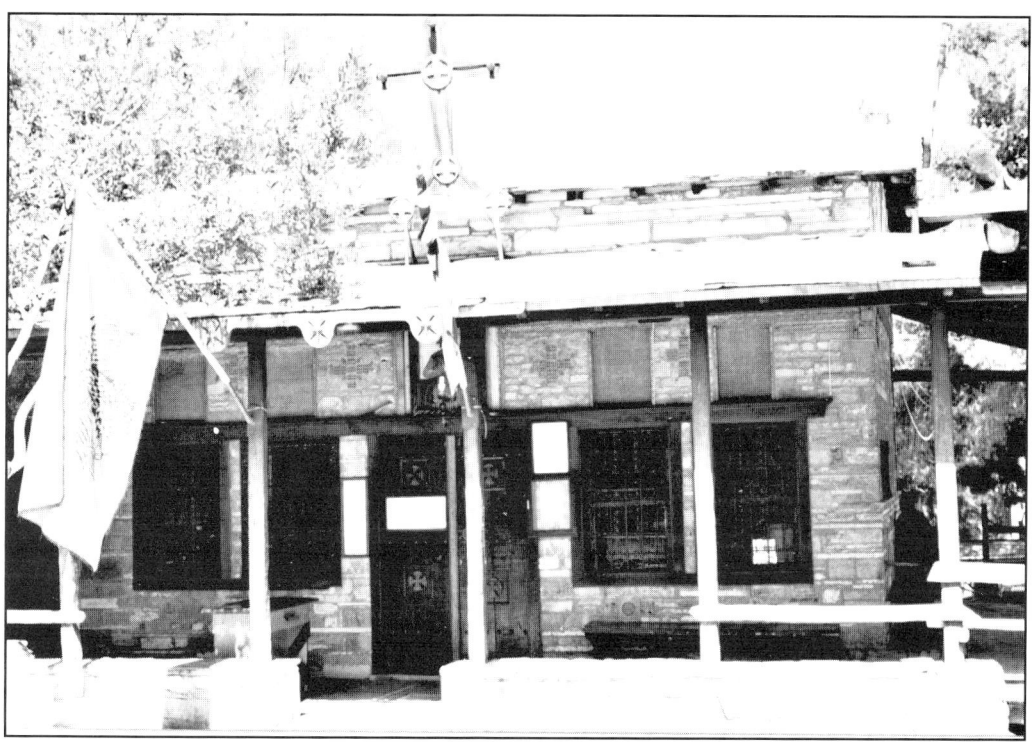

The church of Saint Dimitrios the Bombadier

49

During the night before the festival a fierce storm blew up. A bolt of lightning struck the Propylaia, exploding the store of gunpowder which had been placed there ready for the planned massacre. Aga's own house was destroyed, and he and most of his family were killed in the blast. The life of his daughter, a Christian, was spared, because she happened to be staying at her mother's house in the lower town. Naturally, the Christians of Athens considered this to have been an act of divine intervention.

Since that time, this church has been known as Saint Dimitrios *Loumbardiaris,* or Saint James the Bombardier, after the great cannon. It was extensively restored in 1955, and furnished with an unusual wooden veranda and walkway. When it is examined closely, the fabric of this church can be seen to incorporate a great many, and a great variety, of pieces of carved marble.

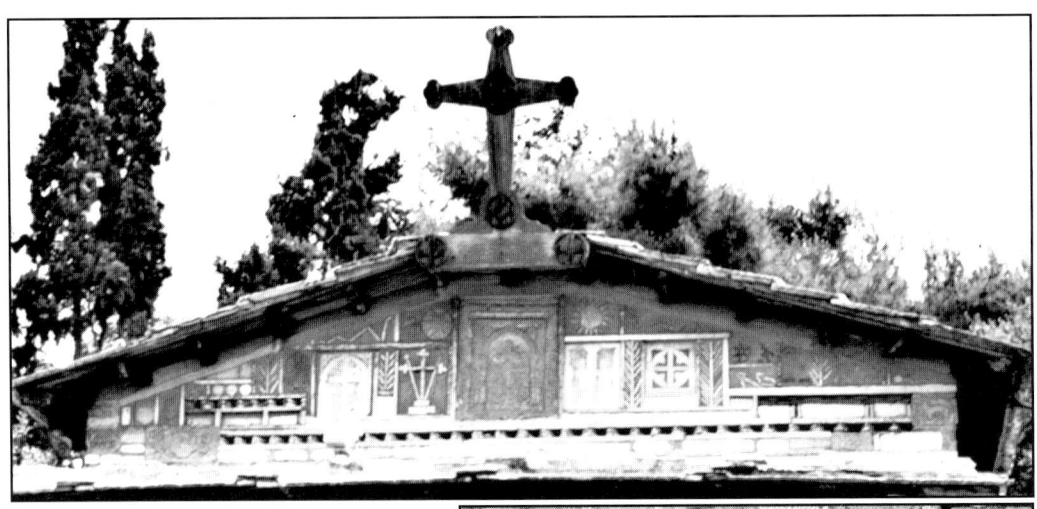

Details showing some of the elaborate carving in the fabric of this church

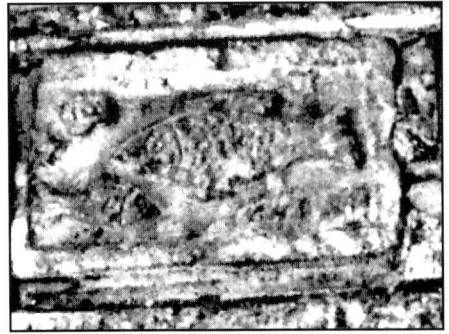

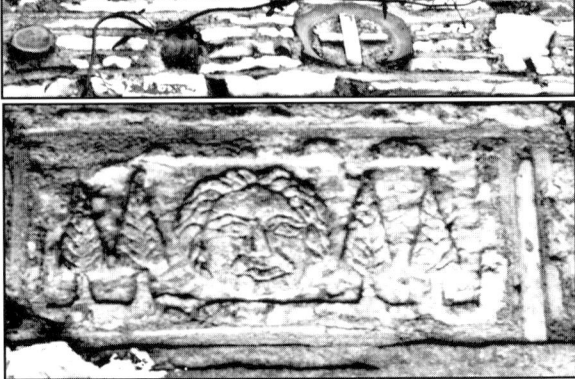

The Museion Hill

A Failed Marriage Broker

According to the archaeologists, the prominent monument which crowns the summit of the Museion Hill, sometimes called the Hill of the Muses, was erected in AD 114-6 over the tomb of C. Julius Antiochus Philopappus, a Syrian prince who was consul of Rome and an Athenian citizen. The Athenians of the newly-independent Greece of the eighteenth century had quite another explanation for this striking landmark, one which illustrates the way in which the folk imagination can build an entertaining little story upon a few merely verbal associations.

The folk-hero Diyenis Akritas once came to Athens and asked his friend, the Athenian Philopappus, a professional go-between in the arrangement of marriages, to secure for him as his bride the lady Syriazi. Philopappus duly went to see the young woman's mother. When she learned of his purpose, instead of answering with the customary polite form of refusal: "No doubt he is good and worthy, but it is not yet time", she simply laughed scornfully: "I would give my daughter to him? Get out of my sight!" Thus Philapoppos was forced to return and confess his failure.

Diyenis' pride was hurt and he blamed his friend. Harsh words were exchanged, and soon the argument descended to mutual challenges to single combat. They climbed the hill on which the monument now stands, and first shared the labour of the digging of a grave for whichever one of them would be the loser. Then they set to with their weapons. All day long iron clanged upon iron until darkness fell. At last Diyenis prevailed, and Philopappus fell, mortally wounded, into the waiting grave. The birds gathered to sing his lament, and the monument marks the site of his grave.

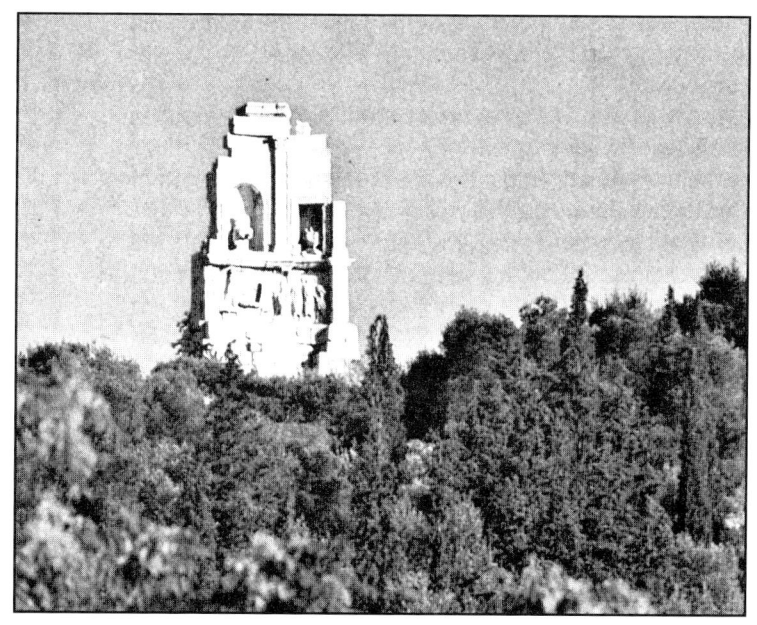

The grave monument of Philopappus on the Mouseion Hill

The Ilissos Quarter

Beside and underneath the busy dual carriageway of Kallirois Street, which takes heavy traffic past the town centre between the southeastern and northern suburbs, lies the bed of the River Ilissos. In ancient times, this was a famous beauty spot.

The North Wind

The ancient Greeks personified some of the winds. They told that the wind god Boreas, who lived in the North, fell in love with some mares grazing in the fields of Attica. Transforming himself into a dark-maned stallion, he covered them, and as a result twelve stallions were born. Boreas did not confine his amorous attentions to mares. For a long time he courted Orythia, daughter of King Erechtheos of Athens, and frequently begged the king to give her to him. When he despaired of a favourable response, he decided to take her by force. One day he saw his chance when she was playing by the river Ilissos, gathering flowers with her friends, and carried her off.

Because of this, he always felt that he owed the Athenians something and so, many years later when the navy of the Persian king Xerxes threatened Athens, and the Athenians begged his assistance, Boreas sent a great storm in the Aegean, with the result that four hundred Persian ships were lost.

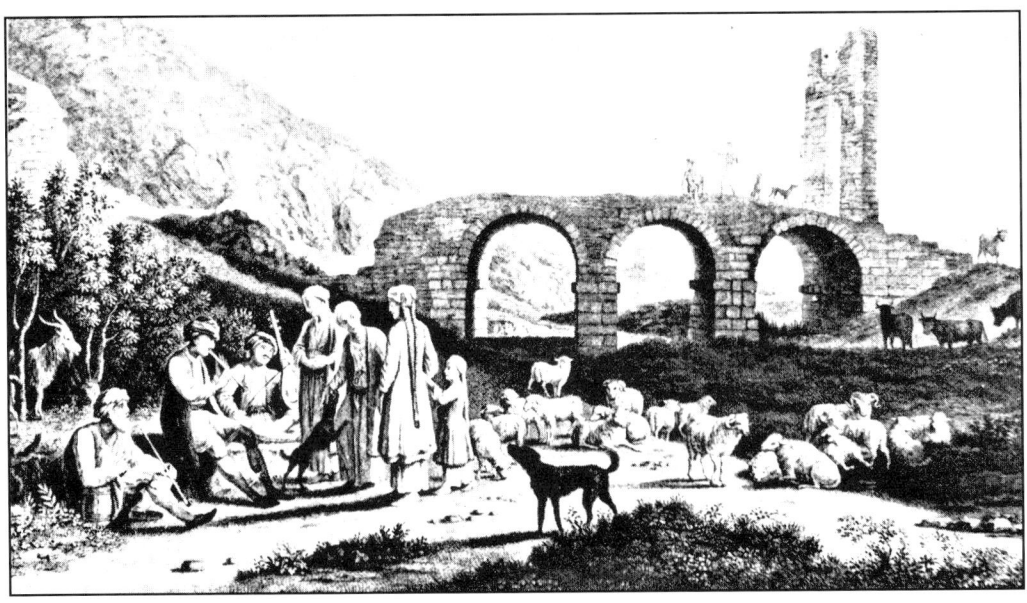

The Bridge over the Ilissos erected by Herodes Atticus (Stuart, 1794)

Hidden Treasure "At The Columns"

In the eighteenth century it was believed by many that a treasure in gold coins was held by a Moor who lived in a brick hut on the top of the ruins of the temple of Olympian Zeus, at that time usually known as "The Columns". It was said that he could sometimes be seen after dark leaping from column to column.

Praying for Rain

During 1809-11, John Galt visited Athens during a severe drought, and found the temple of Zeus, the rain-god of the ancient Greeks, being used by the Turks to invoke Allah to send rain.

"On my return to Athens, I found the price of corn rapidly advancing. The alarm with regard to this crop is becoming general, and some of the pious Turks are every morning heard praying at the dawn of day, among the ruins of the temple of Jupiter [Zeus] Olympius, where they usually assemble for this purpose when the drought happens to continue long. . .

Public prayers for rain are now ordered for nine successive days, and this morning they commenced among the ruins of the temple of Jupiter Olympius. A flock of ewes and lambs was driven together in the neighbourhood of the worshippers, and soon after the close of the sermon, the lambs were separated from their mothers, and all the Turks standing up began a loud and general supplication, in the most pathetic tones. The divided flock at the same time began to bleat. It is not easy to convey to you by words the effect of this simple and effective accompaniment, which infinitely, in my opinion, excelled the lead and leather popery of all the organs of Christendom. Viewing the dry bed of the Ilissos, and the blasted appearance of the grass, and beholding the sun, which at this moment arose from behind Mount Hymettos, red and arid, like a shield of polished copper, it seemed to me as if all nature, feeling the destructive thirst, seconded the supplication of man, and sympathised in his fears."

This curious method of conveying the people's needs to God was also used at that time by the Christians.

Burying the Carnival

In the days immediately following Independence, this area was he scene of the strange ceremony of "burying of the carnival," which took place before noon on the first day of Lent, known as "Clean Monday".

"The spot, which from time immemorial has been chosen for its celebration, would alone give an unspeakable charm to this characteristic scene, independent of the invariable accessories of a cloudless sky and a brilliant sun, which the Greeks may at any time so confidently expect, that they wisely hold all their festivities in the open air. The fifteen majestic columns now alone remaining of the mighty temple of Jupiter Olympus, are usually abandoned to a solitude and stillness so intense, that there seems to hang around them a very atmosphere, of desolation, which singularly enhances the awful sublimity of these stately ruins; but on this day, before even the rising of the sun has been announced by the long shadows of the three lone pillars which stand apart from the rest, and have so long been as a gigantic sundial to that wide plain, the stern silence of this kingdom of the past is broken in upon by every sight and sound that can indicate life moot busy, stirring, and gay.

The whole population of Athens, men, women, and children, followed 'by their asses laden with provisions, carpets, and other indispensable luxuries, pour out of the town at this early hour, and assemble under the deserted columns: nor do they confine themselves to this spot alone, but spread in all directions along the myrtle-clad banks of the Ilissos, over the stadium, as entire in form to this day as when it shook with the roar of the wild beasts and the shouts of the combatants in those terrific games; and round the classic fountain of Calleroe, usually so still and quiet that the most timid of nymphs might use its limpid waters for her mirror, as the stars do every night.

Thus, clustering in groups that are almost always strikingly picturesque, they establish themselves for a long day of enjoyment; the Little infants, strange-look-ing diminutive mummies; swaddled from head to foot, and with long streaming black hair, are laid among the green corn to

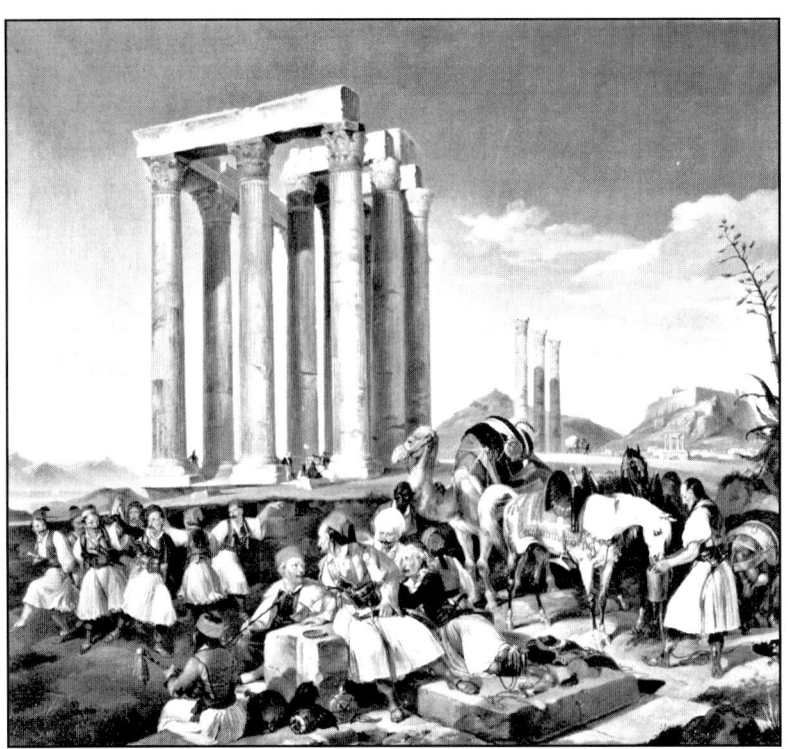

Festival at "the Columns" (Perlberg c. 1835) The first modern celebration of Clean Monday by citizens of an independent country

54

sleep or scream as the case may be; the young girls arrange their little coquettish red caps to the best advantage, and look out from under their long eyelashes at the fierce cavaliers, who, with a self-satisfied air, and an incredibly small waist, keep continually careering at full gallop up and down, over rocks and stones in a reckless manner, more amusing to themselves than agreeable to their horses. Meanwhile the more sedate of the party seat themselves in a circle, and give their serious attention to one of their number, who either regales them unwearied for hours together with the most lamentable music produced by the rattling of a quill on the jingling wires of a sort of mandolin, or else chants, in a monotonous voice, a never-ending story, which, to my infinite delight, is generally word for word one of those we know so well in the "Arabian Nights." Altogether it would be impossible to conceive a gayer or more animated scene, brightened as it is by the effects of the sunshine on the vivid colours of their dresses.

At noon a grotesque figure, representing the late carnival, is carried to his grave in procession, with a great deal of merriment and glee, where he is ignominiously decapitated and buried. From that moment the Greeks enter with all sincerity on the practice of the fast enjoined by their church ..."

The Gospel Riots

The new state of Greece faced a language problem. The language spoken by the people had evolved considerably from its ancient forms by the simplification of many grammatical structures and by the introduction of many words of foreign origin, some of them Turkish. Given the conservative and pedantic educational and linguistic traditions of the time, the normal development of any language was usually seen as the corruption of an earlier purer form. This was true of English, but it was particularly liable to be true of a language whose ancient form had such interntional cultural prestige as Greek. People compared ancient Greek to marble and modern Greek to mud; arguing that as you could not build monuments out of mud, so you could not create a literature in the modern tongue.

It was perhaps equally inevitable, given the romantic nationalism characteristic of the nineteenth century, that many would desire to return to the older "purer" form, closer to its roots in classical literature. The result was the adoption by the new state, as its official language, of a deliberately purified version of Greek known as *katharevousa*, created by a Smyrniote Greek, Adamantios Koraɛs. This was a language which no one actually spoke, except on official or formal occasions, but which came to be used for writing. Naturally, *katharevousa*, since it was known only to those who had been formally educated, carried great prestige as compared with the spoken form of the language, *demotiki*. Thus literate Greeks wrote in a different language from that which even they almost always spoke; and most people were considered unable to read or write "properly" at all. It is only against this back-ground that the remarkable riots known as the *Evangellistria* can be understood.

Since the New Testament was always used in its original untranslated version in the churches, it was not readily comprehensible to the great mass of the people, who understood only *demotiki*. Evangelical considerations clearly called for a translation into the modern form of the language. At the end of the nineteenth century, Queen Olga supervised a project, approved by the archbishop of Athens, to produce an authoritative translation of the Gospels into the form of modern Greek used by the mass of the people in their everyday life. Initially, one thousand copies of the *Gospel according to Saint Matthew* were published in 1900. The print run was sold out within a month.

This enterprise aroused considerable opposition among conservatives. The Gospels were originally written in a form of Greek called *Koine*, then the common language of the entire Near East, and it was objected that by using a modern version, the translators were undermining the unique connection between Greek culture and the Gospel, as well as substituting an inferior version for the inspired original.

When excerpts were published in a newspaper, indignation reached a crescendo. Rival journals published headlines such as "Burn them alive," and enraged students took over the University. On 8th November 1901, together with other opponents of the new translation, the students held a protest meeting among the columns of the Temple of Olympian Zeus. A student speaker demanded the excommunication not only of those who had made and published the new translation, but of all who had dared even to read a copy. Another declared: "The Turks did not do by the sword so much harm to Greece as the pen and the book are doing to her during the present day." Then they resolved to march into the city. The government, which had forbidden the demonstration, ordered the Columns cleared, and soldiers fired blanks at the crowds. During the riots which ensued, Prime Minister Theotokis was shot at while riding through the streets in his open carriage , and when he fled to his home his house was attacked. In the end, eight were left dead and over one hundred injured.

As a consequence of these disturbances, the government, the chief of police and the archbishop of Athens all resigned. The Holy Synod of the Greek Church forbade the use of all translations. Even today the text of the Bible is constitutionally "protected" in Greece. It may not be translated without the prior approval of the Orthodox Church of Greece and of the Patriarch of Constantinople.

What has all the appearance of an example of extreme obscurantism probably concealed more substantial issues. Most of the demonstrators were university students. A tiny minority in Greek society, they had a vested interest in preserving the artificial form of the language, which only graduates understood, since rendering most of the population illiterate in the official language of the country served to entrench their privileged social and economic position. For example, their services were required, and had to be paid for, to transact any legal business, to fill in any official forms, etc. What was really at issue for many of the demonstrators was not so much the breaking of a link with the past as the entrenchment of the social and economic privileges of a small, educated middle class.

The First Modern Olympic Games

The Panathenaic Stadium was the venue for the first modern Olympic games in 1896. The revival had been stimulated by the discovery of the ancient site of Olympia buried under river-silt in 1766. During the late 1820s the area began to be excavated, but serious work began in 1875, when the German archaeologist, Ernst Curtius, gained a permit for the excavation of the site. Amongst the treasures he uncovered was a magnificent statue of Hermes, sculpted by Praxiteles. His discoveries aroused considerable interest in the Games, and led to several attempts at imitation.

Early Revivals

Twice during the 1830s, Gustav Schartau, a professor from Lund organised a 'Scandinavian Olympic Games at Ramlosa. Annually from 1849, a Shropshire surgeon and magistrate, Dr W. P. Brookes, acted as "archon" in the "Olympic Games of Much Wenlock," an English rural festival which mingled mock-Grecian and mock-medieval elements. One Baron Pierre de Coubertin attended the Wenlock Games of 1890.

Meanwhile a wealthy Greek from Northern Greece, Evangelos Zappas, inspired by Alexandros Soutsos' idea of reviving the ancient Olympics Games, proposed to the Greek government to finance the foundation of a modern Olympics organisation. But A. R. Rangaves, the Greek Foreign Minister and a classical scholar, objected: "Today's spirit is different from the one of ancient times; the nations are competing in industry and artefacts, and not in stadiums." According to Rangaves, any modern Olympic Games should focus on agricultural and industrial progress, not on athletics. So, he proposed to Zappas the holding of agricultural and industrial competitions together with athletic games. In fact the industrial part in the Zappian Olympics was held regularly, and got more attention and far more money, than the athletics.

The Games of 1859 took place in what is today Kotzia Square in the centre of Athens on Athinas Street. The Royal Family and members of the Government attended. The athletic competitions were designed for entertainment rather than serious competition. As there were no trained athletes in Greece at that time, the organising committee invited the participation of workers, who were attracted by money prizes. A policeman who was present on duty left his post and took part in one of the races, as did a beggar who usually pretended to be blind.

The Games of the 1870s were held in the restored Panathenaic Stadium. The organisation of these games was more sophisticated. The competitors enlisted some time before the events and were required to follow a special regimen in preparation. Thirty-one athletes were chosen to participate in nine competitions for nominal money prizes. The judges were university professors. A band played a specially composed Olympic Hymn. These Games were an enormous success with the public.

A third Olympiad was organised by the Director of the Public Gymnasium, Ioannis Phokianos in 1875. He believed that the ideal of gymnastics should expand from the upper classes, down through the educated and cultured classes. Thus he initiated the selection and preparation of students of high schools and universities, who were trained in the Public Gymnasium in Athens. The athletes were impressively dressed in white trousers and shirts with a wide blue sash. In spite of the careful preparations these games were a disappointment. The Royal Family failed to attend, and there was not enough space for the crowds who turned up to watch.

The International Movement

Towards the end of the century the idea of a revival of the games on a worldwide, rather than on a merely pan-Hellenic, scale was born. Baron Pierre de Coubertin had dedicated his life to the idea of promoting peace through friendly competition, and in the process came to admire the British public [i.e. private] school tradition of classicism and organised games, which he saw as a means of achieving this.

In 1896, de Coubertin said:

"The idea of the revival of Olympic Games was not a passing fancy: it was the logical culmination of a great movement. The nineteenth century saw the taste for physical exercises revive everywhere... At the same time the great inventions, the railways and the telegraph have abridged distances and mankind has come to live a new existence; the peoples have intermingled, they have learned to know each other better and immediately they started to compare themselves. What one achieved the other immediately wished also to endeavour: universal exhibitions brought together to one locality of the globe the products of the most distant lands; Literary or scientific congresses have brought together, into contact, the various intellectual forces. How then should the athletes not seek to meet, since rivalry is the basis of athletics, and in reality the very reason of its existence?"

For this reason, de Coubertin championed the cause of "competitions at regular intervals, at which representatives of all countries and all sports would be invited under the aegis of the same authority, which would impart to them a halo of grandeur and glory, that is the patronage of classical antiquity. To do this was to revive the Olympic Games: the name imposed itself: it was not even possible to find another."

He invited all the sports societies of the world to send delegates to a congress in Paris in June 1894 to consider a worldwide revival. He expected ridicule from the delegates, but to his surprise they unanimously agreed to his plan. De Coubertin wished the first Olympiad to open in Paris to coincide with an international trade fair planned for 1900, but Demetrios Vikelas, a merchant from Syros, representing the Panhellenic Gymnastic Society, suggested that Athens should be the site of the First International Olympic Games in 1896. De Coubertin warmed to this idea, but at first hoped to use Mount Olympus, but this was quickly seen to be unrealistic. Thus Athens became the site of the first international Olympic Games, and Vikelas the first president of the new International Olympic Committee.

Although the decision was received enthusiastically in Greece, the Government, which knew that the state was bankrupt, at first opposed the idea. Only the arrival of M. de Coubertin in Athens, a chorus of enthusiasm from the Greek Press and the offer of royal patronage overcame their misgivings. As sports historian Michael Biddiss observed: "King George and the princes could prepare to emphasise their particular delight at Hellenic victories and thus employ those gestures of nationalistic identification which might serve to convince their often sceptical subjects that the family was now more Greek than Glucksburg."

A Dream Realised

A provisional Committee was formed to undertake the project, with the heir to the throne as its honorary president. The Panathenaic Stadium in Athens was chosen as the venue. Originally constructed for the Panathenaic Games in 330 BC, the original straight track was centred in a natural gully between two hills, and the only seats were marble thrones for important visitors and officials. In Roman times it had been used for barbaric gladiatorial contests. When the Emperor Hadrian visited, a thousand wild beasts were baited there. The billionaire Herodes Atticus had installed rows of marble seats [see volume two in this series, *Athens: The Suburbs*], and erected a bridge across the Ilissos.

After the abolition of the ancient games the fine marble-seated stadium became a source of building material for the rest of the city. In time the entire area was covered with a layer of earth, and all that remained above ground was the ancient vaulted entrance, known as the "stone with the hole". In the popular mind this spot was a notorious haunt of witches after dark. The sick of the town would be passed through the "hole" in the "stone" in order to effect a cure.

In 1864, the archaeologist Ernst Ziller purchased the site to excavate it. Then King George I became interested, paid off Ziller, and had the excavations continued at state expense. The site was hardly suitable for a large audience, and the state did not have the money to rebuild it. Commemorative stamps were commissioned and a public appeal launched, but only $165,000 was raised. The Committee then turned to a wealthy Greek philanthropist, George Averoff of Alexandria, who had already, at his own expense, erected the Athens Polytechnic, the military academy, and juvenile prisons. He refaced the site with pentelic marble following the original plan of Herodes Atticus' stadium, although only the lower tiers, were ready for the Games of 1896.

The revival of the Games was received with outright antagonism in some quarters. Some nations chose to disregard it completely, while a few offered grudging support. By later standards, not many countries were represented. Many competitors used their own money to support their travelling and accommodation expenses. A few contestants were tourists who happened to hear about the games while they were in Greece, and decided on the spot to take part. Thus the First Modern Olympiad took place in an atmosphere of genuine amateurism and informality. The American hurdler, Thomas P. Curtis, wrote:

"... when we arrived at Athens on the day preceding the opening of the games - after crossing Italy by train, spending twenty-four hours on the boat from Brindisi

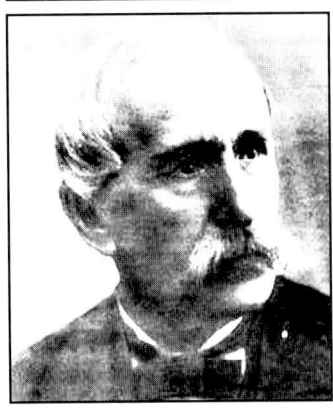

*Public benefactor
Evangelos Averof*

or Patras, and then crossing Greece by train - we were not exactly in what today's Olympic coaches would call the pink.

Nor did our reception at Athens, kind and hospitable as it was, help. We were met with a procession, with bands blaring before and behind, and were marched on foot for what seemed miles to the Hotel de Ville. Here speech after speech was made in Greek, presumably very flattering to us, but of course entirely unintelligible. We were given large bumpers of the white-resin wine of Greece and told by our advisors that it would be a gross breach of etiquette if we did not drain these off in response to the various toasts. As soon as this ceremony was over, we were again placed at the head of a procession and marched to our hotel.

I could not help feeling that so much marching, combined with several noggins of resinous wine, would tell on us in the contests the following day...

"The first day of the games was the 25th of March, the day of the Greek national celebration. The manifestations of the crowds were beyond description, from the early hours in Stadium and Hermes Streets and in Constitution Square, all of them festively decorated. At every moment the cheerful sounds of the various philharmonic bands, from Zakynthus, Leukas, Laurius, Patras etc. echoed everywhere. The visit of the Royal Family with their foreign guests and their retinue to the Metropolitan Cathedral for the doxology, and their return was made triumphantly midst the most enthusiastic cheers.

The crowds, however, were most excited at the inauguration of the International Olympic Games in the Stadium. All hastened from early morning to procure tickets. Ticket-sellers in the streets were surrounded by thick and noisy throngs. All hustled and vied to obtain the best possible seats, while the police were supervising them to see that there was no profiteering.

At noon started the massive going to the stadium. From all sides of the city set out dense crowds of citizens of all classes, ages and of both sexes. The density of the crowd around the area of the Zappeion was indescribable. Order, however, was maintained excellently. In the interior of the Stadium, order was enforced by armed soldiers placed at intervals in front of the stairs leading to the tiers.

The crowds entered long before the starting hour and by 3.30 pm. most of the stadium had been filled... One tier had been reserved for Members of the Parliament. Another was reserved for the officers, and a third for official guests and press representatives. The spectacle was magnificent: The variegated dresses of the ladies, their hats and the undulations of flags in the midst of the black mass of tens of thousands of spectators, the resplendent uniforms and the plumes of the officers, the waving flags, the line of spectators without tickets, perched on the tops of the surrounding small hills ... all contributed to a unique ... spectacle.

The decoration of the Stadium was exceptional. At the entrance very tall masts had been erected and on them hang standards and escutcheons [coats of arms] and a replica of an ancient tripod on each side. The members of the various committees were gathered on the track of the arena, together with curators and other officials. After that, the various bands made their entrance playing, and took their seats. The Royal Family sat on the royal marble thrones with purple-coloured coverings and greeted those present. To the right were seated the cabinet ministers, the members of the Holy Synod, and the foreign clergy in Athens. To the left were the diplomatic corps, the royal retinue, the foreign representatives etc.

Then, the Crown Prince advanced respectfully towards the King and delivered a speech while the spectators rose. The King then arose and with a sonorous voice answered: "I declare the opening of the first International Olympic Games in Athens. Long live the Nation! Long live the Greek People!" He raised his right hand. Immediately after, thunderous cheers echoed from the vast area of the stadium, answering the royal words."

The crowd of 100,000 which assembled for that first opening ceremony was one of the largest peaceful assemblies ever held up to that date anywhere in the world. The Games were held over ten days. Not many of the contests were genuinely "Olympic." There were forty-two events in ten sports but only the running events, the long jump, the discus throw and wrestling had been held in the ancient Games; the rest were unknown to the ancients or were not included by them in the original Olympic Games.

There were a large number of Greek contestants and many Americans from ivy league colleges. A handful of Oxbridge men and a tourist, together with two employees of the embassy who were nearly barred as "servants", made up the British contingent. Germany sent thirteen athletes and the Hungarians eight. The remaining states which participated were represented by even smaller numbers.

Thomas P. Curtis recorded an account of the contest he took part in: "As we stood on our marks, I was next to the French man, a short, stocky man. He, at that moment, was busily engaged in pulling on a pair of white kid gloves, and having some difficulty in doing so before the starting pistol. Excited as I was, I had to ask him why he wanted the gloves. 'Ah-ha!' he answered, 'zat is because I run before ze Keeng!'"

It was April, and that year spring was late. The temperature was unseasonably low. The sole American swimmer, having jumped into the water, instantly leapt out with an oath, and adamantly refused to get back in again.

On Thursday, 9th April the Greeks enjoyed two gymnastic successes. But Curtis recorded that: "The Greek hopes ... centred on two events, the discus and the marathon run. For the first they had the classic example to study and analyse, and for the second they had the precedent of the runner, who had run over almost identically the same course to announce the victory before dying."

"In the discus they were doomed to disappointment by a performance which illustrates as well as anything else the naivete of the contests. We had on our team a Princeton representative, Robert Garrett, a very powerful, long-armed athlete who had never seen a discus, let alone thrown one, but who decided to enter the event just for the sport of it. When the moment came, the Greek champion assumed the attitude of the Discobolus, which incidentally is a very trying and complicated attitude, and proceeded to make three perfect throws in the classic manner.

"Garrett, with no knowledge of form or of how to skim the awkward discus, caused infinite merriment by running up to the mark and completely flubbing his first two attempts. On his third attempt, aided by his great strength, great length of arm, and an enormous amount of good luck, he succeeded in 'sailing' the discus to a new record, beating the champion by almost a foot. This was a tragedy for Greece, but high comedy for us."

The marathon race was the highlight of the Games, and the Greeks took two of the first three places. [For an account of the first marathon race and a portrait of the victor, see volume two in this series, *Athens: The Suburbs*].

On the tenth and last day, the crowds in the stadium were about as many as on the day of the marathon race. The Royal Family was present, together with the Egyptian prince Mehmet Ali Pasha, brother of the Khedive. An English professor from Oxford University, recited an Olympic Ode which he had composed in ancient Greek in the manner of Pindar. After this, the King handed out the prizes: a branch of wild olive, a branch of laurel, the diplomas within blue and white circular rolls, the medals, silver for the first and bronze for the second, and a silver cup for the winner of the marathon race. The Olympic winners all had morning suits, except for the winner of the marathon, who wore a white foustanella. Finally there was a parade of the Olympic victors around the stadium. In the evening the Acropolis was illuminated with torches. The series of festivities was sealed by a banquet offered to the foreign athletes on the following day at Kifissia by the Municipality of Athens.

The sense of national self-confidence which the successful hosting of the Games engendered may not have actually provoked the Cretan crisis and a war that Greece launched and lost against Turkey in 1897, but as Michael Biddiss points out, "...the atmosphere of nationalistic fervour which they encouraged may well have hastened that conflict."

The Intercalary Olympiad

After this excellent start, the next two Olympiads, held in Paris in 1900 and St. Louis, USA, in 1904, were overshadowed by trade exhibitions. The Olympic movement received fresh impetus when an intercalary games was held in Athens in 1906. The Greeks had been lobbying to have the Games held permanently in their home country, but Baron de Coubertin would not agree, as he felt that this would undermine their international character. The Games of 1906 were a compromise.

At the opening ceremony on April 22nd, in addition to the Greek royal family, the British monarchs, King Edward VII and Queen Alexandra, were also present. For the first time, the contingents of the various nations marched into the stadium behind their national flags. This practice was to be repeated at the Games of 1908 in London, and has been continued ever since.

At that time, some of the political divisions which were later to rend Europe so tragically in 1914 and afterwards were already becoming apparent. The Greek members of the team from the Ottoman Empire would represent only their cities or islands of origin. The Hungarians and Bohemians from the Austro-Hungarian Empire fielded separate teams from the Germans. Several Irish athletes demanded not to be counted as part of the British team, asserting that they represented only Ireland.

It was originally intended to repeat these games in the home country every four years, but in 1908 and 1912 the disturbed situation in the Balkans would not allow it. In 1914 the nations found themselves involved in the Great War, and afterwards the situation in the Aegean precluded the revival of the Intercalary Games, and the idea was forgotten. It was not to be until 2004 that another Olympiad would be planned for the country in which the Olympic Games had their origin.

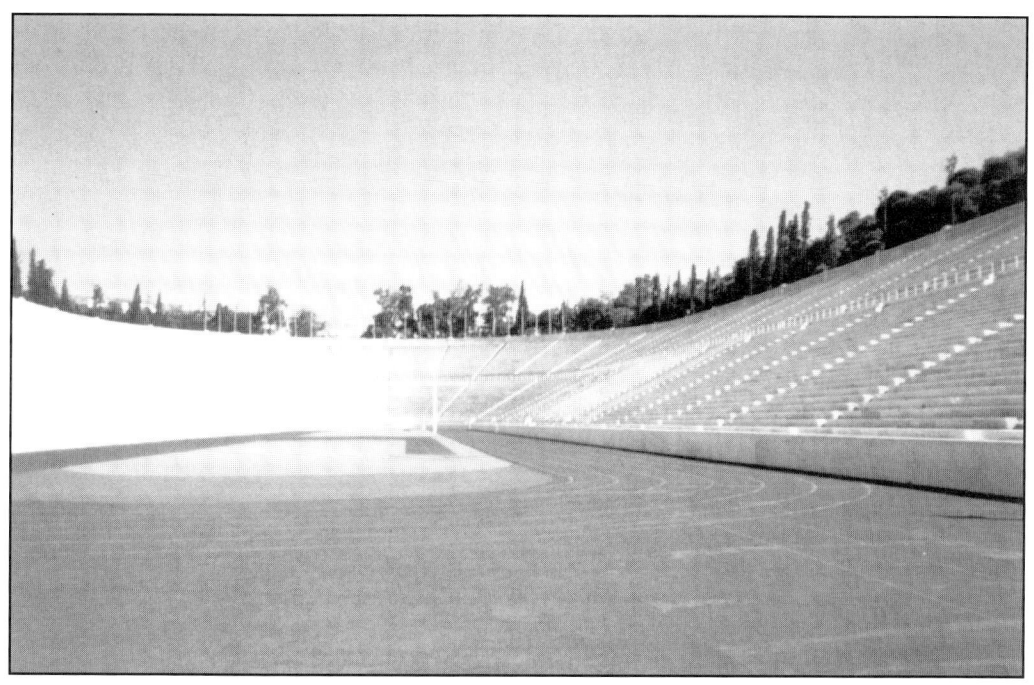

The Panathenaic Stadium, Athens,
site of the first Olympic Games of modern times.
Today it is more usually known to Athenians as
the "Kalimarmara" or "Beautiful Marble" Stadium

An Open-Air Gallery of the Sculptor's Art

Wealthy modern Athenians, no less than their ancient ancestors, have been inclined to erect magnificent grave monuments. The First Cemetery is the chief burial place of the City of Athens, and contains the grave monuments of many of the most famous citizens of the modern state, designed by its most highly-regarded sculptors, many from the island of Tinos. Today it is an open-air museum of the sculptors' art.

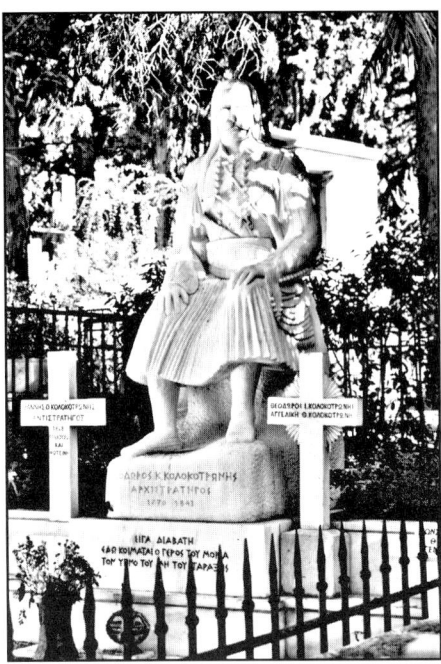
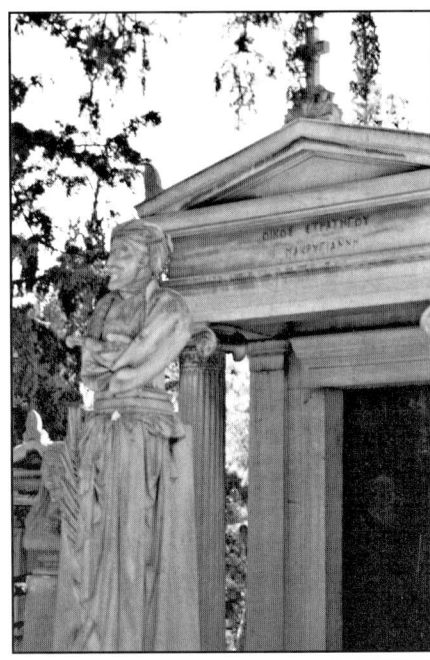

Tombs of the rich or famous:

Top left: Theodoros Kolokotronis

Top right: Ioannis Makriyiannis

Bottom: Evangelos Averof Tositsas

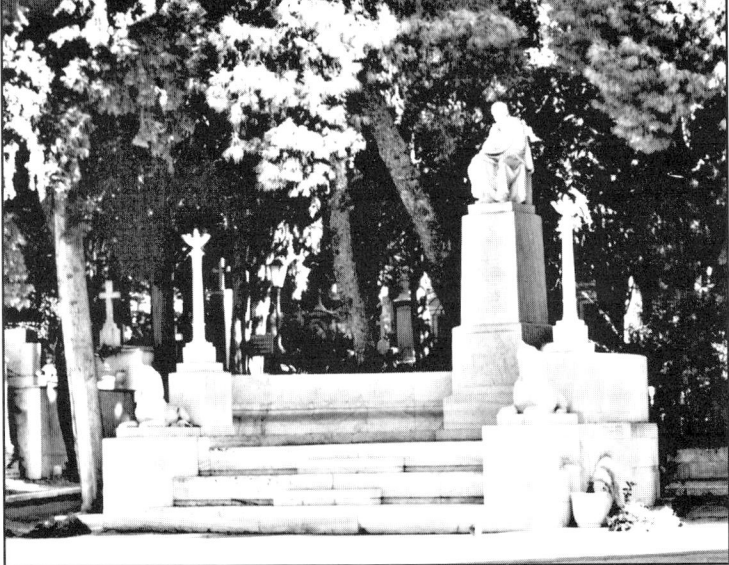

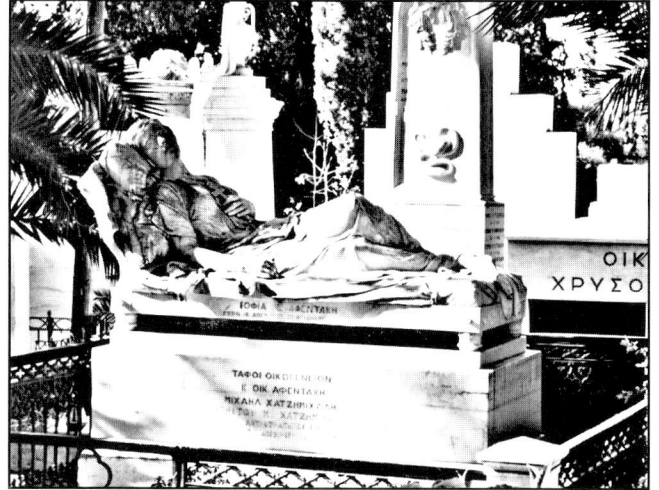

A common theme
of the
nineteenth century
monumental
stonemasons' art
was that of
the sleeping female figure,
known a "Koimomene",
which represented death.

*Above: The most popular
example of "Koimomene":
the tomb monument of
eighteen year-old Sophia
Aphentaki, by Yiannouli
Halepas (1851-1938).
Halepas was an artist
tormented by poverty and
progressive mental illness*

*Right: Another example:
the Spathari tomb (1895)*

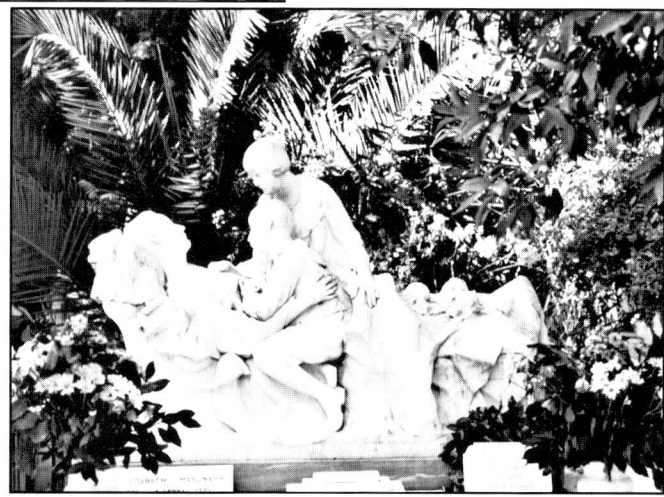

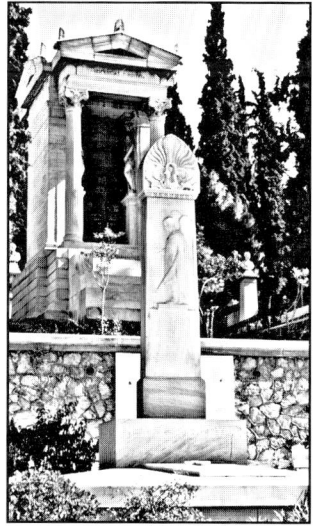

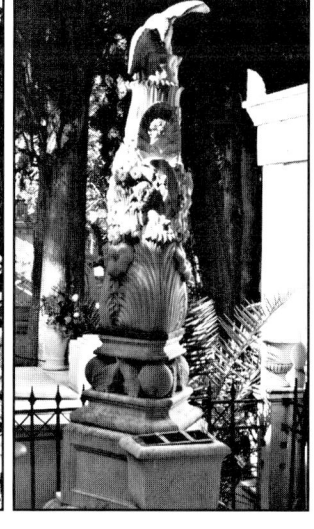

*Far left:
Melina Mercouri
(Koupi behind)*

Near left:Mitropoulou

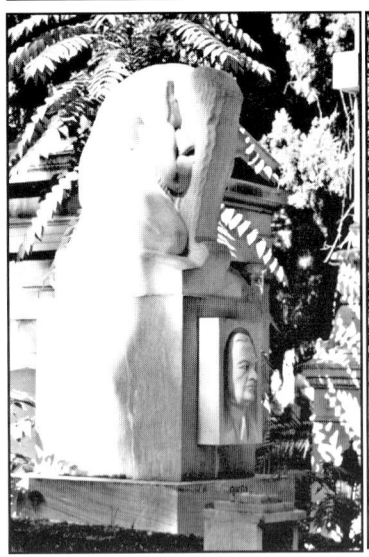

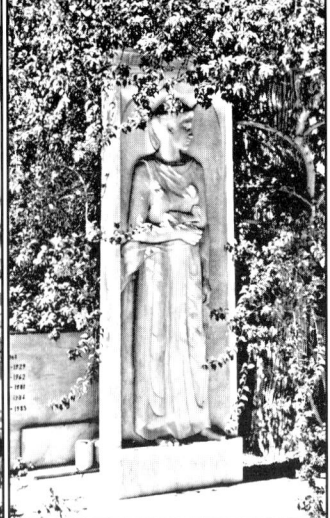

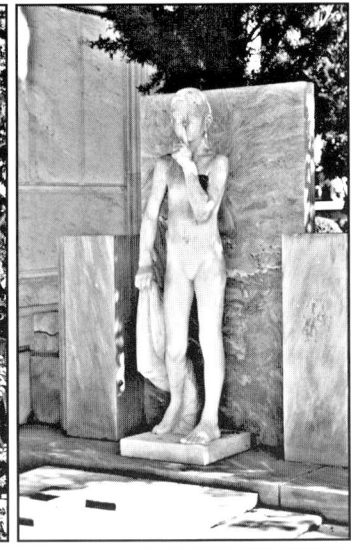

Above left: Papayannopoulou

Above centre: Georgopoulos

Above right: Belli

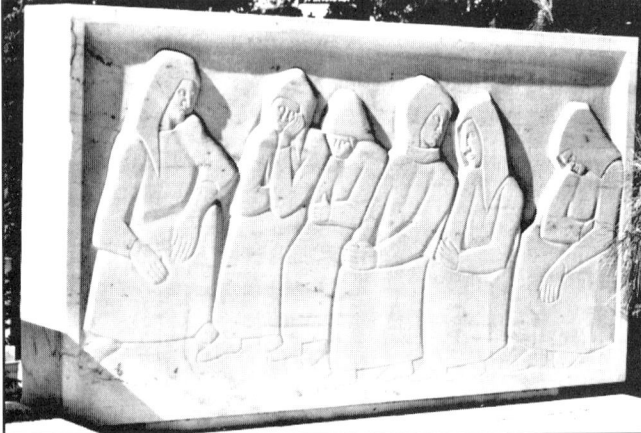

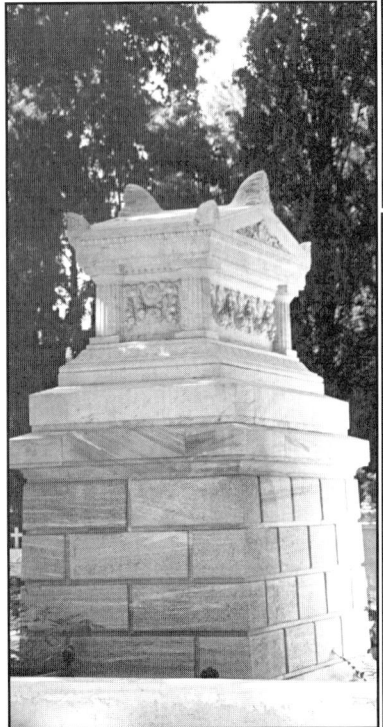

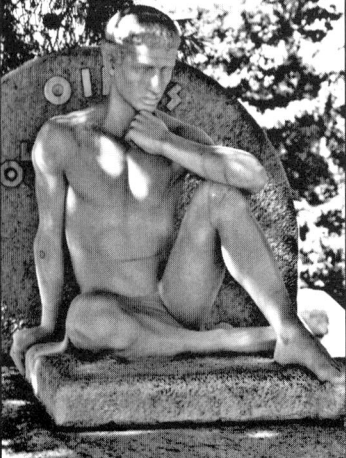

Above:
  Mandyla

Far left:
  Kakomanoli

Left:
  Theodoraki

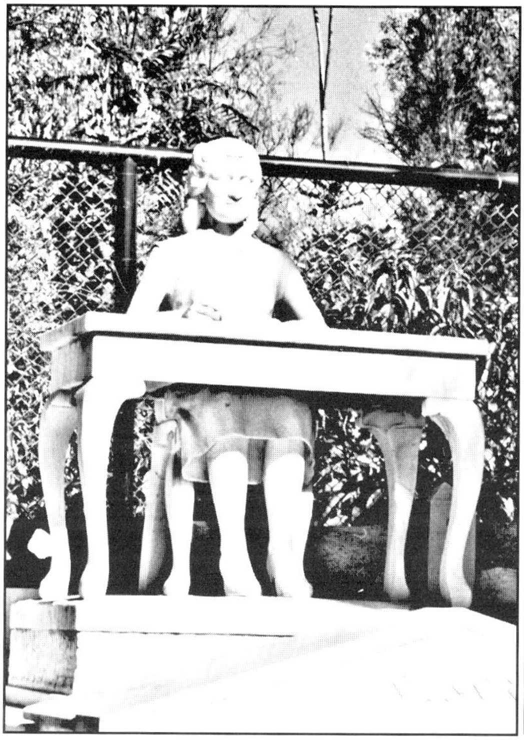

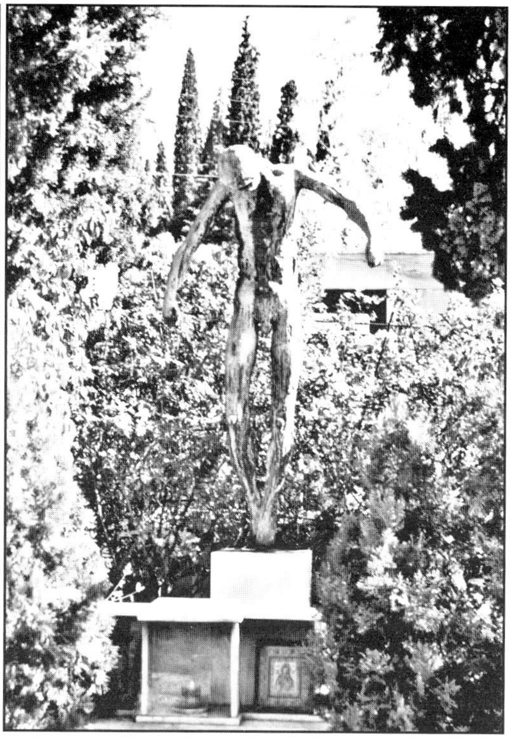

Some of the more recent tomb monuments are less traditional in style
Above left: Grammatopoulou   Above right: Goulandri
Below: Bentouratos

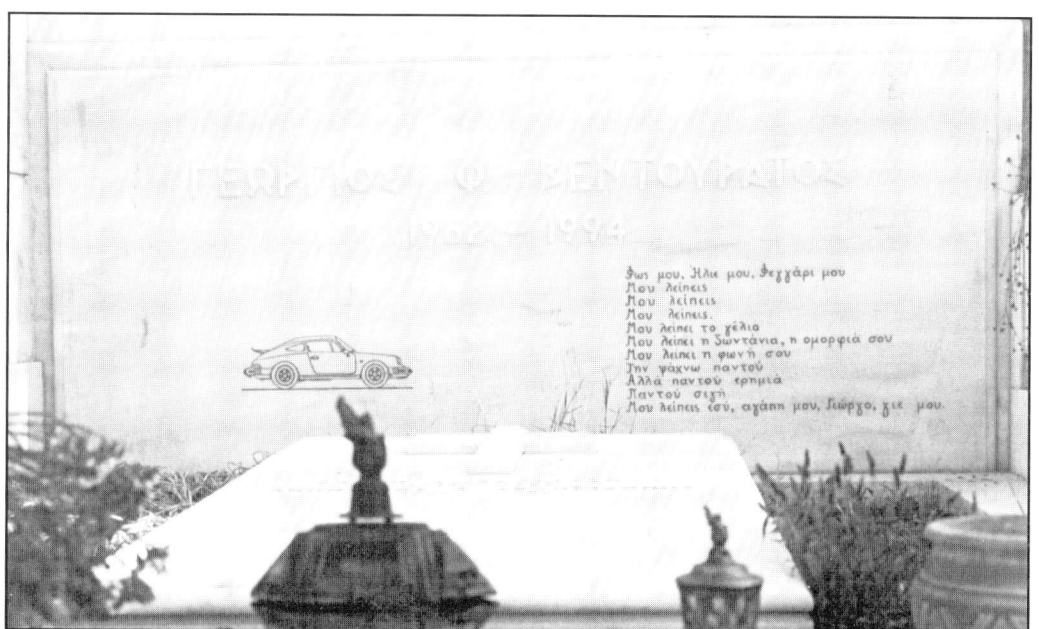

How to Get a Husband

The area of the Ilissos sooms to have long been connected in the public mind with courtship and marriage. The eighteenth century traveller John Galt heard of a method by whch girls would seek to ensure themselves a good marriage by leaving offerings on the banks of the now vanished stream.

"On my return to my lodgings ... the friar ... mentioned to me a curious practice of the young girls here when they become anxious to get husbands. On the first evening of the new moon, they put a little honey, a little salt, and a piece of bread on a plate, which they leave at a particular spot, on the bank of the Ilissus, near the Stadium, and muttering some antient words, of which the meaning has been forgotten, but which are to the effect that fate may send them "a pretty young man", they return home and long for the fulfilment of their charm. Above the spot where these offerings are made, a statue of Venus [Aphrodite], according to Pausanias, formerly stood. It is therefore highly probable, that what is now a superstitious, was antiently a religious rite."

The "Getting Married Place"

The process of getting married was frought with difficulties, and before the accessbility of easy divorce, couples would need to be very sure indeed that they were suitably matched. Sometimes this quest for peace of mind would take a long time, as a story from the district known as Metz clearly shows.

In 1870 the area above the Panathenaic Stadium and the First Cemetery was almost bare of buildings. There were only the windmills of Yeorgakis on the Hill of Ardittos, where the was manufactured. (The last of these was demolished only in 1986.) In 1870 a Bavarian entrepreneur opened a beer hall in this area, to which he gave the name "Metz" in honour of the victory over the French that year in the Franco-Prussian War. In time, the district which grew up around it took its name from this establishment.

It also became known at the turn of the century as the *Pantremenadika*, or "Getting Married Place". This name was used ironically, as the result of an event which took place there towards the end of the nineteenth century. An eighty year old man named Yiannis Marinos finally got married to his long-time fiancıe after a stormy sixty-year courtship, which had included many fierce quarrels, and several bitter partings and tearful reconciliations. By the time that he actually took the plunge and got married, his bride was seventy-five years of age. The celebration of their long-delayed nuptial revels was said to have been so enthusiastic and abandoned that both the "senior citizens" had to be carried to their beds on stretchers.

The name "Getting Married Place" continued to be used for some time after-wards in ironic reference to the many houses of ill-repute in the area.

City of the Intellect

The Schools

Athens became the chief centre of the Greek intellectual revolution as a result of the development of democracy; for it became necessary for the wealthy young man with political ambitions to develop skills of argument and persuasion. Teachers, called "sophists", sprang flocked to Athens to meet this need.

Socrates kindled the spark of critical thinking by developing the practice of philosophical dialogue. He devoted his time to discussions with aristocratic young men, insistently questioning their confidence in the obvious truth of conventional opinions. The parents of his students were displeased with the effects of his persistent and corrosive questioning, which undermined the plausibility of their own certainties. In 400/399, after some of them had been involved in an anti-democratic coup, he was brought to trial for failure to worship the gods and corrupting the young by criticism of democracy. Sentenced to drink the hemlock, he became a martyr for reason.

Plato, one of his disciples, set up a school on land sacred to the Muses, in the olive groves and the *gymnasion* of Hekademos (Akademos), north-west of the city. There he wrote and gave regular instruction to students for forty years. Young men from all over Greece converged on the Academy. They listened and took notes as Plato walked about lecturing. This was the world's first university.

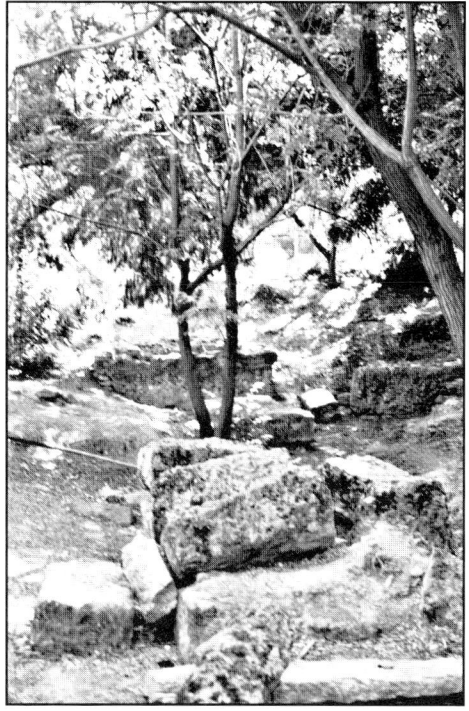

The most famous student of the Academy, Aristotle, in 335/4 founded his own institution in the sanctuary of Apollo Lyceus, which became known as the Lyceum, near the present Byzantine Museum. His students were known as Peripatetics (from the word for "walking") on account of their practice of engaging in their discussions while walking up and down a covered ambulatory.

Another school known as Cynics (dogs) was founded by Antisthenes, who taught in the gymnasium of Kynosarges (the dog's tail). Like all academic communities, Athens was not without its eccentrics. The cynic Diogenes taught that animal life was a model for mankind. An enemy of all conventions,

The Academy today

he advocated holding wives and children in common. Given to outrageous public gestures, he called himself "the Dog" and for a time lived in a barrel placed on its side, like a dog kennel, in the *agora*.

Zeno of Citium, in Cyprus, lectured in the Painted Stoa, and founded the school of the Stoics there. Materialists, who believed all knowledge to be founded on sense-perception, they taught that moral freedom from the passions is the basis of ethics. Epicurus of Samos opened a school in his garden and taught that all things are made of atoms in space, and that the goal of all human endeavour is ultimately pleasure. Finally, Pyrrho of Elis founded a school of sceptics, based upon the belief that knowledge is unattainable. We cannot know how things are, only how they appear to us.

The World's First University Town

With the spread of Greek learning throughout the Roman Empire, other centres of teaching and research sprang up, particularly Alexandria, in Egypt. No longer a centre of political power, Athens came to resemble the older provincial university towns of the modern world, such as Oxford, Cambridge or Heidelberg. Enlightened emperors were benefactors. Hadrian built a great library with a roof of alabaster sustained by one hundred marble columns. Professorial chairs were endowed, with truly academic impartiality, for each of the schools.

Edward Gibbon wrote:

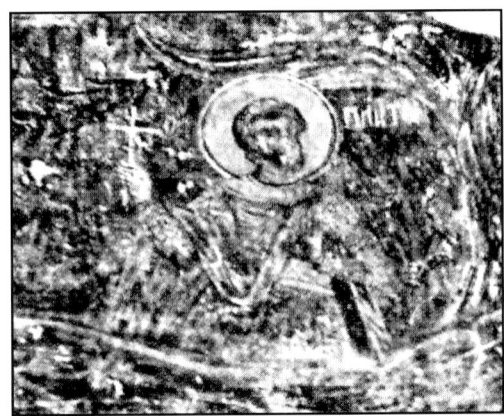

"Athens, though situate in a barren soil, possessed a pure air, a free navigation, and the monuments of ancient art. That sacred retirement was seldom disturbed by the business of trade or government; and the Athenians were distinguished by their lively wit, the purity of their taste and language, their social manners, and some traces, at least in discourse, of the magnanimity of their fathers. In the suburbs of the city, the *Academy* of the Platonists, the *Lyceum* of the Peripatetics, the *Portico* of the Stoics, and the *Garden* of the Epicureans, were planted with trees and decorated with statues; and the philosophers, instead of being immured in a cloister, delivered their instructions in spacious and pleasant walks, which at different hours were consecrated to the exercises of the mind and body. The genius of the founders still lived in those venerable seats; the

Above: "Saint Plato" (Ayios Platon): Faded sixteenth century wall painting in the chapel of the Archangels (Taxiarches) in the suburb of Maroussi. The church initially opposed the philosophers and closed down their schools. Later, the philosophy of Plato, the most amenable of them, became a source of pride, and he was occasionally accorded sainthood..

ambition of succeeding to the masters of human reason excited a generous emulation; and the merit of the candidates was determined, on each vacancy by the free voices of an enlightened people."

Yet Athens was hardly a dull city. Students flocked from all over the ancient world. They would group themselves around a teacher, to whom they would profess passionate loyalty, while developing an enthusiastic rivalry with other groups. Like all such groups, they developed bizarre initiation rites, and like the students of modern university towns, they frequently engaged in rags and demonstrations. New students arriving at Piraeus would be met at the quayside by rival groups of recruiters in an ancient "Freshers' Fair", who would try to press-gang the newcomers into joining their own groups. Inevitably there would, from time to time, be disturbances as members of one group fought, or even kidnapped, those of another.

In the end, it was not the violence of barbarians, but the rise of dogmatic Christianity, which spelled the end to this civilised way of life, for intellectual freedom was incompatible with the fierce dogmatism of the Church. In 529 AD, the pious emperor Justinian finally closed all the schools, and with it silenced the intellectual ferment sparked into flame by Socrates more than nine hundred years before.

A group of Athenian teachers, believing the emperor of Persia, Chosroes, to be an enlightened monarch, decamped there *en masse*. To their chagrin they discovered there what they had fled in Athens, and more: "haughty nobles, servile courtiers, unjust officials and an intolerant and dogmatic priesthood." Returning disillusioned, they ended their lives in obscurity, and the flame of learning quietly expired.

The Quick-Witted Shepherd

The Athenians never quite lost their awareness of their former intellectual pre-eminence, as is illustrated by the following folk tale:

The fame of the wise men of Athens was so great that it irked those of other cities. At one time the intellectuals of rival cities gathered together and determined to travel *en masse* to Athens, to see for themselves whether they might challenge and outdo the Athenians, and so put an end, once and for all, to their reputation.

Hearing of their purpose one of the wise men of Athens, named Thodoros dressed up as a shepherd, took a shepherd's crook and a flock of sheep, and went down to Piraeus to await the visitors. When they landed, the first person they saw was this man, whom they took to be a shepherd, and they determined to make a preliminary investigation by testing his wits. They quickly gathered around him, and one of the philosophers abruptly questioned him: "Whence, where, who and how many?"

Without any hesitation, and with equal alacrity, the "shepherd" replied: "From Athens, to graze, Thodoros and five hundred."

Shocked at the speed of this response, especially from one they considered to belong to the lowest intellectual level, the visitors decided that if a mere shepherd could demonstrate such quick wits, they would stand no chance at all against the real intellectuals of Athens. They called off their plan and promptly sailed away.

Two Athenian Saints

Despite its strong association with pagan learning, Athens seems to have been the birthplace of a surprising number of Christian saints, although little is known of most of them. They include, however, no less than three early martyr-bishops of Rome, or popes: Anacletus, (103-112), Hyginos (154-158) and Sixtus II (257-8). The first bishop of Athens, Ierotheos, Pouplios, bishop during the second century, and Leonides, bishop during the third, were martyred. Others appear in the lives of the saints which formed much of the reading matter of the Middle Ages. Many travelled far from Athens for their faith. A councillor who was converted by Saint Paul and became a missionary to the French, is better known as Saint-Denys. Another apostle of the French is known to the Scots as Saint Giles, and the great cathedral of Edinburgh is dedicated in his name. Just two are included here: one an example of the tales of extreme asceticism beloved by the Byzantines, the other which illustrates the problems which a Christian could encounter under Muslim Turkish rule.

A Hirsute Ascetic

In the middle of the fourth century two ascetics named Serapion and John lived in the desert of northern Egypt. One evening, Serapion had a dream that a man came to him with a command from Christ to go to a particular mountain in Ethiopia. After four days he reached the city of Alexandria. There he was told that there were two ways to get to his destination, one was to follow the coast road, and the other was a very dangerous inland route across the desert. Naturally, being an ascetic, Serapion chose the more difficult option.

He had been walking through the desert for thirty-five days when he settled down for the night outside a cave. As he was lying there, he heard a human voice raised in prayer to Christ. Then a man appeared in the darkness at the opening of the cave and greeted him by name. This stranger told a remarkable tale. He was named Mark, and he was an Athenian. Raised as an idolater, he had studied in the famous schools of Athens; but at the age of twenty he had been baptised, and after the death of his parents he had given his inheritance to the poor and left for Alexandria. Dissatisfied with life in the city he had chosen to move deep into the desert. He claimed to be one hundred and thirty years old, and said that Serapion was the first living person he had met for ninety-five years. After some conversation, the two slept.

When the sun rose next morning, Serapion was shocked to discover that the body of the man he had been talking to in the darkness was covered in a thick coat of hair, like an animal. The stranger told him not to be afraid, for that was the way in which Christ had protected him from the extremes of temperature in the desert. He asked whether the persecution of Christians had ceased, and Serapion replied that it had. Mark than said that God had sent Serapion to him on the last day of his life to bury him. He spent the rest of the day in prayer, finally saying farewell to the plants and animals that had been his companions for so many years. Then he re-entered his cave and asked God to receive his soul. A supernatural light lit up the scene, and the air was filled with the perfume of flowers. When Serapion saw two bright angels bowing before the ascetic, he fainted with fear.

When he awoke, he took stones and blocked up the entrance to the cave and went on his way, telling everyone whom he encountered of his strange meeting with Mark, the hairy Athenian hermit.

A Modern Martyr

Although the early centuries under pagan Roman rule were the great period of Christian martyrdom, rule by the Mohammedan Turks ensured that martyrs would not be unknown among modern Greeks. The story of Anthony of Athens illustrates how difficult life could be for poor Christians, without influence or wealth, under the arbitrary rule of the Turks. Although the Muslims tolerated Judaism and Christianity as "religions of the book", Turkish tolerance had severe limits. In any case, to be converted from Islam to another religion carries the death penalty even today in any country where the Sharia, Islamic Law, is strictly enforced.

Born of poor Athenian parents, Anthony began work for some Muslim Albanians who lived nearby when he was twelve years of age. At the age of sixteen they sold him to a Turk who lived in the Peloponnese. He tried to get Anthony to convert to Islam, and beat him when he resisted. This Turk sold him in turn, and Anthony passed successively through the hands of several Turkish owners, each of whom who beat him for the same reason. Finally he was sold to a Christian who employed him in Constantinople, and at last his life seemed to have improved somewhat.

But then one of his former owners complained to the authorities, alleging that Anthony had at one time actually converted to Islam, and then had subsequently apostatised. Anthony was arrested and brought before judge Murat Moulan. Eschewing any flattery, Anthony admitted his Christian faith, but maintained that he had always been a Christian, and that he had never wavered in this. Affected by his transparent honesty, the judge sought to free him, but he was afraid of the scandal that this might cause if it became public, and so he passed the problem on to the vizier, Mehmet Melek. The vizier was similarly inclined to release Anthony, and for the same reasons, but he also was afraid of the consequences of this decision for his own career, and so he referred the matter directly to Sultan Hamid. The Sultan, himself feared that Muslim fundamentalists would provoke riots if Anthony was released while still an unrepentant Christian, so he ordered that he was to be given one final opportunity to renounce his faith and accept Islam. If he accepted, he would be freed; but if he still refused, he was to be beheaded. When Anthony declined to surrender his faith, he was duly executed.

Three Athenian Empresses

Although under Byzantine rule Athens was a provincial backwater, Athenian citizens were occasionally catapulted into the centre of the maelstrom of Byzantine politics.

A Pious Convert

When the young Theodosius II, came to the imperial throne, his older sister, Pulcheria, a woman of strong character, determined to keep a close influence over her brother and over imperial policy. When the time came for him to seek a wife, Pulcheria carefully guided his choice. At that time a young Athenian woman, Athenaos, daughter of the famous pagan philosopher Leontius, was in Constantinople seeking to press a dispute with her brothers over their inheritance. Somehow, she was brought to the attention of Pulcheria, who decided after investigation that Athenaos would be a suitable bride, and that her family were sufficiently obscure to be no threat to her. Born in 401, Athenaos had already been educated in grammar, rhetoric and philosophy. She was a pagan, but she was quickly baptised, taking the name Eudocia.

At first Eudocia was subservient to Pulcheria, but during the 430s as she gained in self-confidence her influence increased. Despite the quarrel over their inheritance, she placed her own brothers in important positions. Always proud of her Greek blood, she profoundly influenced the gradual transformation of the Eastern Roman Empire into a thoroughly Greek state. When her husband founded the university of Constantinople, under her influence more professorships were established in Greek than in Latin. Under her protection, Cyrus, the Imperial Prefect, discarded Latin in official edicts and documents, and began issuing decrees in the Greek language only.

In 438 Eudocia went on a pilgrimage to the Holy Land as a result of a misunderstanding over an apple. One day, as the emperor was going to church, someone in the crowd presented him with a particularly large and beautiful apple. The emperor presented it to Eudocia. She gave it to Paulinus, the emperor's friend from his youth, who was ill in bed. Without knowing where it came from, he gave it to the emperor. Theodosius immediately suspected his friend and his wife of having an affair. Paulinus was executed, and the emperor's love towards his wife turned to hatred.

Naturally, Eudocia's influence waned sharply. One of her brothers was beheaded "for plotting against the emperor," and her protégé Cyrus dismissed for paganism. To save his life, Cyrus consented to become a cleric. He was consecrated bishop of Colyaeum, a see whose last four bishops had been murdered by their reluctant "flock".

When Eudocia returned to Constantinople she seemed to weary of politics, and asked to be allowed to return to Jerusalem in retirement. Although this was granted, she was not left in peace. Saturninus, sent to spy on her, had two priests in her household beheaded. When Saturninus was himself murdered, Eudocia was accused of paying to have him eliminated, and was deprived of her right to a train of attendants. Even so, she still had a generous allowance, which she used to build churches and monasteries. She died peacefully in Jerusalem in 460.

According to a popular tradition in Athens, at some point Eudocia returned briefly to the city of her birth as empress and erected no less than twelve churches there.

The Sainted Empress who Murdered her Son

During the eighth century the Byzantine Empire was riven by a fierce and bloody controversy over the veneration of icons. Influenced by Muslim ideas, many Asiatic Christians wished to ban their use. These "iconoclasts", as they were called, gained the support of the emperors. Constantine V Coprynymos ("name of manure"), earned his insulting nickname by rigidly enforcing this policy, bitterly resented by the monks, and probably by a majority of the population. His son Leo showed signs of willingness to compromise. At least, he chose to marry Irene, an orphan of the Sarandapichos family from the Plaka, in the strongly iconophile city of Athens. Before the wedding, however, he had her swear never to venerate icons again.

It seems likely that Irene was chosen as Leo's husband in a bridal competition, as was the custom. Talent scouts would be sent across the empire with specifications of the physical and mental qualities worthy of an empress. These included, for example, a particular range of measurements of the head, face and feet, to ensure the correct proportions. The successful candidates were assembled for the emperor's choice. Leo and Irene married in 769, and in 771, Irene bore a son, Constantine.

After his father's death in 775, her husband ascended the imperial throne as Leo IV. Irene was allowed to appoint iconophiles to many posts of state, and even to install her own candidate, Paul of Cyprus, as patriarch. However, when Leo discovered two icons in his wife's quarters, he decided that it was necessary to assert his authority. All those implicated were paraded in chains, flogged and then forced to become monks. The Emperor did not believe Irene's own protestations of innocence, since the icons had been discovered in her bedchamber. She was officially disgraced and barred from marital relations with her husband.

According to a rather suspicious official account written by iconophile clerics, six months later Leo conceived an insane passion for a crown studded with pearls which the emperor Heraklion had donated to the church of Ayia Sophia over a hundred years before. He stole it, but when he put it on, boils broke out on his head and he died shortly afterwards, in September 780.

His son, Constantine VI, was only nine years-old, and Irene became regent for him. In 786 she summoned a council of the Church, which met in the City on 31st July 786 to reinstate icon worship, but a group of soldiers burst into the church and broke up the meeting. Biding her time, she had the iconoclast troops moved to Asia Minor, and replaced them with iconophiles from Thrace. In May 787 she called the council again, this time in Nicaea. This meeting, attended by three hundred and fifty bishops is the seventh and last ecumenical council recognised by the Orthodox Churches. The veneration of icons was declared to be true doctrine, and iconoclasm a heresy.

Some historians consider Irene to have been a secret iconophile who cleverly overcame the opposition by guile. Others see her as a Machiavellian character who simply used the religious controversy as a means of gaining the support of the many discontented iconophiles.

Disgruntled iconoclasts soon began to gather around her son, who began to resent his mother's exercise of the imperial power. Sensing growing opposition, in spring 790 she required the army to take an oath of allegiance to her as senior ruler. But elite army units in Asia Minor refused, proclaiming her son as sole ruler. Her gamble had failed. Irene had to acknowledge the rights of her son and was banished from the palace, although in January 792, her son unwisely allowed her to return.

He then divorced his popular wife, chosen for him by Irene, and took a mistress. When he married her and crowned her empress, he offended the monks and much of the population of the city. At the height of his unpopularity, on 15th August 797, Irene struck. Her son was cornered in the porphyry room, where he had been born, and was blinded, and formally deposed as emperor. Shortly afterwards, he died of his wounds.

The first woman ever to rule the Roman Empire in her own right, she styled herself *emperor* rather than *empress*. Unusually dark weather for seventeen days which followed the blinding of the emperor was interpreted by the people as mirroring his loss of sight. So in an effort to court popularity, Irene drastically reduced the taxes, which was certainly very effective in achieving its immediate aim, but over time it ruined the state finances.

Irene's triumph was not to last. First, her late husband's five brothers conspired against her. The eldest had already lost his eyes, and the other four their tongues, for an earlier plot. On this occasion, they were sent to Athens, where they were isolated from potential allies and could be watched by Irene's countrymen. When even there they plotted with the Slavs, the four tongueless brothers also lost their eyes.

The irregularity of a woman sitting on the imperial throne in Constantinople was the pretext which led the pope to crown Charlemagne, King of the Franks, as emperor in Rome on Christmas Day 800, creating a new and rival "Roman Empire" in the West, and increasing the rift between the divided parts of Christendom. In 802 Charlemagne offered to marry Irene to reunite East and West, and a delegation visited the city for that purpose. But the presence of a woman on the imperial throne was seen by many as an unnatural perversion of the proper order of things. Shortly after the delegation from Charlemagne arrived, Irene was deposed by Nicephorus, her minister of finance, who became emperor in her place. She was first exiled to the Princes Islands in the Sea of Marmara, and then to Lesbos, where she died.

During her reign, Irene is said to have founded many churches in Athens, including many in the Plaka, the neighbourhood from which her family originally came.

A Dying Husband and a Castrated Monk

The Emperor Nicephorus I had a son and a daughter, the daughter, Procopia, being married to Michael Rangavı. On December 20th 807, a beauty show was assembled in the palace to select a consort for his son, Stauracius. Nicephorus' choice fell on Theophano, an Athenian girl who was a distant relation of the empress Irene.

On July 26th 811, the imperial army was disastrously defeated by the Bulgarians, and the emperor killed. Stauracius was rescued, but he suffered severe spinal injuries and was not expected to live long. Yet no time was lost in having him proclaimed emperor, in order to prevent the situation from deteriorating even further. Stauracius had no children, and as his condition worsened, he wavered between two alternatives. One was to make his wife his heir, ruling in her own right as Irene had done. The second was to repeal the ancient and forgotten law which centuries before had passed the supreme authority in the Roman state from the Senate and people of Rome to the emperors, and reintroduce some form of democracy.

To the alarmed patriarch, neither the ambitions of Theophano nor the idealistic ravings of her dying husband appealed as solutions to the pressing problem of the immediate security of the Empire. He proposed that the death of the emperor should be anticipated and his son-in-law, Michael Rangavı, placed on the throne. When, on October 1st, it appeared that the emperor was about to have Rangavı blinded in order to pre-empt this option, the conspirators moved. The troops were assembled in the Hippodrome to acclaim Michael. To protect what remained of his life, Stauracius was tonsured and arrayed in monk's costume on his bed, rendering him legally unable to function as emperor. Thus his life could no longer be seen as a threat by the usurper. Similarly, Theophano prudently expressed her desire to retire to a cloister. Stauracius lingered for three months, but after a while the stench from his wounds grew so bad that no one would approach him, and he died on 11th January 812. Rumour in Constantinople suggested that his sister had helped him on his way with poison. He was buried in the monastery of Braka, which Procopia had founded for Theophano, who spent the rest of her life as abbess of the monastery.

Michael Rangavı was not to last long as emperor. In 813 Leo the Armenian seized the throne and sent the old royal family into exile. As a form of insurance against a counter-coup, Michael's son, Theophylact, who had been married to Adelinda, bastard daughter of Charlemagne in an attempt to unite the two empires, was castrated to make him ineligible as emperor in the future. He became a monk and retired to a monastery in Athens.

It was he who, according to a local tradition, founded the church of Saint Nicholas Rangavı in the Plaka, in an area which he had purchased, and which came to be known afterwards by his family name.

The church has been extensively rebuilt at some time, but traces of the older building are visible. It boasted the first bells in Athens after Independence; and it was the first to ring for the liberation after the departure of the Germans in 1944.

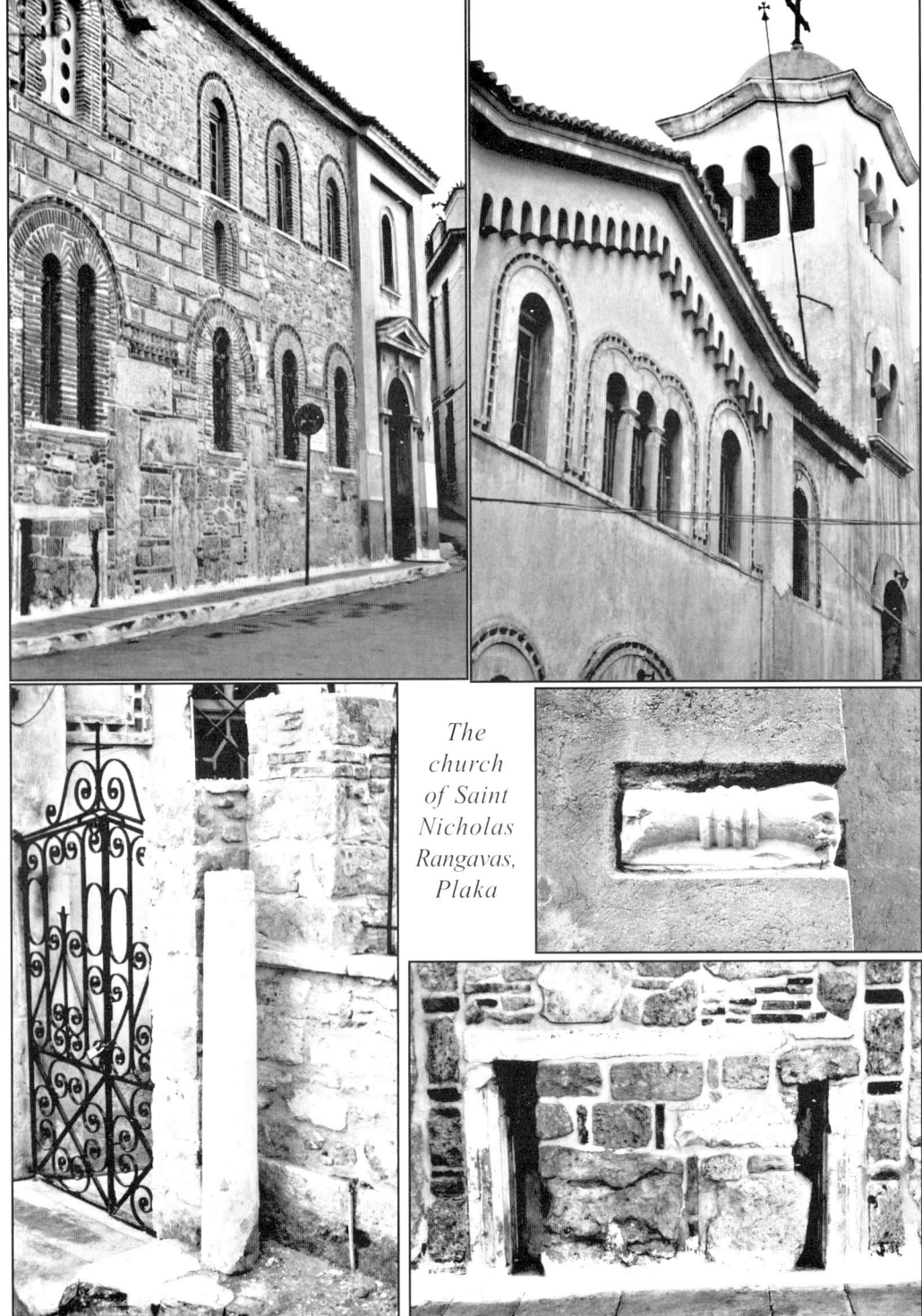

The church of Saint Nicholas Rangavas, Plaka

Saracen City? - A Historical Mystery

A document lying in the former Imperial Library in St. Petersburg, and dated to the sixteenth or seventeenth century, describes a strange anachronistic "Persian" invasion of Attica. This document takes the form of a lament, and pictures Athens as a woman grieving. It records that attackers burst into the city, killed the leaders of the community and the priests, destroyed the houses of the people, defiled the icons, polluted the churches, and raped the women and boys: " ... and Athens subsides and groans and weeps, and simply cannot endure it."

Scholars have always assumed that this manuscript refers either to the fall of Athens to the Turks in 1456, or to an earlier Turkish raid. But the famous historian of Athens, G. Kambouroglou, argued that it reveals an unrecorded, and hitherto unknown, Arab occupation of Athens during the late ninth or early tenth centuries.

The *Lament* also says that the peasants of Sepolia, to the north-west of the city, had lived in freedom and great joy before the attack. Kambouroglou argues that this could hardly refer to the Crusader period, which preceded the Turkish occupation.

During the late ninth and early tenth century, settlements on the Aegean were constantly harassed by Saracen raiders from Egypt. In 827 they captured Crete and founded Kandak (modern Iraklion). They seized Aigina, raided the Peloponnese and Euboea, and held Volos, before being expelled by emperor Nikephorus Phocas.

Kambouroglou pointed out that there are no Greek inscriptions in Athens surviving from this period, while there are for the periods immediately before and after; and that all the oldest churches in Athens were rebuilt shortly after this period. He also draws attention to a variety of inscriptions to be found in Arabic, incorporated into the fabric some of the older churches. Animal reliefs showing eastern influence are found in the walls of other churches. An Arabic inscription found on the site of the Asklepeion seems to have been part of an inscription adorning a mosque.

Cufic inscriptions found in Athens

(Byzantine Museum, Athens)

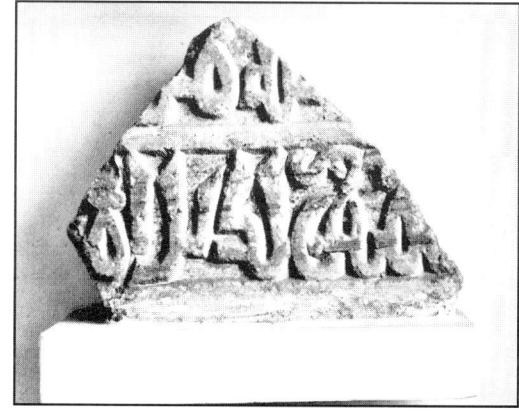 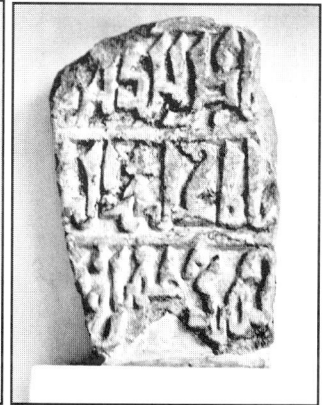

79

A Midsummer Night's Dream

Although Shakespeare's Midsummer Night's Dream is ostensibly set in ancient Athens in the time of Theseus, its real setting is medieval Athens as conceived by the Elizabethan playwright. The leading character of the play, Theseus, is "Duke of Athens" surrounded by a medieval court enjoying an idyllic environment.

In 1204 the Fourth Crusade was diverted to sack Constantinople, causing the temporary eclipse of the Byzantine Empire. The Norman adventurers dismembered it, carving out fiefdoms, where they established their courts and fought among themselves. Attica fell to a Burgundian knight, Otho de la Roche, who initially bore the title *Grand Seigneur* of Athens and Thebes. The Orthodox were ejected from the best churches and replaced by Catholic immigrants. In a remarkably short time, many of these would-be crusaders made themselves at home in Greece.

The Dukes of Athens

In 1246, William of Villhardouin Prince of Achaia, found himself at war with the Venetians and called upon his vassals to assist him. Guy de la Roche, the "Great Lord" of Athens, technically his vassal, not only refused to aid him, but assisted his enemies. In retaliation, William crossed the isthmus and confronted Guy's army at the pass of Mount Karydi. Guy fled the field of battle, leaving many of his warriors dead, and was forced to appear before the High Court of the barons of Achaia.

But when Guy stood before the court, he asserted that William and the barons of Achaia were not his peers, and incompetent to judge him. He appealed over their heads to the most respected monarch of Christendom, King Louis IX of France. At this, the assembled barons agreed to defer to the judgement of the saintly king.

Guy duly appeared at the court of King Louis, who decided that he had been guilty of a technical offence, but a minor one, and that his journey to Paris was penalty enough in itself. The king told Guy he could not return empty-handed, and asked what favour he might desire. Guy requested the title "Duke of Athens", and his wish was granted.

The title was enshrined in literature when Dante, Boccaccio, Chaucer, and later, Shakespeare, each anachronistically used it to describe Theseus. All of them, with the exception of Shakespeare, were contemporary with the duchy, and it was natural for them to think of the ruler of Athens as duke.

In 1308, the ambitious Walter of Brienne inherited the dukedom. Having alienated many surrounding princes, he called in a company of Catalan mercenaries to his defence. They proved an even greater threat than his enemies, and when he attempted to drive them away, he was defeated. In 1311 the Catalan Company took Athens and Manfred, the second son of Frederick of Sicily, became duke in his place.

The Catalans were never popular, and in time the Florentine Nerio Acciajuoli, lord of Corinth and Megara decided to add Athens to his dominions. He had alliances with the despot of Mistra, and the Imperial viceroy of Thessaloniki. When the Navarrese threatened Mistra, Nerio gathered an army. His forces ready, he required only a pretext. In the county of Salona, a fief of the Catalan Duchy, lived the widowed countess Helene and her daughter, Maria. Nero made her the offer of marriage to his brother-in-law, Pietro Saraceno. The dowager countess was a descendant of a Byzantine emperor and scornfully refused to give her daughter to a "Florentine tradesman".

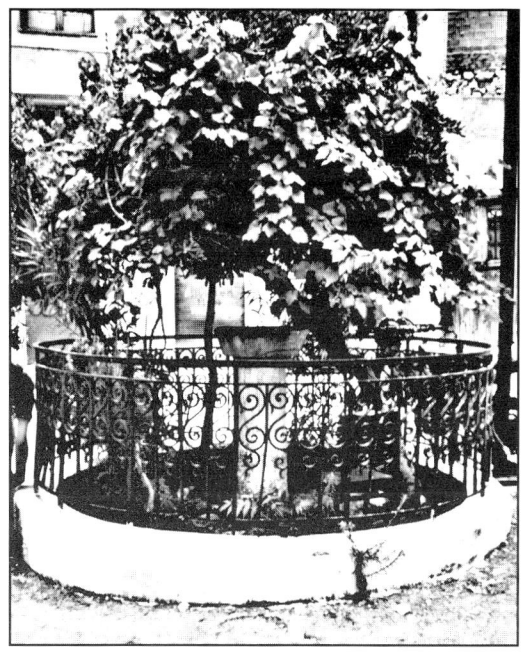

Outside the church of the Archangels (Taxiarchoi) in the Plaka is the base of an ancient column surmounted by a marble slab. It was part of the altar of the now-vanished church of Profitis Elias, chapel of the Sicilian-Catalan dynasty which ruled Athens from 1311-1388. It is a rare relic of those Western mercenaries

Nerio invaded Attica, and by 1387 he was in Athens. Despite their loss, the kings of Aragon and Sicily continued to style themselves Dukes of Athens. The title was inherited by the kings of Spain and continued in use until the end of the seventeenth century.

The easy going nature of Nerio's rule endeared him to his Greek subjects. When he died, he left his income from the city, together with that earned from his famous stud farm to replate the doors of the Parthenon with silver.

His successor Antonio was as Greek as he was Italian. There was no antagonism between the Greeks and the small Florentine community, which boasted names like Medici and Machiavelli, for Florentine rule was infinitely preferable to Burgundian or Catalan. The city of Athens, which had dwindled to the size of a large village, enjoyed a brief revival. Despite occasional Turkish raids, "agriculture blossomed under the care of Albanian peasants and the wooded mountains were used for hunting and hawking." Nicolo Machiavelli wrote to a cousin: "You have never seen a fairer land nor yet a fairer fortress than this."

Many of the Florentines remained in Greece after the Turkish conquest. The Medici hellenized their names to Iatros.Some returned to Italy when the Turks conquered the city, but others stayed on and intermarried with Greeks. One hundred and fifty years later, the Iatropoulos family, which flourished in Athens and Nauplion, claimed descent from them.

The Plaka

The Capuchin Monastery

One of the most striking of the sights of Athens is the choregic monument of Lysikrates. Erected to commemorate a series of plays for the Greater Dionysia, it was originally but one of many such which lined the street now named Tripodon.

The Jesuits had a house next to it until 1658, when the Capuchins, an order of Franciscan friars, purchased. In 1669, friar Simon decided to acquire the adjacent property, which contained the monument, which was converted for use as a Catholic chapel. The former owner decided to get it back, citing a law that no foreigner could own a historical monument. Despite the fact that he had become a naturalised citizen, the court, headed by the archbishop, awarded the monument to its previous owner. The friar appealed to a Turkish judge, who returned it to the priory, provided only that access was provided to visitors. The monument was later converted into a library.

In addition to introducing the tomato to Greece and providing a burial place for Catholics, the friars also offered hospitality to foreign visitors. Chateaubriand visited in 1806, and later Byron fled there to escape the matchmaking mother of Teresa Makri, where he wrote part of *Childe Harold*. John Galt described his quarters thus:

"I have taken up my lodgings in the Capuchin convent, belonging to the Propaganda of Rome. The choregic monument of Lysicrates...is attached to it and serves as a closet to the friar who has charge of the house. He has given me the use of it, and I have no less a pleasure, at this moment, than writing in one of the oldest and most elegant buildings in Europe."

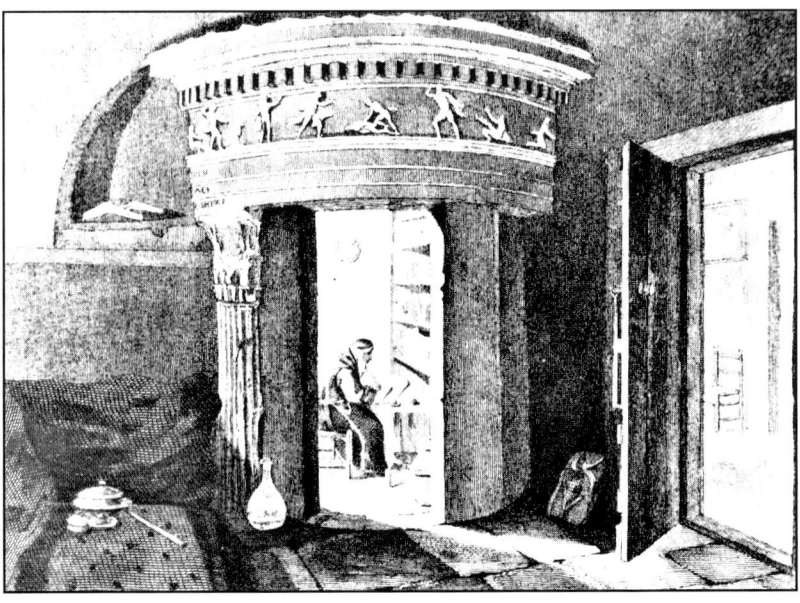

The choregic monument as a library (Pomardi, 1819)

An Island Village at the Foot of the Acropolis

We normally regard squatters as threatening the beauty of any area into which they move, but in nineteenth century Athens, squatters created a settlement which is today one of the most charming and picturesque parts of the city.

The area of the Plaka situated immediately at the foot of sheer northern face of the Acropolis, now known as Anafiotika, was called in ancient times as the "Black Stones". The Delphic oracle forbade the building of houses there, perhaps because it was the site of ancient sanctuaries, but during the Peloponnesian War refugees from outside the city initiated a long tradition of illegal settlement there.

During the Turkish period African slaves from Ethiopia lived in this district. They originally found shelter in the caves at the foot of the Acropolis, but later they built out from the base of the rock. They were still living there in 1841, when Hans Christian Anderson visited Athens. But shortly afterwards, the area immediately at the foot of the Acropolis was cleared of dwellings for archaeological investigation.

When Athens was chosen as the new capital city, islanders were drawn to it in large numbers, seeking work in the construction industry. There were builders from Skopelos, diggers from Naxos, carpenters from Andros and marble-masons from Tinos. Because of their low wages, they were unable to buy land on which to build homes for themselves. Then one night, two craftsmen from Anafi, Damigos and Sigalas, a mason and a carpenter, who were working on repairs to the walls of the Acropolis, each built himself a house at the foot of the rock. Others soon followed. The erection of dwellinghouses on this land was illegal, and would take place overnight. By the time that the authorities noticed another building in the morning, a family would already be installed in their new home.

The steep and rocky nature of the ground was not a problem for the islanders, who built exactly as they would have done on their own islands. For that reason, today the steep, narrow, whitewashed lanes still resemble a village on one of the Cycladic islands, rather than the concrete city all around.

On the eastern boundary of their settlement the islanders took over and rebuilt a dilapidated church dedicated to Saint George. Inside they hung embroideries in the style of the islands from which they had come, and tiny votive offerings in the form of houses, in thanksgiving for the new homes they had managed to build. On the far, western end, they took over the church of Saint Simeon, where they installed a copy of the miraculous icon of Our Lady Kalamiotissa from the island of Anafi, together with more ex-votos in the form of houses. A priest from Anafi administered both churches.

Although the houses in this area closest to the foot of the cliff face were all demolished during the 1950s at the behest of the archaeologists, a remnant escaped and remains as a tiny secret "island village", tucked away beneath the Acropolis. Appropriately, given the origin of many of the inhabitants, it has come to be known as "Anafiotika".

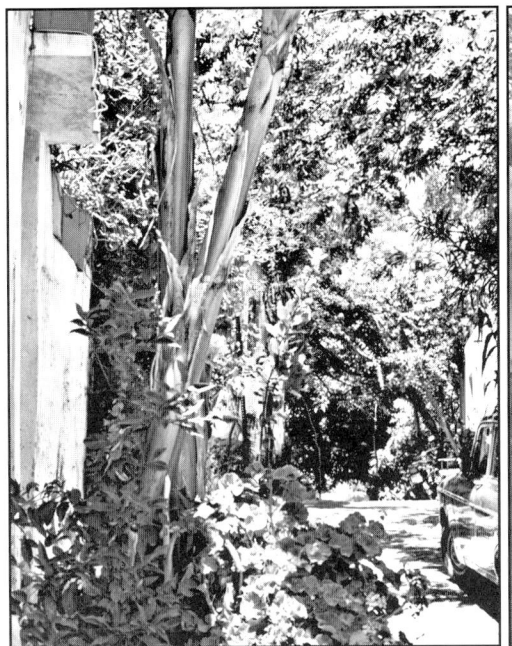
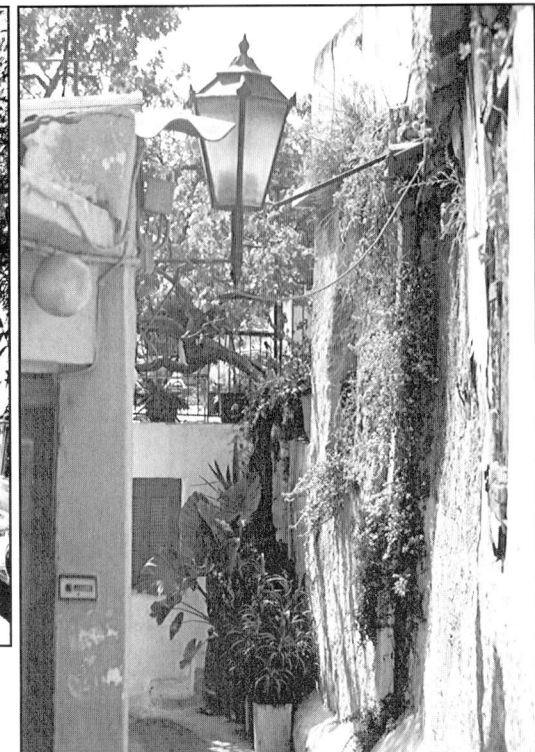

Not an island village!
Anafiotika, in the heart of the Athens

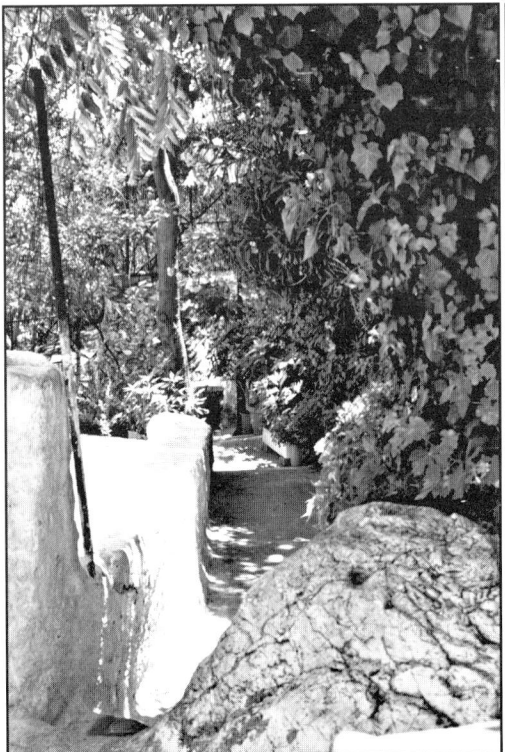
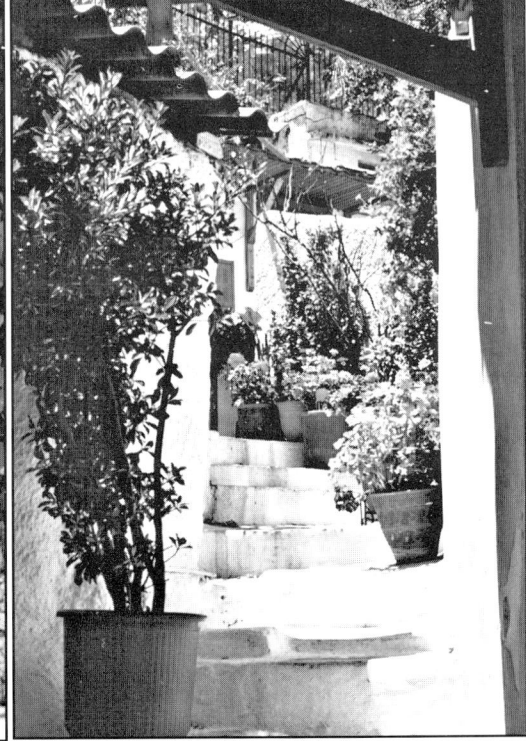

The Holy Sepulchre and the Holy Fire

In 1651 a rich Athenian priest, Dimitrios Kolokynthis, repaired the small church of *Ayoi Anargyroi,* said to have been founded by the empress Irene, whose family formerly lived in that neighborhood, in order to use it for a new monastery he was setting up. The church was ruined soon afterwards, probably in the Venetian campaign of 1687 led by Morosini, and remained in ruins until it was purchased by the Monastery of the Holy Sepulchre in Jerusalem in 1760. Today the church is the seat of the representative of the Orthodox Patriarch of Jerusalem to the Athens archbishopric.

Pilgrims would go to Jerusalem on pilgrimage to visit the site of the Holy Sepulchre, after which they would attach the prefix "Hadji" to their names. The Jerusalem church required a base in Athens in order to administer property and other bequests left by pilgrims in their wills to the Holy Sepulchre.

This church is the scene of a remarkable ceremony which begins in Jerusalem, and which takes place each year on the day before Easter. It has for centuries been the custom that the celebration of the resurrection of Jesus in Jerusalem is initiated by the patriarch. Just before noon, local time, he descends alone into the Holy Sepulchre, first breaking seals placed on the door after the commemoration of the burial of Jesus, and prays there alone. When he emerges from the tomb at noon, he bears in his hands burning torches and announces that "Christ is risen." The flames of the torches, which symbolise the risen Christ, are passed on from believer to believer until the church is full of light. In times past simple people believed that the fire was miraculously kindled each year from heaven, and that their annual ceremony constituted a repeated miraculous proof of Jesus' resurrection. The church took great care not to disurb them in that belief, and some orthodox still hold it today.

The Holy Fire is brought to Athens airport by a government minister in an Olympic Airways jet, where it is met by an honour guard of *Evzones*. From there it is taken to this church in the Plaka, in the early evening, to be used in the Athenians' own celebration of Easter at midnight.

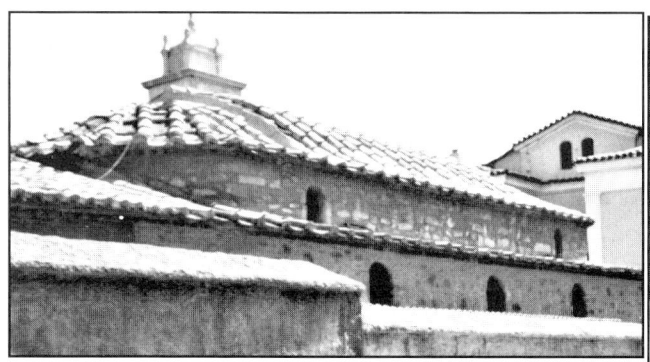
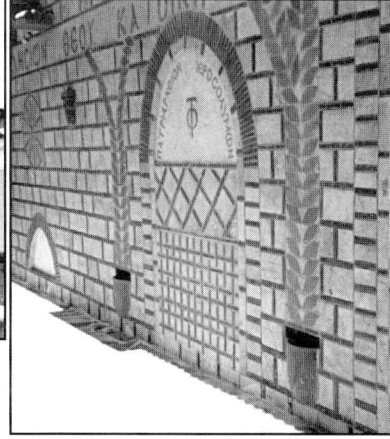

The church of Ayioi Anargyroi,
"the Penniless Ones"

85

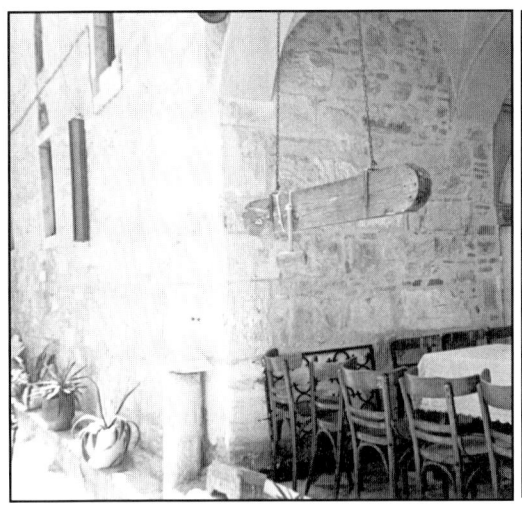
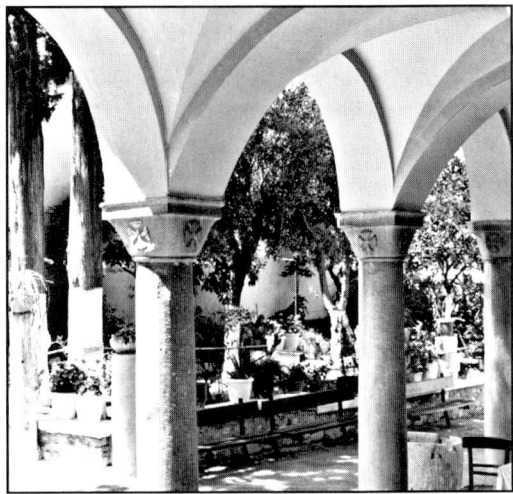

Above: The secluded courtyard of the church
It contains one of the gaslamps which used to illuminate the city.

The Fallen Icon

During the Byzantine period the worship of Athena in the Parthenon on the Acropolis, or "castle", of Athens had been replaced by the veneration of "Our Lady of Athens", represented by an icon known as Chrysokastriotissa ("the Golden Castle"), which was famous for its powers of healing. According to legend, this icon twice mysteriously disappeared from its restng place in the Parthenon, and was later found at a certain spot below the cliff. Each time, it was returned to its place on the Acropolis. On the third occasion that this happened, a church was built for it at the spot below the cliff where it was found.

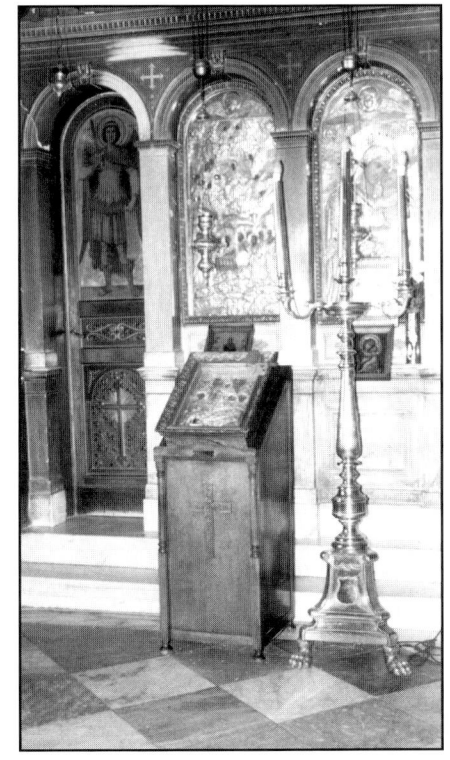

When this church was extensively modernised in the nineteenth century, marble was used to face the wall to a height of one metre or so, to prevent passing goats from damaging the wall when they rubbed themselves against it, as milkmen led them along the narrow alley outside.

The icon of our Lady of
the Golden Castle
"Chrysokastriotissa"

86

An Ancient Meteorological Station

The original purpose of the curious octagonal marble building, now known as the Tower of the Winds was entirely forgotten in the West until a copy of the work of a famous Roman architect, Vitruvius, was discovered in 1486. Then it was revealed to have been a meteorological station dating from the first century BC, built for the citizens of Athens by the Syrian astronomer, Andronikos Kyrrhestes. It was designed to provide information about the time, the weather and the movements of the heavenly bodies.

On each side of the building was a sundial in the form of a rod projecting from each of the walls horizontally, so as to cast a shadow. Incised marks indicated the time of day.

A hydraulic clock, or *klepsydra*, powered from a reservoir on the south side, served as a timekeeper when the sun was not visible. The *klepsydra* was invented in the second century BC by Ctesibus. It consisted of four parts: a vessel for providing a constant supply of water, a reservoir and floatation rod, a display, and a device for adjusting the flow of water into the vessel. Water poured continuously from a reservoir into a vessel, with the overflow escaping from a pipe. As the reservoir filled with water, a notched rod floated up on the surface at a constant rate. This rod was attached to a display which indicated the time of day.

Water was piped from a spring on the Acropolis and fed into a settling tank to remove impurities which might affect the accuracy of the mechanism. From there water was released at a constant rate to run the clock. The time was read from the level of water in the pipe.

The building also functioned as a planetarium, since it housed a mechanical device which represented the relative movements of the sun, the moon and the five planets then known. On top of the building was a weather vane to indicate the source of the wind. A bronze triton, half man and half fish, stood on top of a conical shaped piece of marble, and pointed a wand towards the source of the wind. The stone frieze below represents allegorically the character and effects of the winds which blow from each direction. Thus it was possible to see both which direction the wind was coming from, and the weather it could be expected to produce.

This frieze is perhaps the most interesting surviving feature of the building, since the mechanical contrivances have long since vanished. The north-west wind, Kaikas, is a well-wrapped up bearded old man tipping up a pot of hailstones, indicative of the harsh weather which this wind brings to Greece. Similarly, the north wind, Boreas, is a heavily dressed old man blowing through a conch shell, representing the sound of the howling wind. Although equally well-wrapped up Skiron, the north-east wind, carries a brazier to show the slightly milder weather he brings in winter. Apeliotes, the east wind, is represented as a lightly clad youth bearing the fruit and grain which is the result of the warm moist weather he brings each spring. Euros, the south-east wind has a harsh expression, since he causes storms at sea. Notos, the south wind, is a youth pouring water out, symbolising the rain which falls in Greece with the south wind. The south-west wind (the Italian scirocco), is represented by Lips, a youth who holds a ship's ornament, since his winds filled the sails of the ships. Zephyros, the west wind, which cools down the hot days of summer, is represented by a near-naked youth holding a mantle filled with flowers.

A Magic Building

It is hardly surprising that such a complex building aroused superstitious awe in later, more barbaric, ages. A seventeenth century Turkish traveller, Evliya Chelebi, called it "Plato's tent" and thought that it embodied "the knowledge of all the wise men. He also thought that Philip of Macedon, father of Alexander the Great was buried inside. He described it thus:

"The dome of this tent of marble is capped by a tall rod. They say that in the time of the ancient sages this supported a mirror of the world, similar to the mirror of Alexander the Great, which was designed to give a reflection of an invading army advancing upon the city from any side, but this mirror is now lost. They say also that in those times the wise men who gathered in this town used to perform strange magical tricks here … And they say that this town was never attacked by plague, nor did snakes remain alive here, nor centipedes either, nor scorpions, storks, crows, fleas, lice, bedbugs, mosquitoes, or flies …"

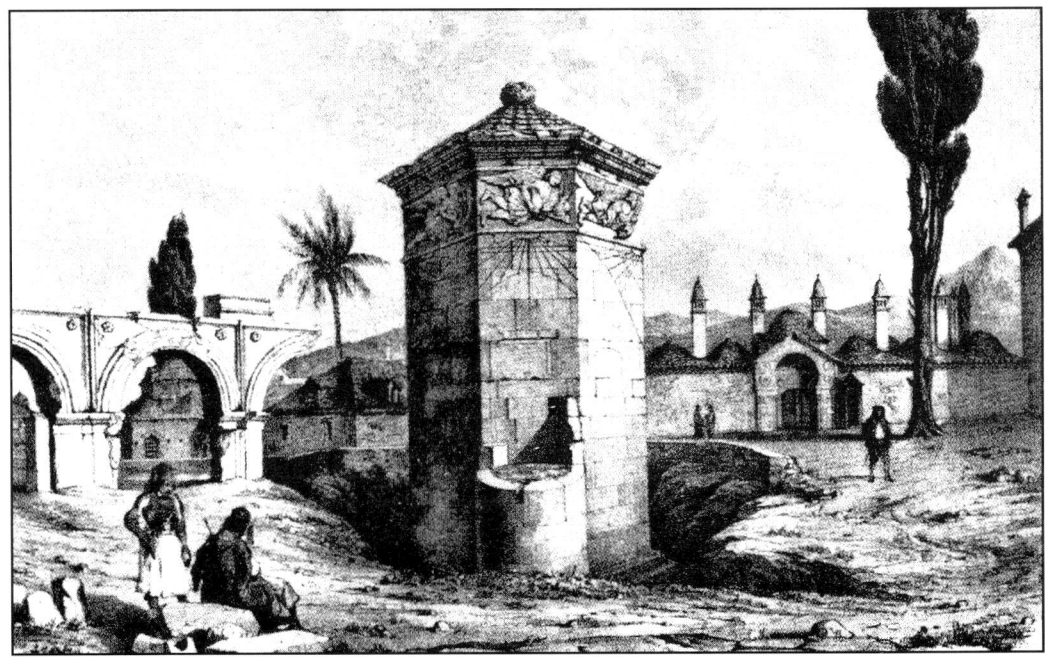

The Tower of the Winds, showing the remains of the reservoir (du Moncel, 1843)
In the background to the right is the Medresse

The Howling Dervishes

In Turkish times the Tower was used as a *Tekke,* or religious meeting house, by an order of the Howling Dervishes. In 1821, Thomas S. Hughes, recorded, in his *Travels in Sicily, Greece and Albania*:

"During the General's sojourn at Athens we accompanied him to that extraordinary exhibition which is displayed every Friday in the ancient tower of Andronicus, called the Temple of the Winds, and converted now into a college of howling dervishes. The frantic gestures, horrible outcries, and inconceivable exertions of these fanatics, urged on by superstitious enthusiasm and stimulated by emulation, made us absolutely shudder at such a degradation of human nature. A sheik or priest presided over the orgies

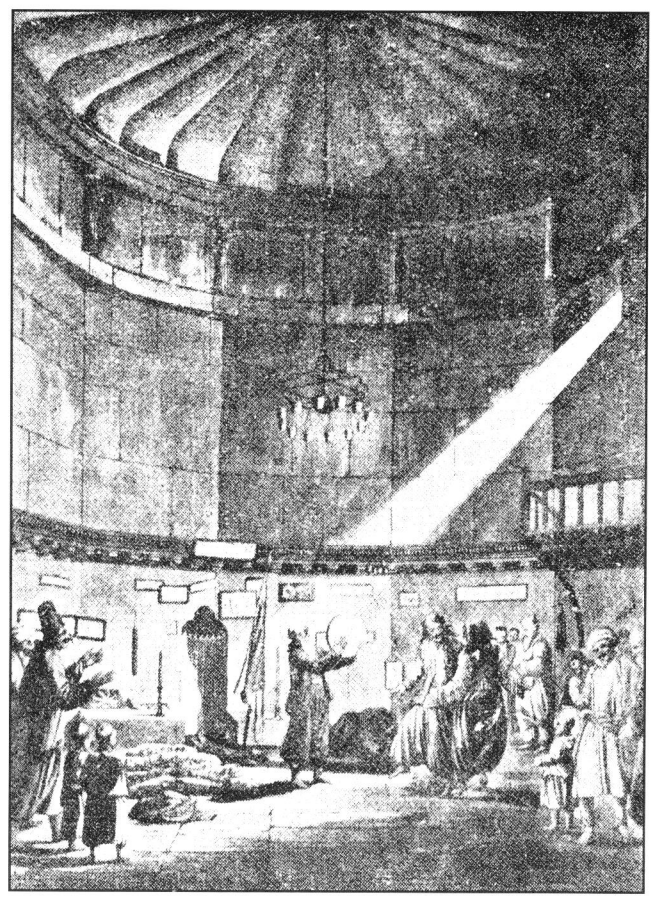

Dervishes in the Tower of the Winds (eighteenth century)

who stood upon a raised step and appeared to limit the time of operation by counting the beads of a rosary; but the movements were regulated by the deafening noise of three small kettle-drums which were beat violently with short elastic sticks. A single person first gets up and goes hopping or jumping round the room, throwing his head backwards and forwards or twirling it like a harlequin, uttering every now and then a hideous noise like the loud grunting of a pig. After a little time another starts up and catching him round the waist accompanies him in his revolutions which soon become most vehemently accelerated; then another and another succeeds until the first is quite surrounded and almost suffocated by the throng; in this manner holding each other with a tight grasp they go round and round leaping up and crying out, as if engaged in a trial of lungs, boo boo, ullah ullah, boo ullah. To this they are excited by a beating of the drums more violent than the cymbals of the Corybantes, as well as by the voice of the sheik who at this time runs over his beads with an astonishing rapidity: their exclamations appear as if uttered by persons in the excruciating tortures of the rack, or even bring to imagination the place of accursed souls: in the mean time their looks become wild, the foam starts from their mouths, their turbans fall to the ground, their hair floats about in disorder, their garments collapse, and some of the performers sink down in a state of perfect insensibility: these, after recovering, generally boast that they have been favoured with celestial visions. When thetumult has at length subsided, a different set of devotees commence that curious, beautiful, and mysterious dance which consists in twirling the body round rapidly like a top, or as upon a pivot, whilst they are moving in a circular orbit with their flowing robes distended like a parachute by the velocity of the motion: nothing but long and constant practice could enable them to perform these giddy revolutions: they seem to feel no fatigue, to make no exertions; but with the head inclined towards the shoulder, and the utmost placidity of countenance they float along as if they were in the enjoyment of a delightful trance. The contrast of this soothing harmony, as it might he called, this graceful ggggkelot, with the horrid uproar of the preceding scene, is extremely pleasing. The mind pictures to itself order and beauty produced out of chaos, or the harmonic revolutions of the planetary system. At the conclusion of these ceremonies some poor sick children were brought before the sheikh who put his hand upon their heads and tied a bit of black silk round their arms, for the purpose of charming away their complaints. He received our donations for the exhibition we had witnessed with great condescension, and politely invited us into his apartments adjoining the temple, where we took coffee and pipes with the actors in this extraordinary pantomime."

Kidnapped by Neraodes

The Greek townspeople told a story about a girl named Klino, who one day shortly after Independence mysteriously disappeared after last being reported by eyewitnesses just outside the Tower. Her parents, thinking that someone had kidnapped her, searched everywhere for her, but could find no clues at all as to her whereabouts.

She was discovered one week later lying unconscious on the ground where she had last been seen, outside the monument, her clothes torn to rags. When she was taken to the doctors she was found to be half mad, and raved about being kidnapped by the neraodes, who had danced around her, then carried her away in a whirlwind.Her parents took her to the church to be exorcised for eight consecutive days, and at last her sanity seemed to return. She said that the neraodes had snatched her away and taken her to the top of a mountain to be one of their company. But she wept every day, and after some time they lost their patience with her, slapped her face, and returned her to the spot from whence they had originally taken her.

Some understanding of the ancient association of this tower with the winds seems implicit in this tale.

The Mosque of the Conqueror

Today the Fetihie Djami stands locked up and forlorn amidst the ruins and tourist *tavernas* of the modern city, but for much of its history it was an important centre of local life, its fate reflecting that of the city around it. In 1456, three years after the fall of Constantinople, a Turkish army took Athens from its Florentine overlords. The mosque was erected during the next two years, probably on the foundations of a Byzantine church which may have been used as a cathedral by the Orthodox metropolitan after his expulsion from the Parthenon. It was built in preparation for the ceremonial visit, in 1458, of Sultan Mehmet II, the Conqueror.

The Sultan arrived some time during the autumn of that year. According to his Greek biographer, Kritoboulos, he was a cultured man and a philhellene. He had already read much about the wisdom of the ancient Athenian philosophers, and was eager to view the places where they had propounded their theories.

After touring the ancient sites, Mehmet granted many privileges to the city. Although he took many of the citizens' sons and daughters for his seraglio, it seems likely that Turkish rule did not become unduly oppressive until some time after his death. Certainly, the monks of Kaisariani and "the elders of the people", who had exercised some authority under the Florentines, retained some of their privileges and obtained important tax-exemptions. In addition, the Catholics were ejected from the Parthenon and the orthodox reinstated. It was probably only after the death of the

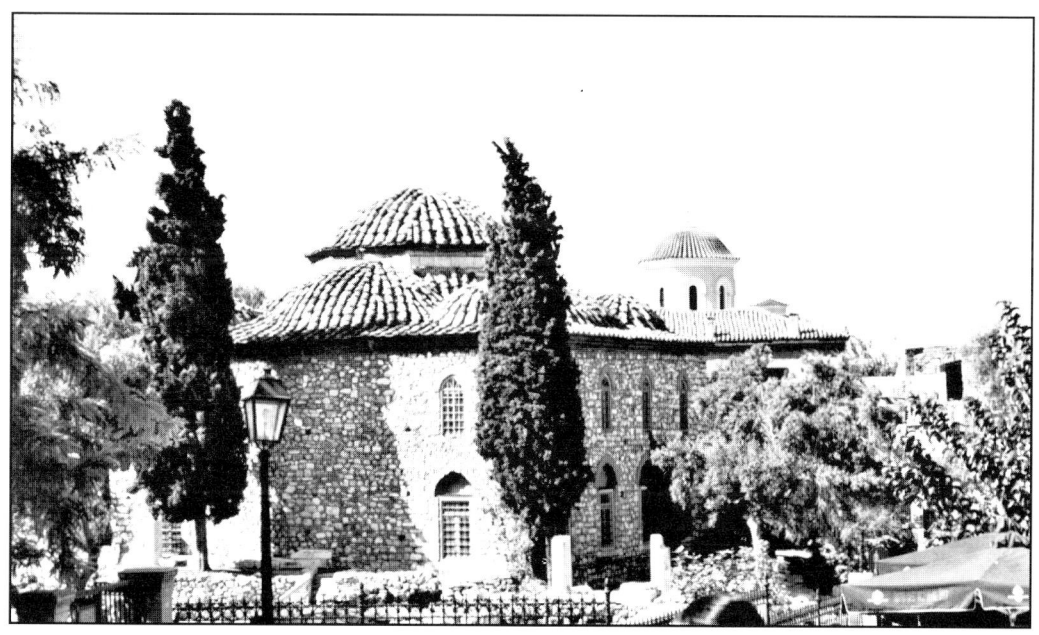

The Mosque of Mehmet the Conqueror,
known as the Wheat Bazaar Mosque, near the Roman agora

Conqueror that the Parthenon was converted into a mosque.

In later years the mosque of the Conqueror came to be known among the people as the Wheat Bazaar Mosque, as it was adjacent to the site of the annual wheat market, in an area used as a commercial centre at least since Roman times. When the Venetians occupied the city for five months during 1687-8, it was converted temporarily into a Catholic church, and a premature *Te Deum*, or thanksgiving, for the liberation of Athens was sung there. After independence the minaret was demolished, and the building was adapted for use as a college for teachers, and then it became an army bakehouse. Today it is used as a store for ancient architectural fragments found in the area of the Roman *agora*, which lies around the mosque.

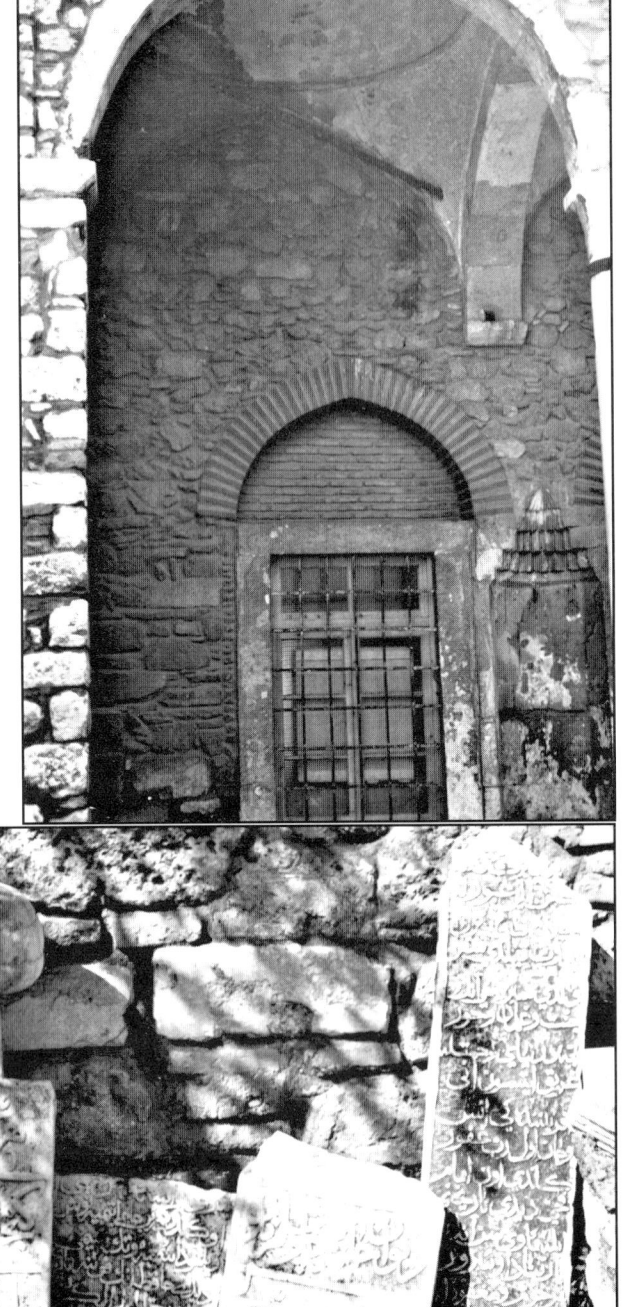

Tombstones in the grounds of the Mosque of the Coqueror The turban on one of the headstones signifies the burial of a male. The nature of the head-dress indicated a pasha, dervish, eunuch or ordinary Muslim.

A Prophecy Fulfilled

Originally a Turkish theological school founded in 1721 by Mehmet Fahri, a palace official during the reign of Sultan Ahmet III, the Medresse, situated opposite the Fetihie Mosque and the Roman Agora, originally consisted of a series of cells arranged around the sides of a colonnaded courtyard, where the students boarded and studied. A large domed chamber contained the lecture hall. This also served as a mosque where the teacher led Friday prayers. In good weather, the lessons would be held under a great plane tree, which stood in the centre of the courtyard. By the time of the War of Independence, the building was used as a prison, and during the struggle for liberation, many Greeks were hanged from the branches of the plane tree. After Independence, the new Greek authorities continued to use it in the same way, and put the tree to the same use.

The place became accursed in the minds of the people, both for the inhuman conditions under which inmates, many of them political prisoners, were confined, and because passers by peering through the gateway could see the corpses dangling from the tree. On the night of 3rd September 1843, the crowd which had just demanded a constitution from Bavaran King Otho released the prisoners. The resentment of the people was given eloquent voice by a poet, Achilleas Paraschos, who foretold that one day the accursed tree would be chopped up and burned.

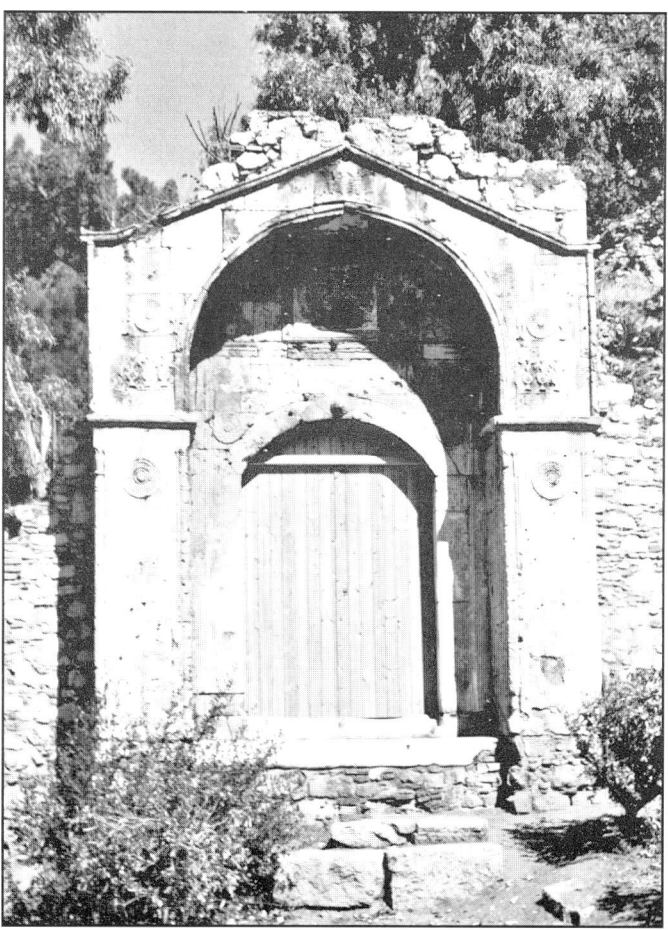

It was struck by lightning in 1919 and, in accordance with the words of the poet, the remains were chopped up and removed for firewood. In the same year, the rest of the building, except for the main gateway, was demolished.

*The gateway
of the Medresse*

The Oldest Distillery in Athens

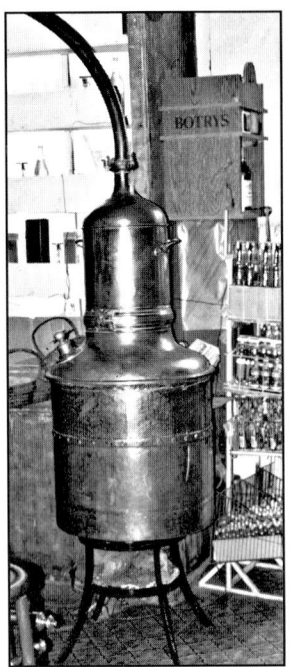

On Kydathneion Street near the corner with Adrianou, is to be found a living relic of nineteenth century Athens: Brettos' liquer store. Coloured bottles line the walls up to the ceiling, together with old barrels full of spirits, and an ancient distillery. A shop rather than a museum, a wide variety of spirits together with Brettos' own products are sold, while at a tiny bar drinks may still be purchased by the glass.

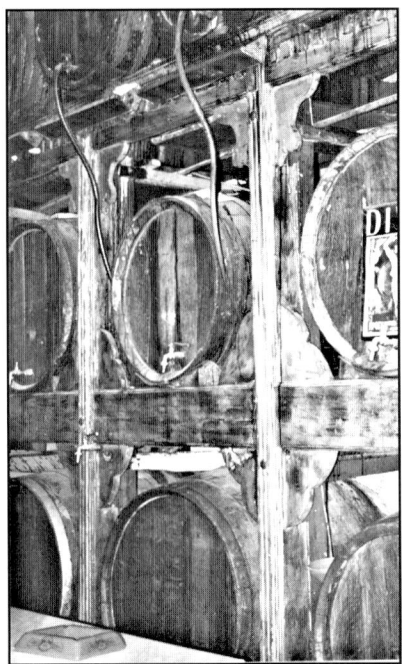

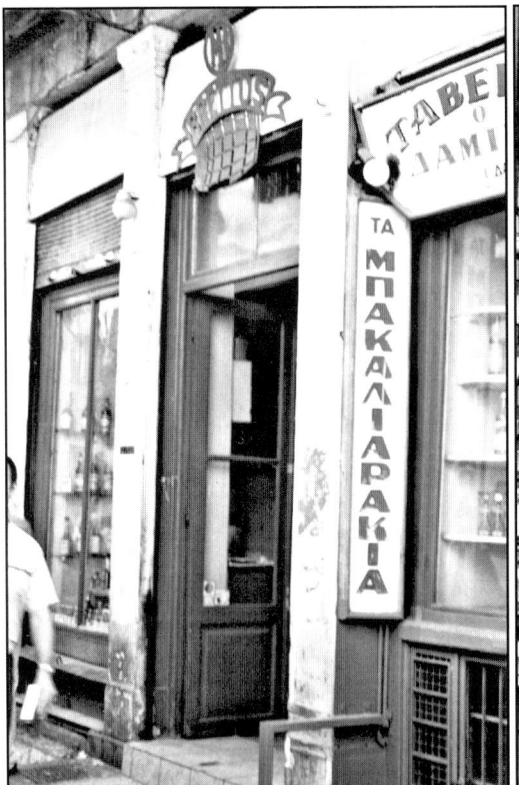

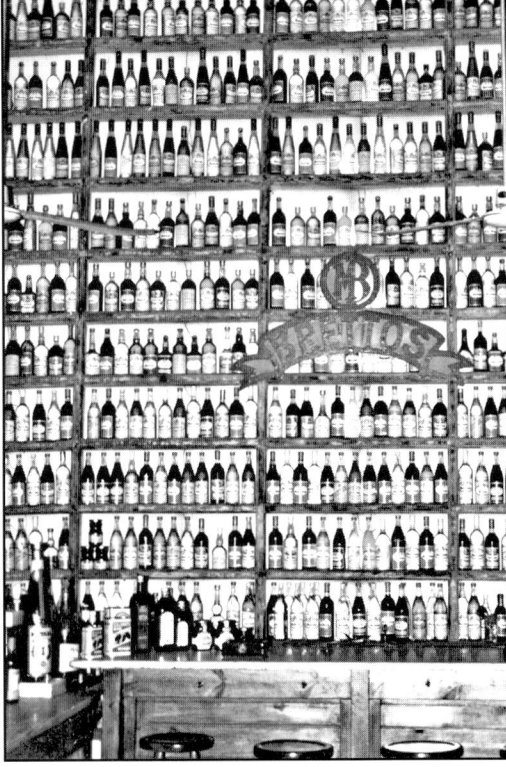

Monastiraki

An Apostle's Curse

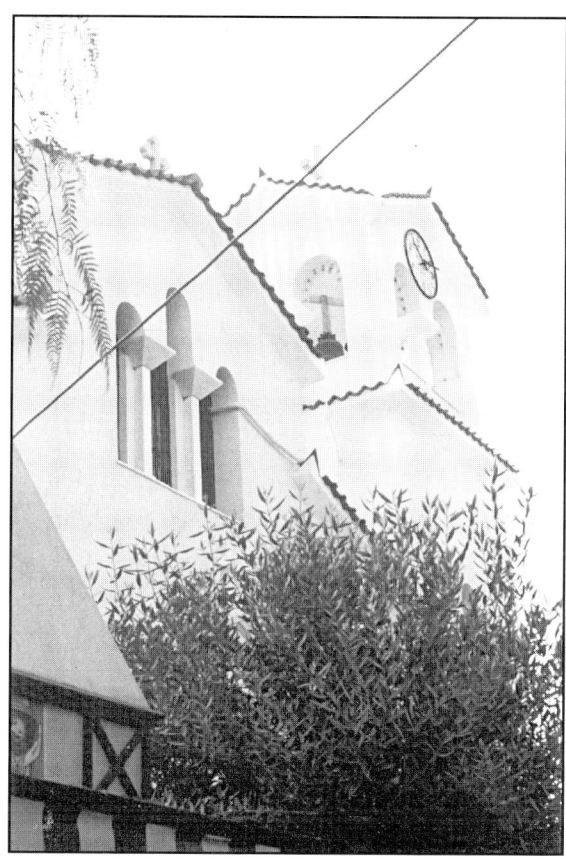

*The church of Saint Philip,
Monastiraki.
The church is now surounded
by the flea-market.*

In addition to the books of the New Testament, which give accounts of the life of Jesus and of his apostles, there are many other books which deal with the same events, but which were never accepted by the early church as "authentic". These are usually full of alleged miracles, and are known as apocryphal books. According to one of these, the *Acts of Saint Philip*, that apostle travelled to Athens, and spent two years in the city preaching the gospel, mainly to the Jewish community. Close on his heels from Palestine came the scribe of the Chief Priest of the Jews, who would constantly contradict whatever he said. At last one day, when he was preaching in the *agora*, exasperated beyond control by this constant carping opposition, the saint lost his temper and cursed hs adversary, causing the earth to open and swallow him up.

A church dedicated to Saint Philip was said to have been founded on that spot to commemorate the event. It was completely rebuilt in the nineteenth century, and stands in busy Monastiraki.

Loosing an Ancient Curse

The Tzistarakis Mosque, erected by the Voivode (or Turkish governor) Tzistarakis during the mid-eighteenth century, in the centre of what was then the market area of Athens, was to prove the downfall of its builder.

Wishing to establish a worthy place of worship, older buildings were ruthlessly raided for material. To finish it off, the Voivode desired some high quality lime to make plaster for the walls, and in April 1759 ordered the dynamiting of one of the remaining columns of the great temple of Olympian Zeus on the far side of the city.

This act of vandalism both annoyed and frightened the Athenians. They believed that each ancient column stood upon a curse, and imprisoned it by its weight. The curse would be released if the column were ever moved or destroyed. When, later that same year, there was an outbreak of plague, the Voivode was regarded as responsible.

Of course, the Turkish governor had little to fear from the subject population. But, unfortunately for him, his actions had also annoyed his superior, the Pasha of Chalkis, in Euboea. According to an old law, ancient monuments throughout the Ottoman Empire were the property of the Sultan himself, and needed his permission before being interfered with. Needless to say, this had not been sought, much less obtained. The Pasha saw his opportunity to remove Tzistarakis, and invoked this law. The Voivode tried to bribe his way out of trouble with 8,000 piastres, then sixteen pouchfuls of coins, but the Pasha was adamant, and ordered him exiled.

Later people said that the remaining columns of the temple nightly lamented their lost sister so noisily that no one could get any sleep, and it was not until some time afterwards, when Tzistarakis had been poisoned, that the clamour finally ceased.

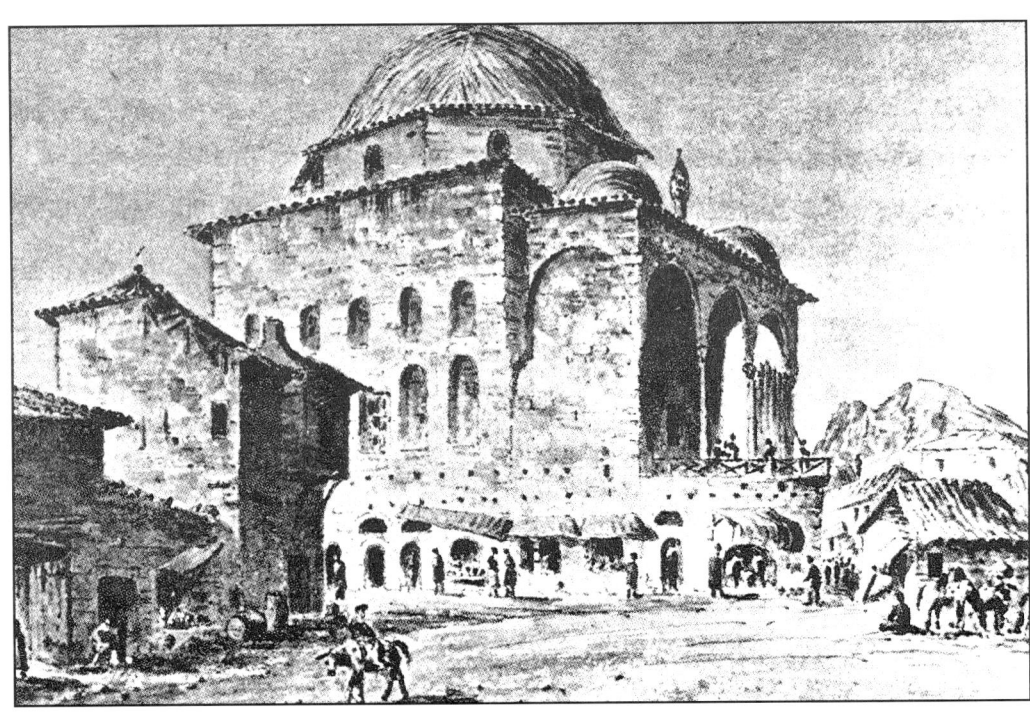

The Tzistarakis Mosque, Monastiraki,
(J. Skene, 1839)

The Kerameikos

An Ancient Burial Ground

The area of ancient Athens known as Kerameikos was named after Keramos, son of Dionysos and Ariadne, who was the hero of the potters. It was the centre of the pottery industry, at which the Athenian craftsmen famously excelled. For archaeologists, it is chiefly interesting as containing the most important cemetery of the city.

The area was used continuously for burials from the twelfth century BC for perhaps a thousand years. For this reason, archaeologists have been able to catalogue changes in funerary customs over many centuries at a single site. For example, in the twelfth century BC bodies were buried with small ceramic objects. After 1100 cremation was the norm. From the seventh century the dead were being buried once more. Initially they were laid in pit graves; from the sixth century under mounds of earth; and from the fourth under cairns of pebbles.

From the fifth century BC, increasingly magnificent grave monuments were erected, while an official State Burial Ground, the *demosion sema,* was laid out for those the state wished to honour. In time, competition in erecting ever more lavish monuments got out of hand, and in 317 Demetrios of Phaleron, a pupil of Aristotle and Macedonian governor of Athens, passed a law forbidding all grave monuments except modest columns (known as *kioniskoi*).

During 1994-5, excavations for a new underground railway line and station brought to light one thousand tombs dating from the fifth and fourth centuries BC, and a single mass grave in a shaft which may originally have contained up to one hundred and fifty skeletons. There was every evidence of hurried burial, since the remains had been thrown in anyhow, with no soil between them. The burial vessels found there were fewer than would normally have been expected, and were inexpensive. It seems likely that this internment, dated between 430 and 426 BC, had been made over one or two days, and that it was a plague burial site. Thucydides, recorded an outbreak of plague in 430, which lasted for two years and which may have killed as many as one third of the citizens.

Archaeologists had to work quickly, for the bulldozers employed in the construction of the station soon destroyed both the tombs and the mass grave. Shortly afterwards, the Government ordered the cancellation of the construction of the station, which had been the reason for the destruction of the site in the first place, and the area was designated for a multi-storey car park.

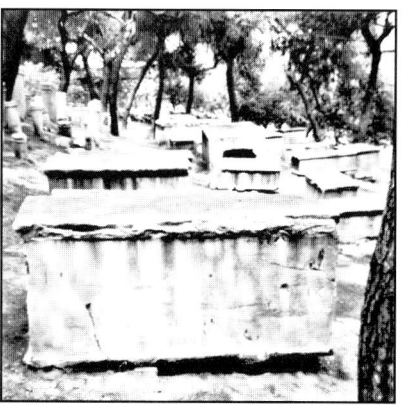

Stone sarcophagi

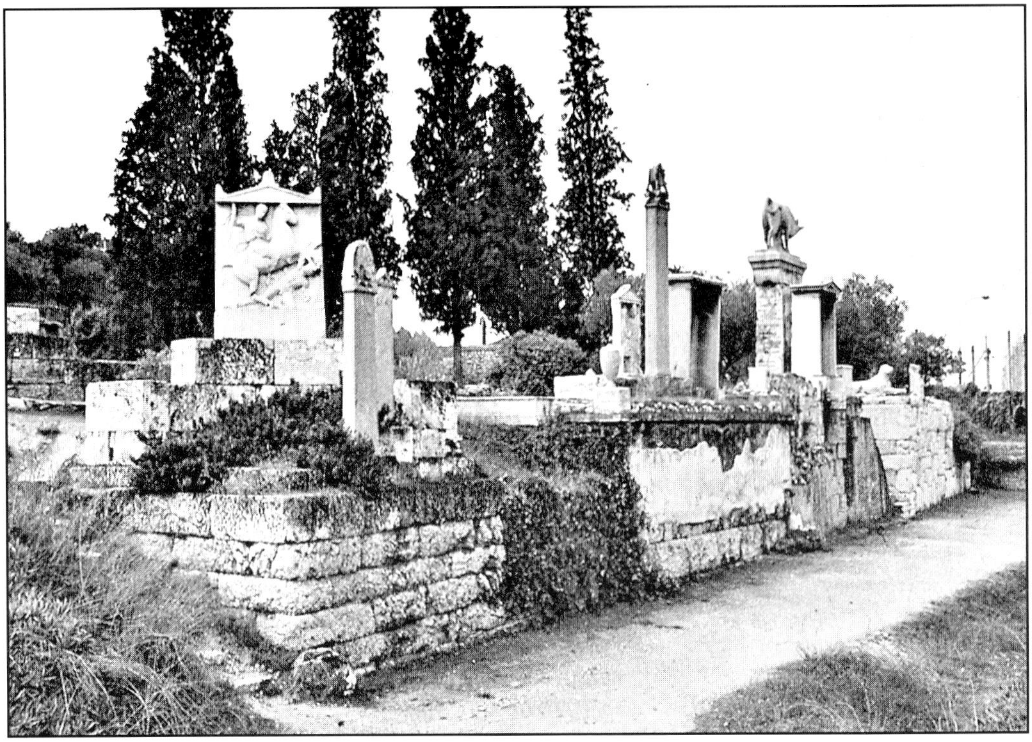

Above: The Street of the Tombs
Below left: Grave relief of Dexileos, 394 BC
Below right: Grave monument of Prokles and Prokleides

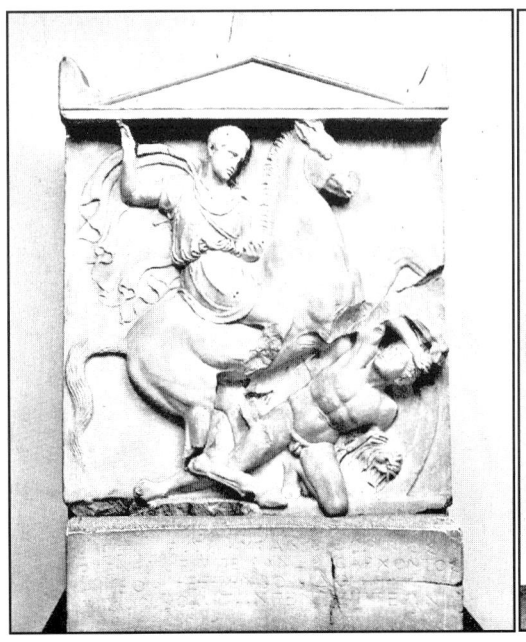 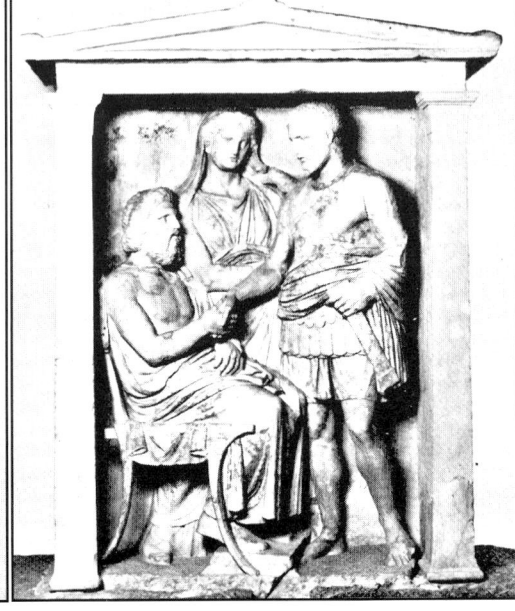

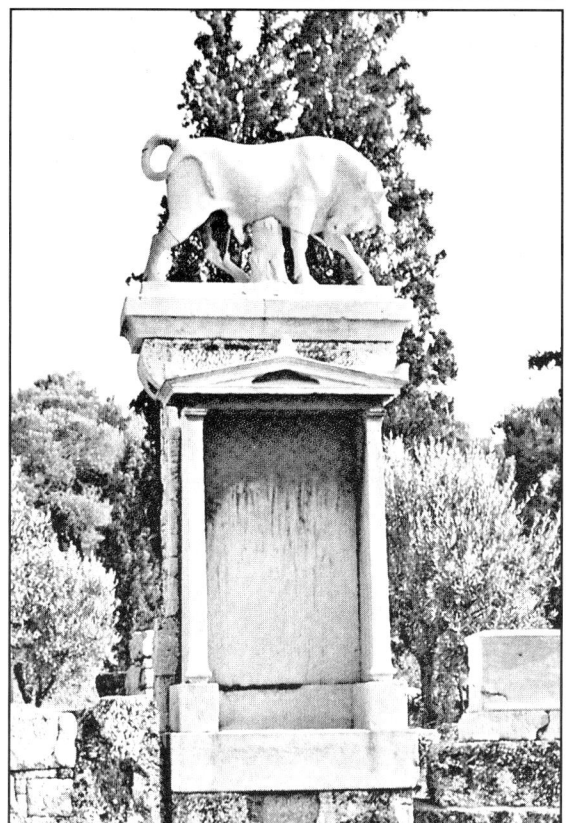

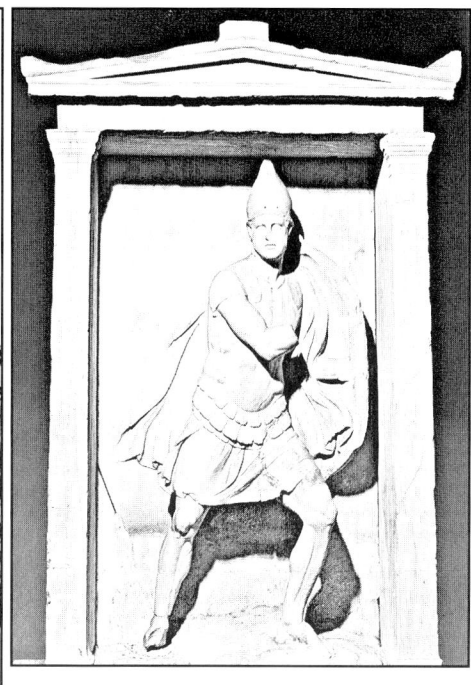

*Above: Grave stele of Aristonautes
(Nat. Arch. Mus., Athens)
Above left: Bull in the grave
precinct of Dionysios of Kollytos*

*Below left: One of the "mini-columns", or kioniski,
to which grave monuments were limited after 317 BC
Below: a field of kioniski*

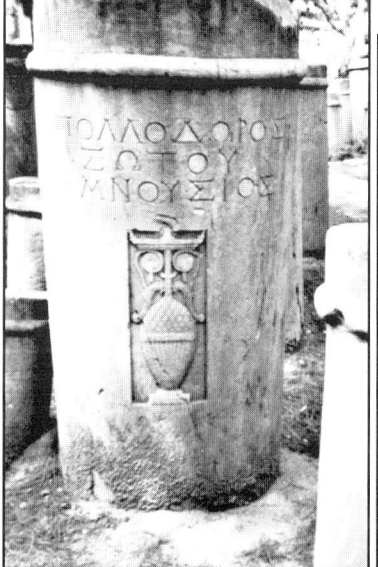

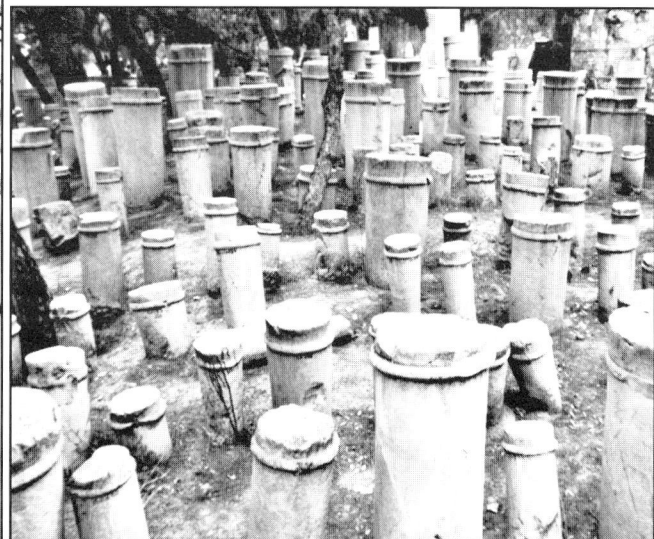

Botanikos (Votanikos)

Figs and Fava Beans

In ancient times, at the crossing of the Sacred Way to Eleusis over the river Kifissos stood several temples and shrines. The medieval church of Saint Savas stands on the site of an ancient temple of Demeter, and incorporates ancient stonework in its masonry. The temple was built to commemorate an incident in the myth of Demeter and Persephone *[See Volume Three in this series: Attica]*. On her travels in search of her missing daughter, Persephone, the goddess was met at that spot by Phylalus, who received her honourably. In gratitude, she gave him the first fig tree, with instructions on how to cultivate it. When Theseus entered Athens, he was supposed to have resorted to this temple to be ritually cleansed of blood-guilt, since he had been forced to kill several people on his journey.

Nearby was a shrine to the hero Cyanites, famous for being the first man to cultivate the large fava bean, now such a prominent feature of Greek cuisine.

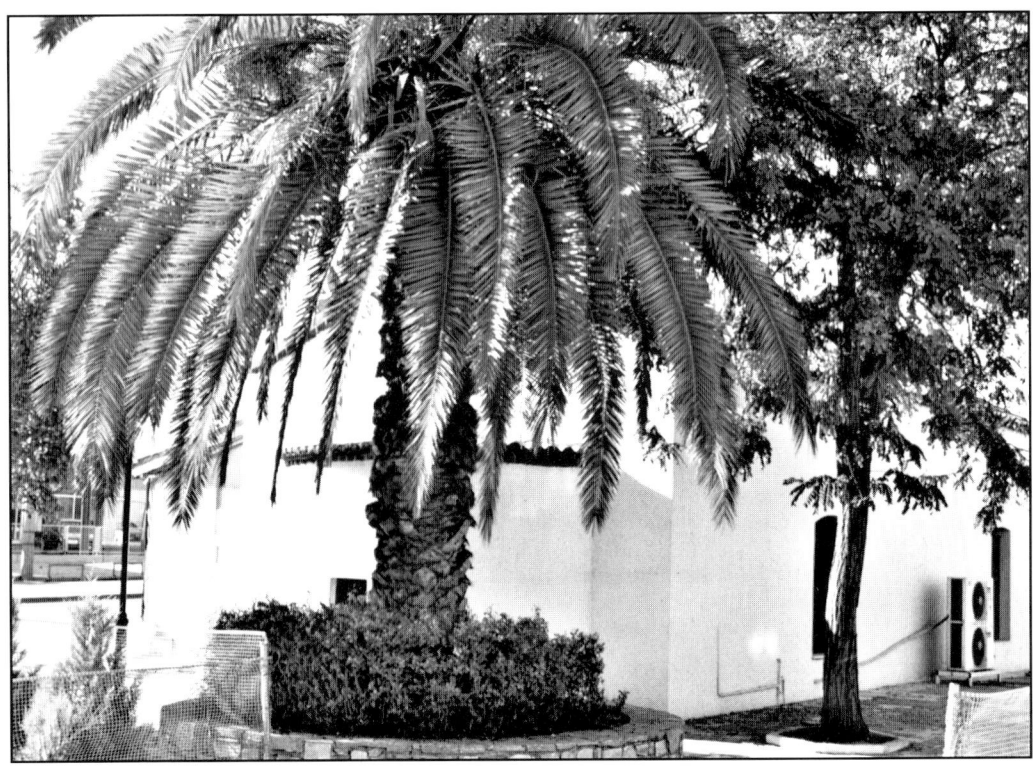

The church of Saint Savas at the ancient crossing over the Kifissos River

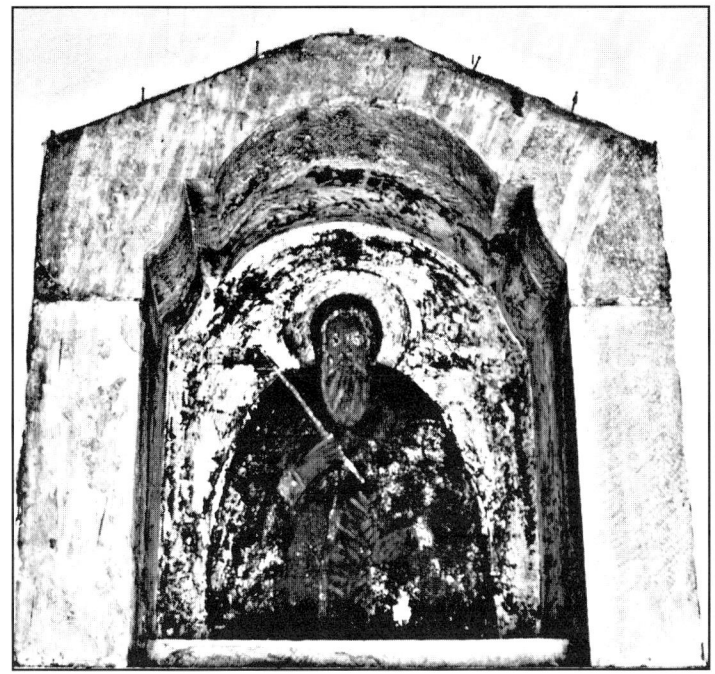

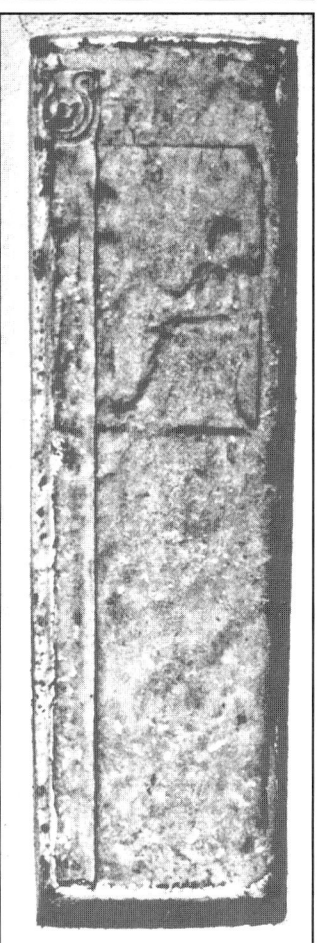

Above: painting over the door
Above right and below:
> *The medieval church incorporates*
> *in its fabric ancient carved stonework,*
> *probably from the temple of Demeter or*
> *from the other shrines in the neighborhood*

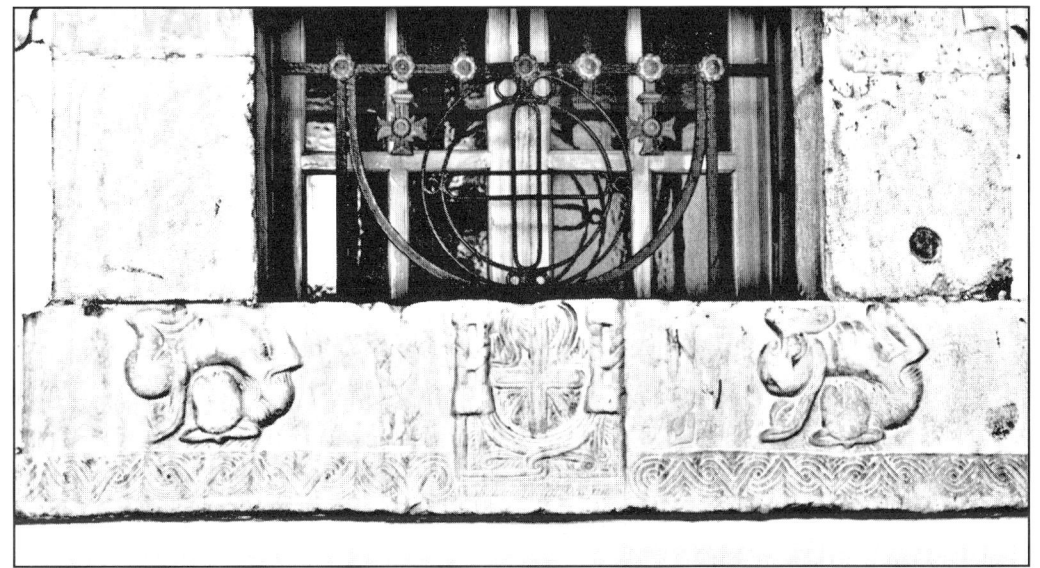

The Worst Tyrant of Them All

The harshest period of Turkish rule was late in the eighteenth century, when Ali Hadji Haseki, was governor (*voivode*). Panayis Skouzes recorded that under his tyranny the Athenians lost everything, and the entire province was reduced to poverty. During this period many Christians emigrated other parts of mainland Greece, the islands, or even to Anatolia.

Hadji Ali was a member of the royal bodyguard from the interior of Anatolia. He arrived in Constantinople and entered the Seraglio while he was still young, and became servant to the sister of Sultan Selim, and daughter of Sultan Hamid. He very quickly made his way up in the palace hierarchy. It was said that his mistress was infatuated with him, took him to her bed, advanced his career, enriched him and protected him. In 1772, when the state land of Athens was sold at auction, she purchased it for 750,000 piastres and gave it to him as a present.

Shortly afterwards, Athens was twice overrun by hordes of Albanian Muslims. In 1778 Hadji Ali and the influential archons of Athens, the hereditary governing families, decided to build a wall around the city, known as the Serpentzes. Many ancient and medieval buildings, including some of Athens' most famous landmarks, were demolished to provide material for this wall: including the Temple of Demeter and Kore by the Ilissos (dating from 449 BC, later converted into the church of the Virgin on the Rocks), the bridge over the Ilissos before the Panathenaic Stadium, built by Herodes Atticus, and the facade of Hadrian's reservoir on Lykabettos.

The wall was conceived originally as a means of defence against external attack, but it soon became the Athenians' prison. As extortionate taxation drove many into penury, Ali set guards at the gates to prevent the citizens from leaving. More than two hundred farmers and tradespeople managed to get out, and hastened secretly to Constantinople to file a complaint at the imperial court. They went to the Grand Vizier and threw down their ploughshares one after the other, shouting that the Sultan should give them land elsewhere to live.

Their protest was effective. Haseki was removed from office and summoned to Constantinople to give account of his government. As he was travelling to the city, an official was sent out with a warrant to arrest him and take him into exile in Cyprus. Hadji Ali bribed him to take him back to Athens instead. There, he announced that he had been pardoned and would retain his post. He then got testimony from his henchmen, the archons, supplemented by some false signatures, stating that those who had complained about him were troublemakers, and requesting that the Government put them in chains. Then he collected a sum of money and sent it, together with the false report, to Constantinople.

Two of the farmers who had gone to Constantinople to complain went on to Alexandria, where Hasan Pasha, Grand Admiral of the Fleet, gave them his sword-bearer, to be their *voivode*. The citizens deposed Hadji Ali's henchmen and replaced the hereditary archons with elected representatives.

When, in 1787, Hasan Pasha died, the archons drew up a report saying that they did not want the new *voivode* because he was a drunkard and corrupted girls, and complained that the new elected archons were not ruling efficiently. They were believed, and Haseki was able to return as governor a third time.

He tricked the new headmen by sending them presents and telling them he would allow them to keep their posts because the hereditary archons had grown old. The more prudent among them were not taken in by this, and fled; while all those who stayed behind were arrested and imprisoned. Then the archons drew up two lists of twelve culprits, recommending that they be tortured and, after being stripped of their possessions, be put to death. One was hanged from a huge olive tree, another was suffocated in the Crusader tower on the Acropolis, a third was hanged in front of his shop after a beating.

Haseki also imprisoned twenty-four heads of well-to-do families who had not taken part in the protest, demanding a large sum of money from them. He showed them sharpened stakes and said that whoever had not paid within eight days would be impaled on them. They sold their wives' jewellery and their farmlands and paid up. Then he called a general assembly of the population from the villages around, where the archons presented the people with a bill for Haseki's expenses during the time he had been in exile. He set guards at the gates and demanded so much from each man according to his property. When they were unable to pay, the prisons filled up.

"The men had to stand upright, there was no room to sit down. When people came to talk to a prisoner through the bars of the window it was not so bad if he was in front. If he was in the back the others lifted him up and passed him over each other's heads, or else he had to fight his way to the front. If someone brought a piece of bread or something else to eat, the others passed it from hand to hand if the prisoner was in the back. And out of the window came a smoke - steam like a black cloud, the stench of the bodily functions of so many people. For the old people it was dangerous; it brought them to their last gasp, and a few were dead by morning. In the men's prison the *falanga* was hung up. Whoever did not pay after eight days' imprisonment had his feet slashed with the rods...

For the women there was a marble column. The guards would tie a woman up with her breast against it and whip her on the behind. Some of these women were widows, others had their husbands hiding in the country or working and sleeping outside the town, in caves and ravines, or some of them had escaped. Indeed it was hard for fugitives to take their families with them."

Between 1788 and 1790 he obtained almost every last possession from the Athenians. Only the archons were exempt from his depredations; the population was reduced to penury. To make matters worse, in 1788 there was an outbreak of plague. People died each day, and those who could left the city.

Finally the tyrant began to realise that he had destroyed the economy of the city. Many had fled secretly with their families. If someone escaped the others were required to pay his tax, but when they broke into the fugitive's house they would find nothing. Haseki began to buy up the fields at low prices, for no one dared refuse him, and acquired a large tract of land. Wherever he saw young olive trees, poplars, lemon or orange trees, he would send workmen to dig up as many as he wanted and transplant them into his own gardens. On Sundays, before the service was over, he would set guards at the church doors to round up the menfolk for work. People began holding the services in the middle of the night, but his soldiers went by threes to every church during the night and waited until the service was over.

In 1796, Haseki's protectress died. He went to Constantinople to find a new patron, but people there wrote to the Athenians saying it was a good time to file a suit against him, because his mistress was dead and it was known to everyone that he had ruined Athens. A report was composed, and Dionysios Petrakis, the abbot of the Petraki Monastery in Kolonaki took it under cover of paying his annual tribute of oil and honey to the mosque. Hadji Ali's henchmen warned him what was afoot. He invited the abbot to his house and offered him poisoned coffee, but the wary abbot did not drink it all down, but quickly excused himself, and promised to return the next day. He managed to vomit up what he had drunk, but his beard fell out and his teeth were damaged. When he was well again, the deputation reported to the Patriarch and all the high officials who would listen to them. Finally, Sultan Selim III ordered Haseki's

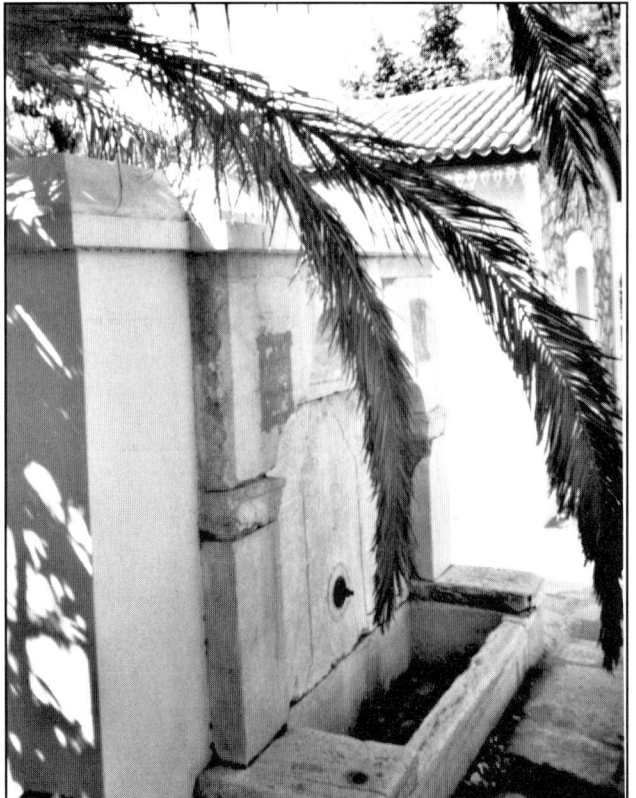

exile to Kos, and summoned the archons to Constantinople. They pleaded that they were afraid to report what was going on. They were arrested and an executioner was sent to Kos, who beheaded Hadji Ali His head was taken to Constantinople and exhibited before the Topkapi Palace.

After that the Athenians began to recover. They elected new headmen and established schools in the city.

Fountain in the grounds of the mansion of Ali Haseki, now the School of Agriculture, where he diverted the River Kifissos to water his enormous orchard

A Rustic Capital

Nothing illustrates the essentially rural nature of Athens when it first became the capital city of the modern state of Greece than some of the folk beliefs of its inhabitants at that time.

Animal Spirits

Many of the churches of Athens were believed to be haunted by a guardian spirit which would emerge and give voice three times at midnight just before the death of someone in that parish. These were usually imagined to have animal form. In one church this spirit took the form of a bull, in another a snake, and in another a black cockerel. Whenever someone in the parish of the Transfiguration of the Lord *(Metamorphosis)* in the Plaka, was about to die, on the night before, a ghostly calf would bellow three times. The church of All Saints was haunted by a large snake with the head of a cat, and people were still claiming to have seen it at the end of the nineteenth century.

Frequently animals were sacrificed at the foundation of buildings, and it is tempting to suppose that the memory of the remains of the creatures buried in the foundations was the stimulus of many of these stories of animal spectres.

The Demons of Christmas

Like people all over Greece, the Athenians believed the festivities of Christmas to be accompanied the haunting of their dwellings by creatures from the bowels of the earth called *kallikantzaroi*. These demonic creatures emerged on Christmas Eve, and remained at large for the twelve days of Christmas, disappearing back into the earth on the eve of the Epiphany, when priests go from house to house sprinkling holy water as a blessing.

They were usually thought of as swarthy creatures with red eyes, cloven hooves and covered with hair. They would pester people in various ways, spoil food, at times and even try to kill people by choking them in their beds at night. They could enter through doors, but mostly they got into houses by way of the chimney. In order to avoid being bothered by them, people would scratch a cross on their doors and keep their hearths alight throughout this period. People would take care to throw onto the fire branches which would crackle and bang, so as to frighten away their unwelcome visitors.

Some scholars have conjectured that these strange creatures are derived from the common practice of masquerading and pestering people at Christmas. Others have identified them with the *silenoi* or satyrs who were thought in ancient times to attend

105

the revels of the god Dionysos. Some, however, consider the *kallikantzaroi* to be the souls of the dead, who in ancient times were believed to live in the underworld and returned to the surface of the earth for a period each year when Hades opened its gates during the festival of the Anthesteria.

The Plague Women

During the nineteenth century the urban populations living on the shores of the Mediteranean Sea were repeatedly plagued by various epidemic diseases, such as smallpox, cholera, typhoid, and others, which frequently caused great mortality. The Athenians used to personify these diseases as old women.

One coach driver claimed that at about midnight one night near the church of Saint Mavros in Athinas Street, he picked up a woman dressed in black who asked to be taken to the Monument of Lysikrates in the Plaka. When they arrived, he turned around only to find, to his amazement, not one but three women, all similarly dressed, getting out of the carriage. None of them turned around to pay the fare as they got out, but so surprised was he that he just sat there and watched them walk way. On the next day he heard that the cholera had broken out in that neighbourhood.

On another occasion, an old woman encountered two mysterious woman who were strangers to her, dressed entirely in white, at the cave below the Observatory, on the Hill of the Nymphs. Curious, she watched to see which road they would take. Soon afterwards, an epidemic of smallpox broke out in the area towards which they had travelled. For the people of old Athens, the implication was clear.

The Visit of the Fates

The ancient Greeks worshipped the Fates or *Moiroi*: three ugly, terrible and merciless old women wearing veils woven out of spiders webs, who controlled the destinies of both gods and men. Clotho, the spinner, spun the thread of a person's life; Lachesis, the apportioner, sometimes portrayed as writing, decided how much time was allowed each person; and Atropos, the inevitable, carried scissors to cut the thread when a person died. Even the Olympian gods feared this terrible trio.

Among uneducated people in Athens, propitiation of the fates continued well into the twentieth century, when it was believed that each person had an individual fate, something like a guardian angel, but that every person's destiny was ultimately controlled by the great trinity of Fates, known as the Fates of all Fates. These terrible beings were only ever mentioned using honeyed words, so as not to offend them, although at the same time it was believed that they were absolutely implacable, and could never be persuaded to change their initial decrees.

Despite this, a black-handled knife, a coin or a Gospel would be placed under a boy's pillow, and ornaments under a girl's, to influence their fates. On the day a mother first rose from childbed, she would remain silent "lest the Fates snatch her speech."

The most fateful time in any person's life was the third night after birth, when the three "Fates of all the fates" were expected to visit the baby in person and seal its fortune once and for all. Elaborate preparations were made, supervised by the midwife, to make their visit a pleasant one, and to avoid annoying them in any way.

That night, the baby would be bathed in scented water using, for example, laurel or rosemary, and then put to sleep by itself in the formal room of the house. The door communicating with the rest of the house would be closed, while that leading to the outside door, which would be unlocked, would be kept open. The dog would be kept securely on its chain, and any obstacles over which visitors might trip in the darkness would be pushed out of the way. A light would burn in the room where the baby was sleeping. Beside the cradle, a low table would be set out surrounded by cushions, for the Fates never learned to eat using modern upright chairs and high tables. On the table would be placed various refreshments: usually honey, three white almonds, bread and a glass of water, and perhaps other dainties as well. Sometimes the family jewels would be set out on a side table for the Fates to take their pick from them if they so desired.

The three Fates would make their visit between midnight and one o'clock in the morning. No other human might be in the room with the baby during that time, but listening mothers sometimes claimed to have detected a low murmuring. Any marks subsequently observed on the baby's face, such as moles, especially on the brow, were called the "writing of the Fates." Despite all these efforts to propitiate them, it was commonly said that the Fates never gave anyone an entirely good destiny.

The writer Kevin Andrewes observed that in the villages immediately outside Athens this practice was still frequently being observed during the 1960s.

When a girl reached the period shortly before marriage, her mother would become uneasy, for once again, rather inconsistently, the role of the Fates would again become crucial. A plate would be prepared with spoonfuls of honey and taken to one of the many caves of the Fates by an old woman who was a member of the family, or trusted by them. She had to be freshly bathed and wearing a new dress. It was important that she should also take myrrh and incense, otherwise the Fates would not accept her offering. She would return to the cave on the next day. If the honey had disappeared, the Fates had accepted the offering and the girl's future good fortune was ensured. If the offering was partly consumed, then good fortune would come in time. If it had been ignored entirely, the old woman would sing a dirge in the face of the girl's evil fate.

Christopher Dodwell found that the cave known falsely as Socrates' Prison on the Hill of the Pnyx was still used to leave offerings to the Fates. He found "in the inner chamber, a small feast consisting of a cup of honey and white almonds, a cake on a little napkin, and a vase of aromatic herbs burning and exhaling an agreeable perfume." His donkey ate some of the offering. This cave was still used for that purpose in 1910. On the Museion Hill several old rock dwellings in the form of caves were employed in a similar fashion.

Metaxurgio

During the period of Turkish rule, in the popular mind ancient columns, when they survived singly, came to be thought of as imprisoning curses. Most of these curses were thought to be epidemic diseases of various kinds.

The fate of a single broken column near the present Piraeus Street was once believed to be connected with the health of the city, in that if it fell, an epidemic would break out. The disease was believed to be trapped underneath it. The column was said to have been erected by forty women who had collected money to purchase a cart, to which they yoked calves. They purchased a silver vessel, wrote down the names of the various epidemic diseases to which the population was liable, enclosed them inside the vessel, and then it, the cart and the calves were buried, and the column placed on top of them in honour of Saint Haralambos, protector against plagues. This column was removed, without an outbreak of disease, in 1835; but a similar column remains standing today, protected by a church.

The Plague Church

Tucked away between two large and featureless modern buildings in the area of the central market is a tiny church built around a large column surmounted by a Corinthian capital, a relic of some ancient building, which protrudes through its roof. The church is dedicated to Saint John the Baptist, but according to the story told by Athenians during the eighteenth century, the Saint John who gave his name to this church was not the Baptist but an ascetic, skilled in art of healing of various types of fever.

When he felt death approaching, he laid the foundations of the column, and then bound to them diseases of various kinds with coloured threads. Then, to ensure that the diseases would stay bound, he set up the column over them, and promised: "When I die, whoever is ill, let him come and tie to this column a thread of the colour of his sickness with three knots in it." He must say: "Dear Saint John, I bind my sickness to the column."

Since medieval times the column has been credited with curing illnesses, especially fevers. A sick person would visit the church, light a candle, pray to the saint and then attach a thread to the column. Threads of different colours were used for different ailments, and attached to the column with candle wax or glue, so that the fever would be drawn through the thread and into the marble. White thread was used for malaria, red for measles and yellow for less specific fevers. Sometimes the afflicted person would first rub the thread over the icon of the saint and then return home, keeping the thread around his waist or right arm for three days and three nights. Then he would return to the church and attach the thread to the column saying: "Take this cursed illness. Take it to the high mountains, to the boulders at the root of the mountains where no cock crows. And as it came with a shiver, let it go with a shiver. As it came unannounced, let it go unannounced."

The column was also used as an oracle. A sufferer would attach a silver drachma to it. If the coin held fast, he would be cured; if not, his case was hopeless.

Although the cult has waned, it still survives, since strings are still tied around the column, and there are many ex-votos hanging from the walls of this frequently visited chapel to bear witness to past successes and present hopes.

Several mosaic floors and no less than six wells have been discovered in the vicinity of the church, suggesting the existence of an ancient healing shrine on the site. According to a tradition this was a monument to Toxaris, a Scythian doctor who specialised in the cure of fevers. When plague broke out in Athens, he appeared in a dream to the wife of an aristo-crat, and through her advised the people to bathe themselves and to throw the water into the sea. Then they were to sprin-kle the streets of the city with wine. They did, and the plague abated. Afterwards, the Athenians went to his tomb, hung it about with garlands and sacrificed a white horse. After that, they venerated him as a hero.

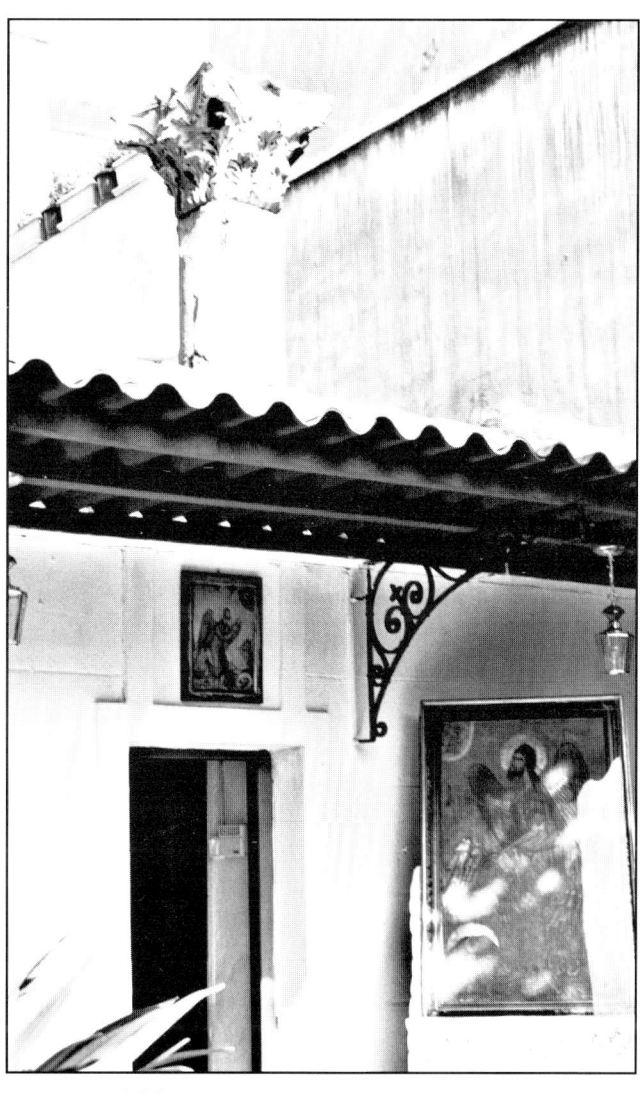

There might be a genuine memory of ancient practice here, because it seems likely that they would have used old or spoiled wine to sprinkle the streets, i.e. vinegar, which has antiseptic properties.

This church has probably been continuously used as the site of a healing cult since ancient times - another unbroken link between modern Athens and its ancient past.

Saint John of the Column, showing the roof of the church pierced by the plague column

Psiri

Lord Byron and the Maid of Athens

In 1809 the famous English poet, Lord Byron, decided to make the Grand Tour in the company of his friend, John Cam Hobhouse. After visiting Spain and Malta, he landed in Greece at Patras. He paid a visit to the court of Ali Pasha of Ioannina, and called at Delphi, Levadia and Thebes, arriving in Athens just before Christmas. In those days there were no hotels in the city, and everyone recommended him to rent rooms. In order to find suitable accommodation, he sought out the Greek citizen who was at that time acting as British vice-consul, who lived in Psiri.

This man had recently died, but Byron met his widow, Theodora Makris, who lived on the site of number 11 Theklas Street. This woman had a sister-in-law, also widowed, named Tarsia, living next door with her three daughters. The entire family spoke English, not merely because of the official position held by Theodora's late husband, but also because they had relations by marriage in Ionian Islands, at that time under British sovereignty. The widows supported themselves by taking in visitors, and Byron was able to rent rooms at what is today the corner of Agias and Papanikole streets. He wrote: "We occupied two houses separated from each other by a single wall, through which we opened a doorway."

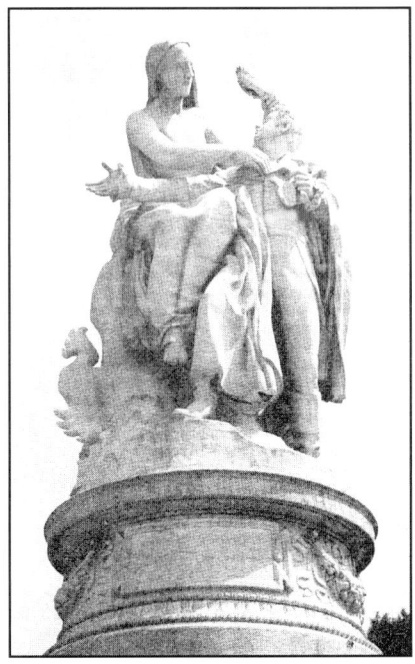

The twenty-two year-old Byron flirted with Tarsia's daughters, Ekaterina, Marianna and Theresa, calling them the "Three Graces." He wrote to his friend, Henry Drury: "I almost forgot to tell you that I am dying for love of three Greek girls of Athens, sisters . . . three divinities, all of them under fifteen." He chiefly teased the youngest, Theresa, who was then but twelve. When he left with Hobhouse on an excursion to Asia Minor and Constantinople, he left her with the words: "My life, I love you."

After his trip, Byron returned to Athens alone, and discovered that the widow Makris had in the meantime resolved that her youngest daughter would be married to the (doubtless wealthy) English "milord", and that she hoped to persuade him to pay six hundred pounds for the privilege. This was a disastrous misreading of the

Statue of Byron in the Zappeion Gardens

110

situation. In a letter to Hobhouse, Byron wrote: "the old woman was mad enough to imagine that I was going to marry the girl, but I have better amusement." Byron was notoriously catholic in his tastes. This "better amusement" was Nicolo Giraud, a fifteen year-old boy with whom he spent all his days at that time riding and swimming. In order to evade the widow Makris' importuning, Byron moved out of his lodgings into the Capuchin Monastery in the Plaka, and when he left for England, he took Nicolo to Malta, where he arranged for his schooling.

Although Theresa was never more than a passing infatuation at most, and the poet's feelings for the twelve-year-old probably no more than a literary fiction, he had nevertheless in a few words immortalised her in poetry as the "Maid of Athens":

"Maid of Athens, ere I part
Give o give me back my heart."

The Makris girls remained unmarried for some time afterwards, since they had only sixty olive trees for their dowry. They made their living by embroidery. During the War of Independence, the Makris family temporarily moved to Corfu to escape the fighting, where they made the acquaintance of another Englishman, John Black. At the age of thirty-two, Theresa married him and had four children by him, three boys and a girl.

Byron returned to Greece and took part in the War of Independence. Although it was the fever which took his life, such was the power of the romantic imagination at that time that he became, in the public eye, a heroic martyr figure.

Theresa Makris was widowed by 1867, and soon found herself in impoverished circumstances. But such, by that time, was her fame, through her brief, tenuous and rather artificial association with Byron, that public collections were made for her in England. With the development of the "Byron legend,"

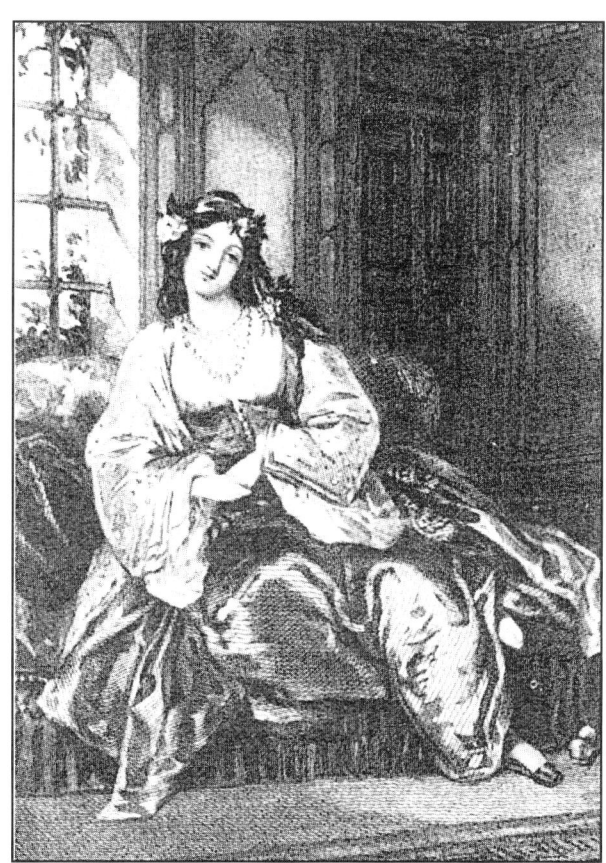

The Maid of Athens (C.R.Cockerell) a figure far removed from the twelve-year-old girl who had inspired Byron

111

particularly after the hero-poet's death, the girl became renowned across Europe, herself a romantic icon, and literary tourists would seek out the house where she had lived, and affect to admire that beauty which had so stirred the heart of the great poet himself. It may be that this cult of "the Maid of Athens" served to legitimate and "sanitise" Byron's reputation in the eyes of the homophobic Victorian public in England. Her reputation, however, was as widely celebrated as that of the poet himself. In 1872 the French composer Gounoud wrote a song for her entitled "The Maid of Athens," and sent her the proceeds of the concert at which it was first performed.

Theresa died on 22nd September 1875 aged seventy-eight seven at 35 Sophokleous Street, not far from her original home. Her daughter, Caroline, continued to live at 13 Kerameikou Street, in nearby Metaxurgeio, until well into the twentieth century.

An International Incident

During the nineteenth century it was the custom of the people of Athens, and had been from time out of mind, to burn Judas Iscariot in effigy on the day before Easter. During Easter 1847 the government issued an order forbidding the practice. They did not wish to offend a member of the French branch of the wealthy Rothschild banking family, in Athens at the time, since they were hoping for a loan from him. Those assembled in Thesion Square to take part in this ancient custom had already been angered by an incident which had taken place on the previous day. Don Pacifico, a Spanish Jew who was consul-general of Portugal, had publicly insulted their religion by refusing to dismount from his horse as a token of respect when the Good Friday procession from the nearby church of Saint Philip bearing the *epitaphio,* the image of the dead Christ woven in cloth, had passed by. The ban on the traditional bonfire was the last straw. The angry crowd in Thision Square made their way to the house of Don Pacifico on Karaoskaki Street in Psiri, and attacked it. They beat his wife, stole his goods and started a fire, while the police, always reluctant to enter this area of the city at the best of times, declined to intervene. One of the looters, who took away a box of money, was said to have been the son of the Minister of War.

Don Pacifico had recently been in financial difficulties, and had borrowed one hundred drachmas from the Duchess of Placentia. He saw the riot as a heaven sent opportunity to recover his fortunes, and claimed the enormous amount of £31,534 1s 11d in damages from the government for his house and property, and a further £500 in compensation for the "personal injuries and sufferings" of himself and his family. When the government refused to pay this huge sum, Pacifico tried to enlist the support of the Portuguese, and then the Spanish, governments. When he failed in this, he used the circumstance of his birth on the rock of Gibraltar, a British colony, to claim British citizenship, and to call upon the assistance of the British Government. He sent a letter to Lord Palmerston, at that time Britain's chauvinistic Foreign Secretary, outlining his plight.

Palmerston bundled this complaint together with several others which the British Government had amassed over a period of time. George Finlay, a Scottish historian who had bought property in Athens, had lost a part of it when it had been arbitrarily seized without compensation by Queen Amalia to enclose within her gardens. Another issue concerned the treatment of some British sailors arrested in Patras. On January 7th 1850, all these matters were drawn to the attention of the Greek Government by Thomas Wyse, the British Minister in Athens, together with a peremptory demand that they be settled within twenty-four hours.

When this ultimatum was ignored, a squadron of British warships imposed a blockade upon Piraeus, seizing a Greek warship and several merchantmen. Public opinion in Greece was outraged at this arrogance. The staff of the British Legation had to move on board a ship lying offshore for their own safety. Palmerston defended his action in the House of Commons, and declared that a British subject, like a Roman citizen of old, who could proudly boast *Civis Romanus sum,* should feel safe anywhere in the world where he might find himself. While predictably supported by his own party's majority in the Commons, in the House of Lords he was censured for his conduct of the affair. On the whole, the British people were dismayed by this outrageous bullying. The influential satirical magazine *Punch* asked why the British lion did not take on someone its own size. Even George Finlay, one of the injured parties, admitted: "The British Government acted with violence and shamed the authority of international law."

After some time, the Greek Government consented to arbitration by a French mediator. Baron Gros was sent to calculate the amount of compensation to be paid to Don Pacifico, but his attitude and conduct alienated the British and his decision was considered unacceptable by the British Government. The French, insulted in their turn, then withdrew their arbitrator.

Some time later, an Anglo-Franco-Greek commission sitting in Lisbon reviewed documentary evidence in the Portugese archives in order to settle the amount of compensation and found that Don Pacifico's claim had been grossly inflated. It was reduced to £150.

The Outsiders

The "Hard Men" of Psiri

From the nature of its establishment by a lengthy war of liberation, the Greek state found itself from the beginning with a large number of armed civilians. Inevitably, many of these men from the countryside flocked to the new capital city. Still wearing their foustanellas or baggy pants, they brought with them the pistols and knives, tucked into their wide sashes, with which they had fought the Turks.

Unemployed veterans and other men from the provinces seeking work gravitated to Psiri, particularly to Iroon Square, in the centre of the warren of narrow alleys. Many of them came from the island of Naxos in the Cyclades. Many who found work and success left the area and settled down to become respectable citizens. But a residue did not. These discontented outsiders often felt cheated, that they had been deprived of their rights in the newly independent state. In time, they came to form an underclass, their numbers constantly being made up by new immigrants.

In time, many of them came to be organised in gangs of "hard men", and were known as *manges.* When King Otto was forced to grant a constitution and hold elections, his Prime Minister, Kollettis, sought to retain control of the state by rigging the vote. In Athens, he employed gangs of *manges* to intimidate the voters. Opposition politicians fought back using the same tactics. The *manges* also came to be known as *trabouki,* from the cigars which they were paid by the party bosses for their work.

Some groups, called *Koutsavakides*, affected a peculiar fashion of dress. In addition to being particularly proud of their long moustaches, they wore slender shoes extending far beyond the toe, with high heels, tight pants, and a black armband which normally signified mourning. The jacket would be worn on the left side only, the right arm hanging over the shoulder, presumably to leave the weapon hand free. Into a broad red sash, they would tuck their various weapons.

These gangs created a "no-go area" in Psiri for the police, whose lower ranks frequently sympathised with them. The gang leaders became well-known as an unofficial local government within the area, and held court at the Acropolis Taverna. These leaders would sometimes go to the local police station to help out members of their gangs who had been arrested.

"Hard Men" to Deal with the "Hard Men."

After forty years of independence, these gangs, whose members frequently engaged in crimes of various kinds, began to be regarded as an anachronism in the Western style society that was slowly evolving, and both the power they exercised locally and their immunity from police action were increasingly unacceptable to ordinary citizens. Since the police seemed unable to protect them, many took to carrying weapons to protect themselves when they went out into the streets.

A succession of capable police chiefs, working from their headquarters in Klafthmonos Square, waged a determined war against the *Manges*, taking the battle into their home ground in the narrow streets of Psiri.

Mr. Vratsanos from Psara, made his arrests in the company of his formidable wife, the fearless Flora, who was said to be able to handle a gun or rifle as well as any soldier. Then in 1893 Prime Minister Harilaous Trikoupis sent in the equally capable and tough Dimitrios Baoraktaris. He cleverly attacked the visible symbols of the *Manges'* subculture. Rounding up those dressed in the fashionable manner, after a blow with a whip, he would systematically divest the *Koutsavakides* of the outward symbols of their way of life. Shoes lost their elongated toes. With his scissors, he would cut off the useless sleeve of their jackets dangling behind their right shoulders. Afterwards, they were released, although most would have preferred imprisonment to the humiliation of returning home in such an "emasculated" condition.

The shame felt by the *Koutsavakides*, and the laughter of the law-abiding citizens, effectively killed the phenomenon. Even Psiri, the heartland of the lawlessness became safe and quiet. Only in literature, the theatre, and later in the cinema, did they linger on. They became a literary phenomenon and featured in many Greek novels, such as *Les Miserables of Athens*, and in the operetta *The Outcasts of Athens*.

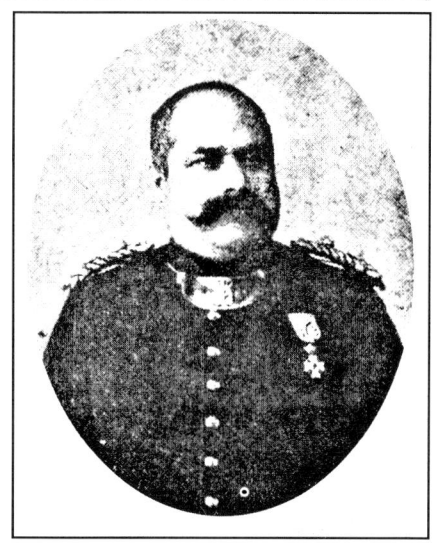

Inspector Baïraktaris

The "Nightingales" Silenced

A less happy consequence of Baoraktaris' regime, which today would be described as one of "zero tolerance" was the disappearance of the nocturnal serenade. By the latter half of the nineteenth century, the Mediterranean custom of young men serenading the objects of their affection on their balconies during the hours of night had taken a firm hold in Athens. As soon as darkness fell, particularly during the balmy nights of high summer, young men clutching guitars would take up their positions below balconies and begin their nocturnal serenades. Unfortunately, not many were naturally talented vocal artistes, and many sought to achieve with persistence what they could by no means attain by tunefulness. The result was a lot of sleepless nights for a lot of irritated citizens, and many complaints. The new ultra-efficient police force declared war on the young nightingales. First the patrol officers would break the singers' guitars over their backs or heads, and then they would march them down to the police station for the night, releasing them next morning with a ticking off. Although the burgers of Athens could sleep sounder in their beds for these efforts, surely something of value was lost in this Victorian crusade for bourgeois respectability.

The "Stone Wars"

Not all the amusements of the poor were so easily suppressed. In the days before organised sports, rivalry between working class districts was expressed in regular stone-throwing battles. Contests between the inhabitants of Psiri, Metaxurgio and Petralona would be held at prearranged times and places, such as Thisio Square, Vathis Square, or the ravine of Kuklovorou. Businesses in those areas had protective grilles fitted to their windows. The two sides engaged in combat would parade and hurl insults at each other before the melie, and spectators would gather to watch in large numbers. The injured would become local heroes afterwards. Towards the end of the century, these *petrapolemoi,* or stone-wars, became so institutionalised that the Athens newspapers would carry announcements of the times and places of the engagements.

The Cathedral Quarter

A Museum in its Fabric

Next to the large, and given its date, inevitably rather ugly, nineteenth century cathedral, is the tiny church once known as *Panayia Gorgoepikoφs* (the Virgin Who Grants Requests Quickly). Said to have been originally founded by the Empress Irene, in its present form it dates from the end of the twelfth century and stands on the ruins of an ancient temple, dedicated to the goddess Eileithyia. It served as the personal chapel of the archbishops of Athens when the bishops were ousted from the Parthenon, by the Crusaders and then by the Turks, and from 1841 it housed the public library of Athens.

On its reconsecration in 1868, it was dedicated to Christ the Saviour, but it is universally known as *Ayias Eleutherios* (Holy Freedom). Since that time a modern bell-tower and other accretions (see below) have been removed, so that the building looks at present very much as it must have done in the twelfth century.

This remarkable building is constructed almost entirely from fragments of ancient buildings, including churches of the sixth and seventh centuries.

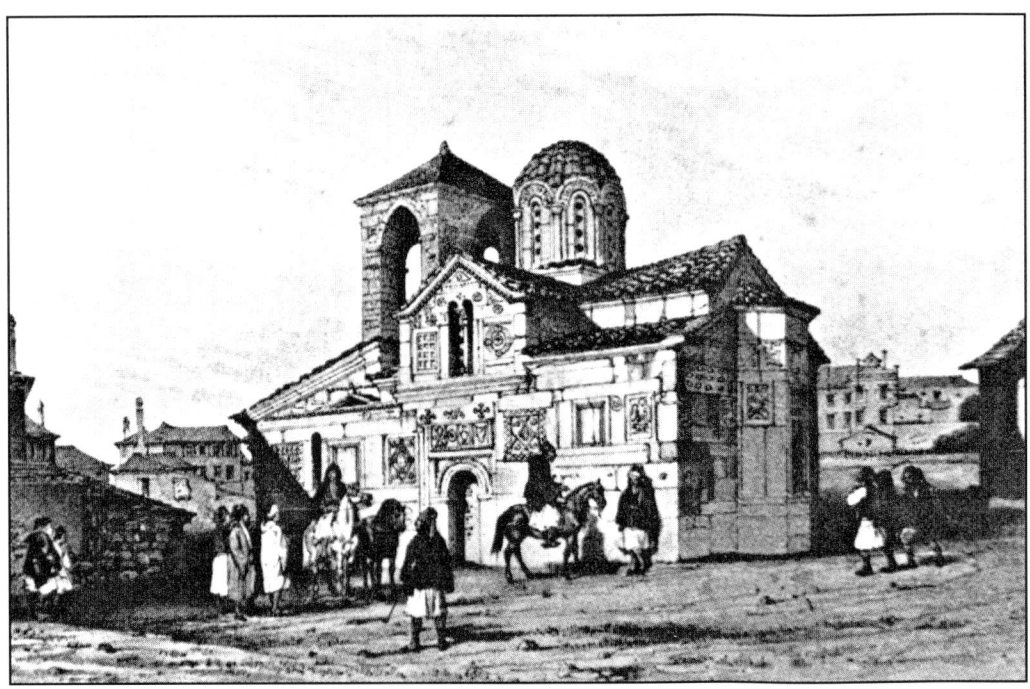

The Church of the Virgin Who Grants Requests Quickly (Du Moncel, 1846)

116

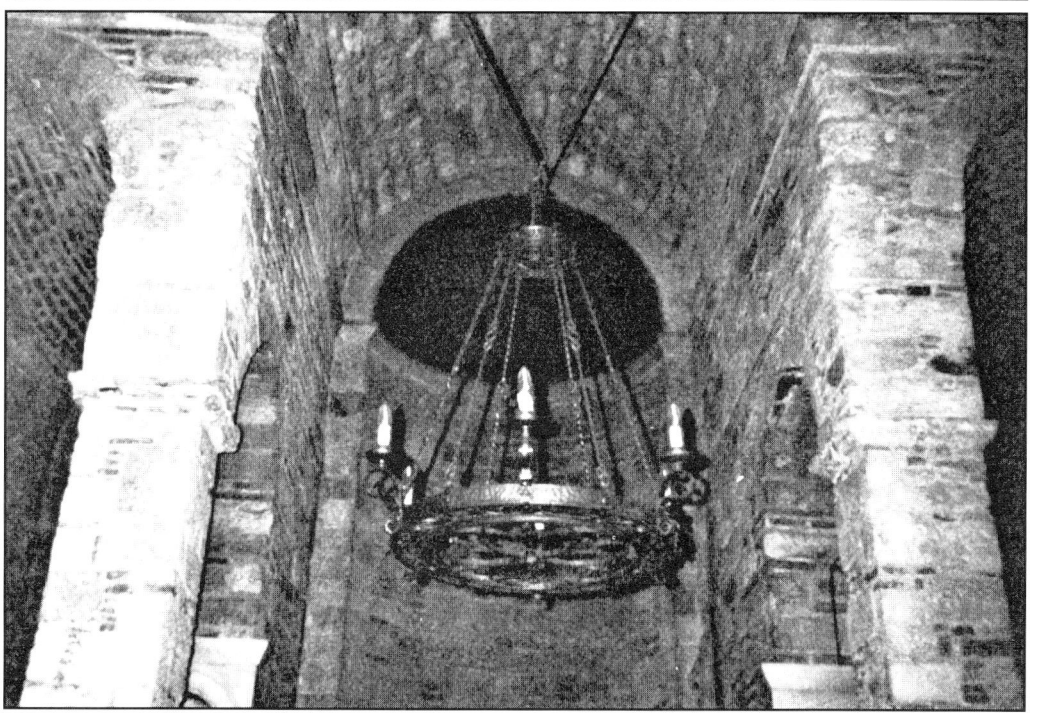

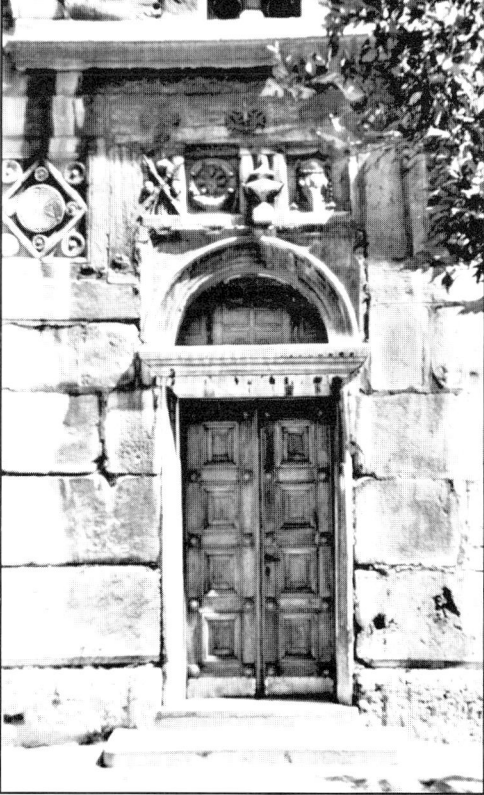

Among these carved blocks one, on the west side over the door, is a calendar of Athenian state festivals which probably dates from the second century AD. Signs of the zodiac represent the sequence of time, while figures in relief represent the various festivals of the ancient calendar.

Most of the carvings clearly date from the Byzantine period, and were probably originally parts of churches which were destroyed in some calamity, either an earthquake or a raid on the city by Saracens or others.

On the south side of the church was a block of grey marble inscribed: "This is the stone from Cana in Galilee where our Lord Jesus Christ changed the water into wine." It was supposed to have been the marble bench on which Jesus reclined at the wedding feast. Inside is the miracle-working icon of *Panayia Gorgoepikoφs* which gave the church its original name.

117

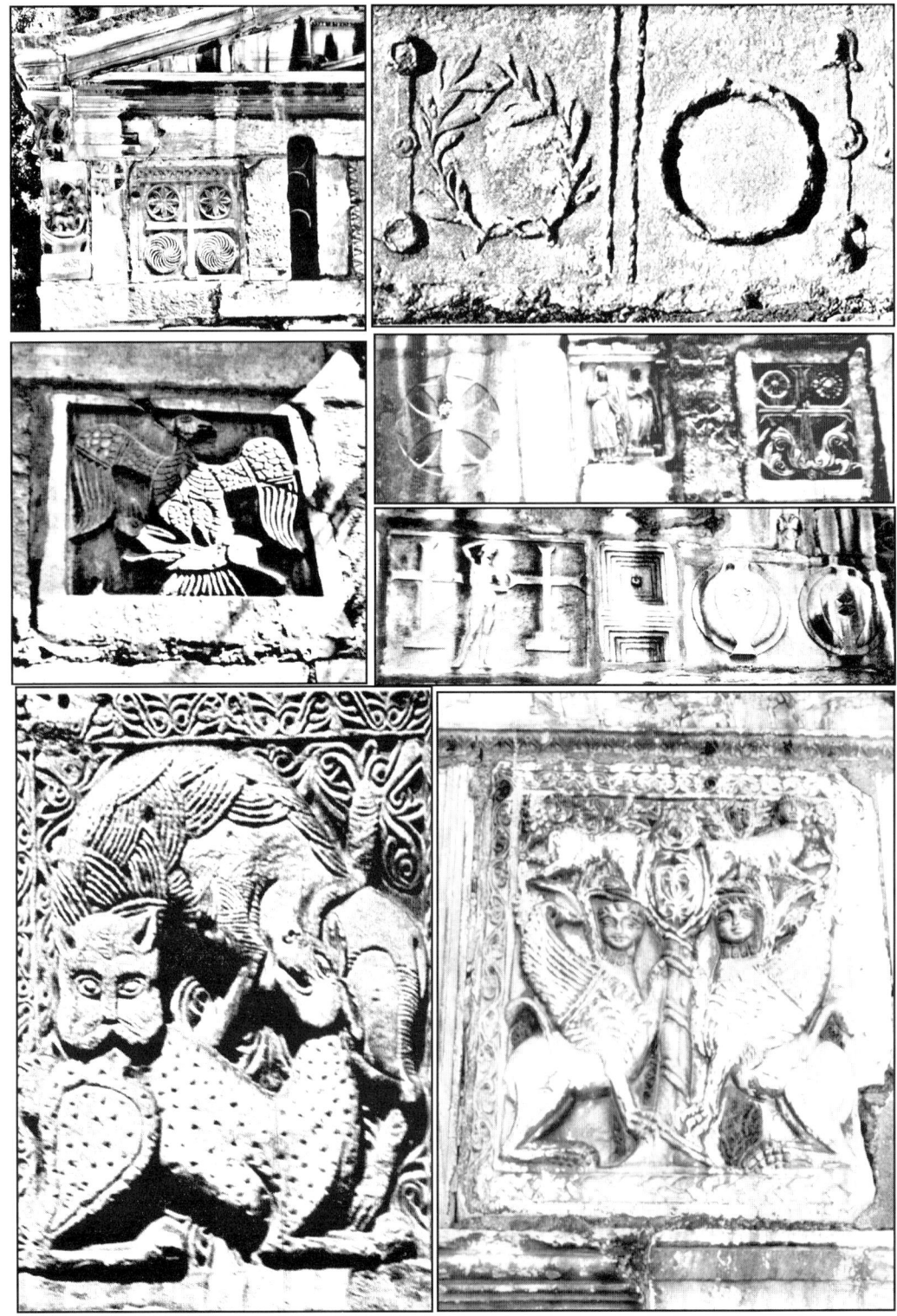

Holy Power

The tiny church of *Ayia Dynami*, or Holy Power, in Mitropoleos Street, which belongs to Pendeli Monastery, looks forlorn today, overshadowed and dwarfed by the massive bulk of the ugly Ministry of Education building which overshadows it. Yet its name suggests, and its history shows, that the importance of a building is not always evident in its appearance.

The Turkish Voivode, Hadji Ali Haseki, had given the monks of Pendeli licence to manufacture ammunition for the use of the garrison on the Acropolis, and the building was used by their armourer as a workshop. Each day, he would hand over the bullets he had manufactured to the Turks, as required; but after darkness fell he would continue working for his own people. From the chapel, through a secret passageway these would be taken into an old house, dating from 1641, which lay adjacent to the back of the chapel. After dark, an old woman, Manolaina Biniari, would creep out from the house with the ammunition concealed under her washing in a basket, to the banks of the River Illisos. There freedom fighters would meet her and take the contents to a house in Menidi, at the foot of Mount Parnes, where revolutionaries were meeting to plot an uprising. With the ammunition from this chapel, the people of Attica rose up during the night of April 25th, liberated Athens and laid siege to the Turks in Acropolis, to which most of them had retreated.

Later, when the Turks had temporarily regained control of the city, an edict was issued forbidding anyone to remove any of his possessions to the islands, to which many of the people had fled. Because of this, the monks of Pendeli secreted all of their valuable treasures in the crypt underneath this church. There Turkish soldiers found all of them: liturgical items, such as vestments, legal documents, including edicts of the sultans and encyclicals of the patriarchs; all were destroyed.

The "holy power" referred to in the name of the church is that of the Virgin Mary to help women in childbirth. For this reason, pregnant women traditionally pray in this church. However, the chapel did serve as a source of strength to the national cause, and for that reason, its unusual name is doubly appropriate.

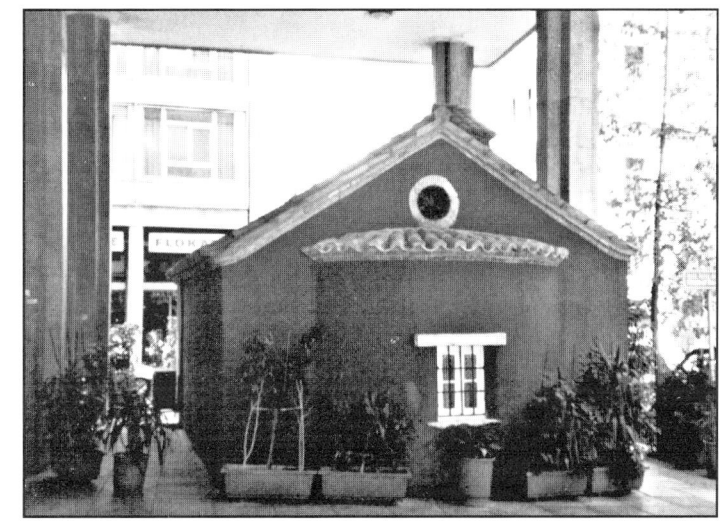

The church of Holy Power (Ayia Dynamis), dwarfed by the offices of the Ministry of Education

An English Parish Church in Athens

Nothing could be more visually incongruous than the typically English church which stands in the centre of Athens opposite the Zappeion Gardens. Saint Paul's Church was erected following a meeting of prominent English residents of Athens, including Sir Edmund Lyons, the British Minister, and George Findlay, the eminent historian. Lord Palmerston was asked for Government aid, which was not generously given. But with private subscriptions, the building was erected, and consecrated by the bishop of Gibraltar, in whose diocese it lies, in 1843.

Although not old by the standards either of Greece or of English parish churches, this building has become the repository of many memorials of the British in Greece.

On the inside wall is the oldest monument to a Briton in Athens, to George Stoakes. It was probably originally a gravestone in the Thiseion which, as the church of Saint George, was the designated burial place of Englishmen during the period of Turkish rule. The inscription reads:

> "Here rests in hope of resurrection the body of Georges Stoakes born at Limehouse in London who after nigh seaven years apprenticeship in Athens unto Consul Lancelot Hobson and learning the Italian Greeke and Turk-ish languages dyed the sixth of August 1685 in the twenty fourth year of his age unto the inexpressable grief of his said patron who hath erected this monument out [of] true [*sic*] unto the deceased's memory. Adjacent lie the bodies of Captain Thomas Roberts comander of [the] Shipp Recopense of Yarmouth who died at Porto Leone in twelth of May 1685.

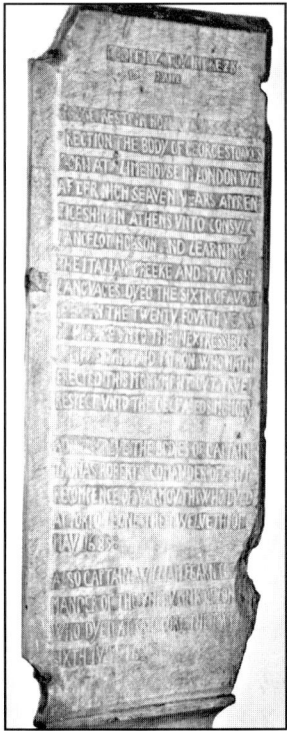

> Also Captain William Fearn Commander of the Unity pink of Lond[on] who dyed at said port the twen[ty] sixth of July 1685."

Clearly, the authorities did not want to waste some free space on the stone slab, and so adapted it to commemorate two other Englishmen who had also died at that time.

Several monuments in the church recall the Philhellenes who arrived in Greece to assist in the struggle for independence. The windows in the north and south transepts are dedicated to perhaps the greatest of them all, General Sir Richard Church, who was appointed to command Greek forces in 1827. A plaque records the spot where the heart of Frank Abney Hastings is immured. He brought the *Karteria* to Greece, the first steam-driven ship to take part in a naval battle, which helped defeat a Turkish fleet in the Bay of Itea in 1827.

The Stoakes Monument

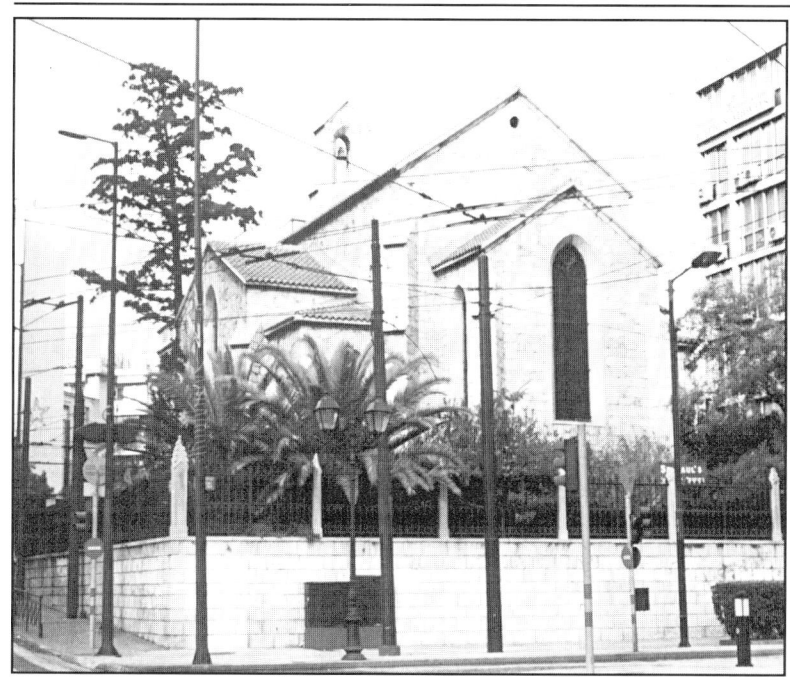

Above: All Saint's Church
Below: The Lusieri Monument

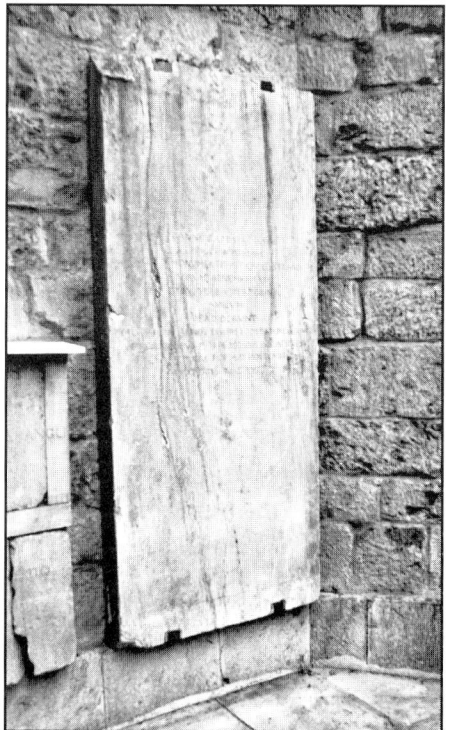

A plaque in memory of one Clement Harris, who died at the Battle of the Five Wells in Epirus, in 1897, shows that philhellenes from abroad continued to support the freedom of Greece with their lives for many years after independence was won. Another commemorates those who died during the Second World War.

Anglo-Greek relations were not always harmonious. A plaque to the memory of chaplain Henry Leeves and his family records that his infant grandson died of cholera, and that his son and wife died on the same day, August 28th 1854. He had a house at Kastaniotissa, on Euboeia, where the pair were murdered by some of the villagers. The culprits, who were caught and guillotined, included the son of the village priest. The east window is dedicated to the victims of the "Marathon Massacre". A group of wealthy travellers visiting Marathon in 1870 were kidnapped by brigands. Some politicians were in league with the brigands, and a bungled rescue attempt led to the death of the hostages. [See volume three in this series: *Attica*].

Among the monuments outside the church is one to John Tweddell, a Fellow of Trinity College, Cambridge, who died in 1799 of fever. Another is the gravestone of John Baptist Lusieri, who died after looting the Acropolis on behalf of his employer, Lord Elgin.

121

The Palace Quarter

An Uninhabitable Barn of a Palace

When Otto Wittlesbach arrived in Greece to take up his throne as king, he was a seventeen year-old youth in a foreign country. His father, King Ludwig of Bavaria, wished to give his rule an air of power and durability. Accordingly, in 1835, he invited the Bavarian State Architect, Friedrich von Gartner, to design an imposing palace for his son. He promised to provide the necessary finance in the form of a long-term loan.

Unfortunately, either Ludwig's benevolence or his pocket could not rise to the design von Gartner produced, and much of the decorative embellishment had to be abandoned. The architect complained that what remained resembled an army barracks.

King Otto and Queen Amalia moved into the building in 1843, although it was not finished for another four years. Many maintained that the building was never really habitable. Some of the rooms had fireplaces, but others were heated by means of porcelain stoves, which roasted those warming themselves on their nearest side, while they shivered from the draught on the other. Lighting was by oil lamps placed on tables or suspended from ceilings. These gave off a thin blue smoke and a strong odour which made the eyes water. Although the palace boasted three hundred and sixty-five rooms, only one was a bathroom. John Van der Kiste notes that no one had ever been known actually to take a bath in it, since the taps rarely produced more than a trickle of water, and when they did, what emerged was usually accompanied by a succession of dead cockroaches and similar fauna.

Queen Amalia busied herself with the palace gardens. A Roman mosaic unearthed was used as the floor of a pergola called the "Garden Room", and the king and queen occasionally held dinner parties there. The public was admitted into the gardens during certain times, but the queen decided that the privilege was being abused, and on 21st June 1851, it was decided to admit in future only those holding special permits. When this provoked public outrage, the idea was quickly dropped.

Paradoxically, the grandeur of the palace and its gardens had the opposite effect than that originally intended. Out of proportion in a city the size of Athens and for the head of a kingdom the size of Greece at that time, the ostentatious palace and its luxuriant gardens served only to stimulated resentment towards its foreign occupants. The French writer Edmund About remarked in 1854: "It will never be known how much work and water is required to maintain a lawn in Athens in July. It is truly a royal luxury. To water her plants the Queen has taken over several reservoirs that supplied the city and satisfied Athenians' thirst. The people of the capital are suffering but the lawn is doing well."

Otto was ousted in 1862, to be replaced by George I of Denmark.

In July 1884, the north section of the building was destroyed by a fire. A second blaze on 24th December 1909 burnt down the main section of the Palace. The royal family decamped to their summer residence at Tatoo and never returned. The Old Palace remained uninhabited until the Asia Minor catastrophe of 1922, when thousands of refugees occupied the by that time half-ruined building and its grounds.

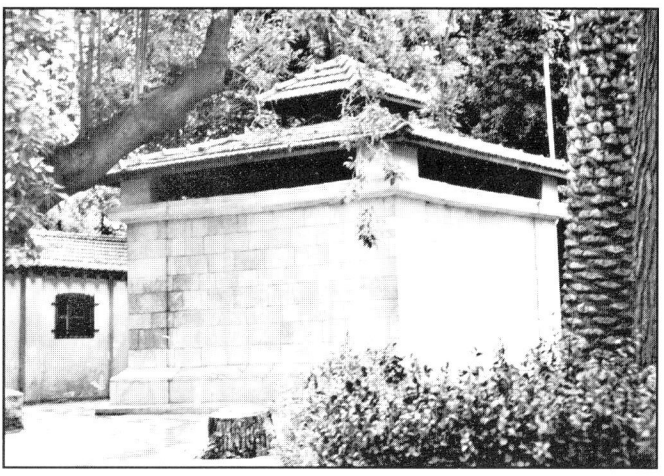

*The former palace cold store
in the National Gardens,
now a public toilet*

The Royal Gardens became public property, and opened to the public in at the National Gardens in 1923. Their heyday was between that date and the Second World War, when they were well-protected and well-maintained. The Senate moved into the building in 1934, and the *Boule* or parliament moved there a year later. The monument for the Unknown Soldier was placed in position before the palace in 1932.

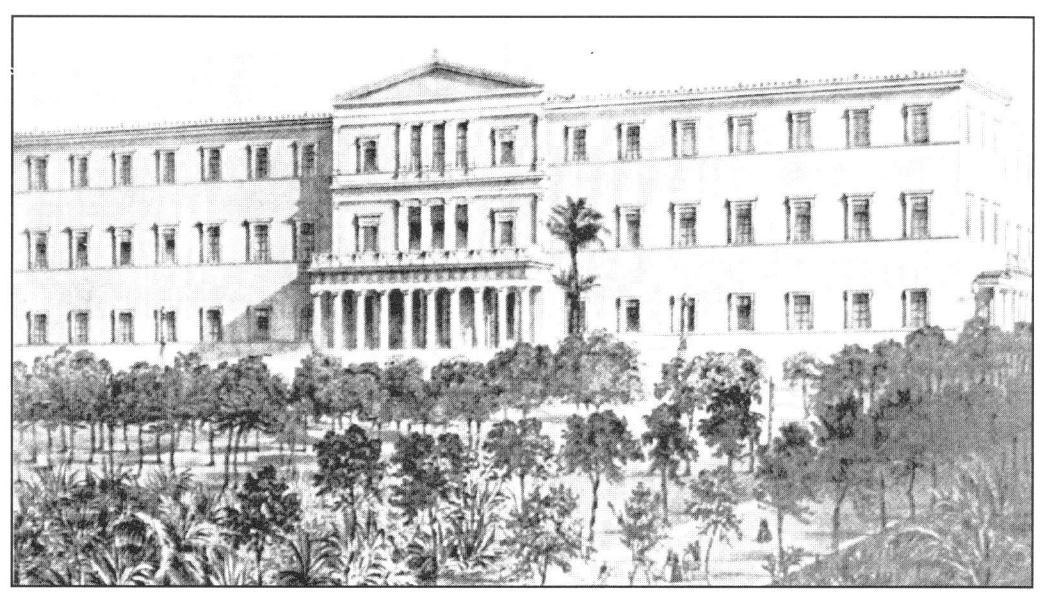

*The palace of Otto and Amalia in the days of royal occupancy.
Today it houses the Boule, the parliament of the Greeks*

The "Well-Belted Ones"

On the far corner of the National gardens from the Parliament building lying on Vasilissis Sofias lies the barracks of the Presidential Guard, more commonly known as the *Evzones*. With their distinctive pleated kilts and pom-pommed slippers, they are one of the most distinctive and recognisable sights of Athens.

The term e*vzone*, which means "well-belted", goes back to Homer, who used it to describe lightly armed soldiers distinguished for their spirit, strength and fighting ability. During the eighteenth and early nineteenth centuries the term referred to a man with a narrow waist. So desirable was a slender waist considered that at that time, that many men wore their girdles or belts painfully tight. In 1824, during the War of Independence, an infantry battalion bearing that name was founded. By 1864 the *Evzones* were recognised as an elite section of the Greek regular army. Made up of men chosen from mountain areas, they had special responsibility for guarding the northern borders of the country.

The most prominent feature of the Evzones' uniform today is the kilt. Properly called the *fustanella,* this was once worn by men in many parts of Greece, most memorably by the *klefts* and *armatoles* (brigands) who fought the Turks during the War of Independence. For that reason, it came to be associated in the national consciousness with the warlike spirit of the freedom fighters.

In those days the *fustanella* was not the clean garment it is today. Containing hundreds of pleats and taking many hours to iron, it would normally be changed only twice a year, once Easter and once at Christmas. Moreover, popular belief had it that a well-soiled *fustanella* offered better protection against fleas, lice and bugs than a clean one. For this reason, the garment was always smeared with a fatty substance before being worn.

The *Evzones* of the presidential guard were originally a royal guard, founded in 1914. Today this elite corps comprises about two hundred members, who enjoy much better accommodation and conditions of service than other soldiers. When they join, they must be under twenty-five years of age and over 1.80 metres tall. They must have been nominated by their division commander for their outstanding character blameless and conduct".

Changing the guard on a Sunday morning

Changing the guard;
the officer carries
the flag of Saint George

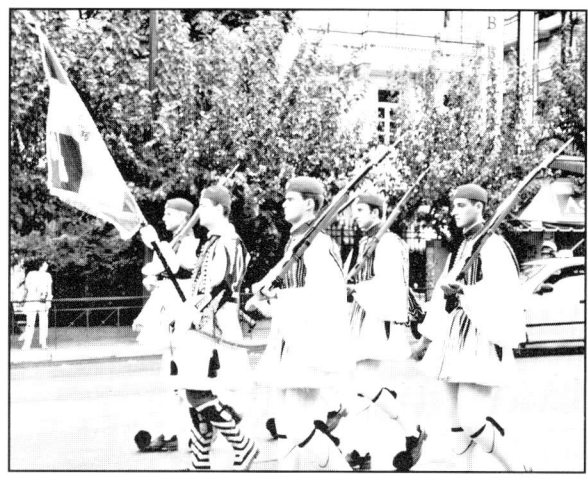

Their duties include mounting the guard on the Tomb of the Unknown Warrior, the Presidential Mansion, and their own barracks, and ceremonially raising and lowering the flag on the Acropolis. Each soldier mounts guard for one hour at a time, three times during each period of forty-eight hours. They do so in pairs, and work with the same partner throughout their service, so as to enable them to perfect the co-ordination of their movements. The Presidential Guard is ceremonially changed at the tomb of the Unknown Warrior in Syntagma Square every Sunday at 11 am rain or shine, when one company relieves the other. In addition, the *Evzones* mount honour guards at many national ceremonies and events, both in Greece and abroad, and engage in military training.

Their uniforms, which take eighty days to prepare, are made and repaired by craftsmen employed in special workshops within the barracks. The full dress uniform worn on Sundays, holidays and special occasions, dates in its present form from 1914. It consists of a red fez with a black tassel, a white shirt and embroidered jacket, a

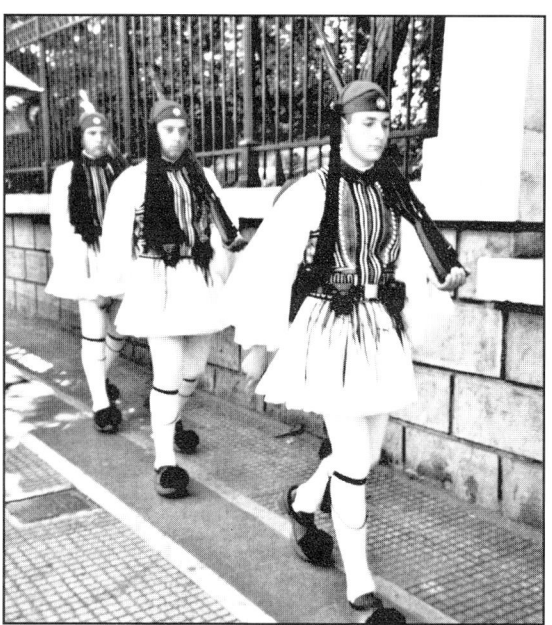

white *fustanella,* a shiny black leather belt and two leather pouches, long white socks and red *tsarouchia*, or slippers, with black pom-poms. The soles of the slippers are covered with metal studs, originally to aid movement up and down steep mountainsides, but now they are equally useful in preventing slipping on wet marble pavements. In rain or very cold weather a black cape of thick wool is also worn. On ordinary days, a plainer khaki uniform, which still preserves the characteristic *Evzone* look, is

Going to mount guard at
the tomb of the Unknown Warrior
(every hour, on the hour)

substituted. Officers wear an older, and more elaborate, form of the uniform. Since the Second World War, *Evzones* from Crete have worn a distinctive dress of blue breeches, and caps and white boots based upon the Cretan regional costume. Off duty, the *Evzones* wear the same khaki uniform as other members of the Greek Army, with a light blue beret and distinctive insignia.

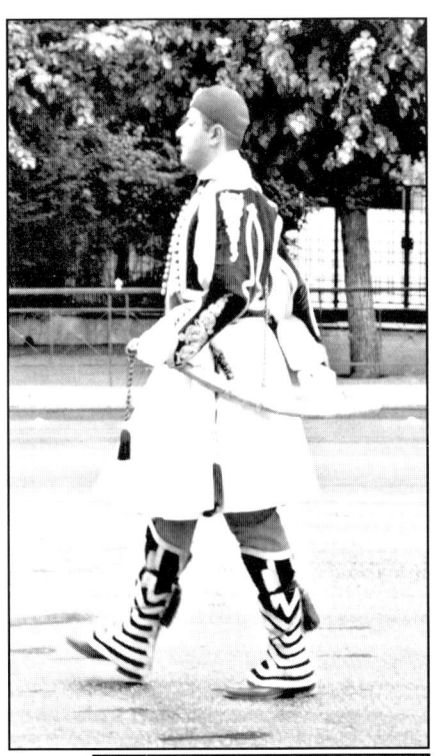

Right: Officer, wearing the older, more elaborate version of the evzone uniform
Below left: On guard duty wearing the "undress uniform"
Below centre: On guard at the evzones' barracks in full dress uniform
Below right: Members of the Cretan Guard wearing their distinctive blue breeches and caps, and white boots.

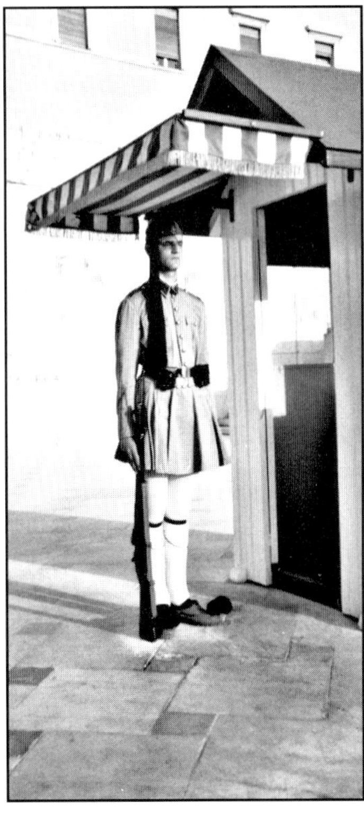

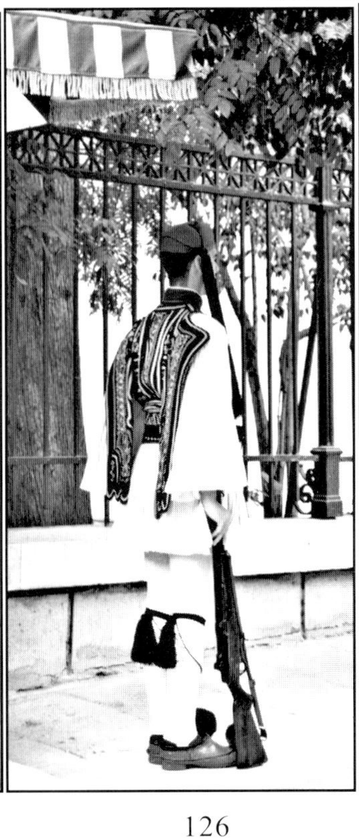

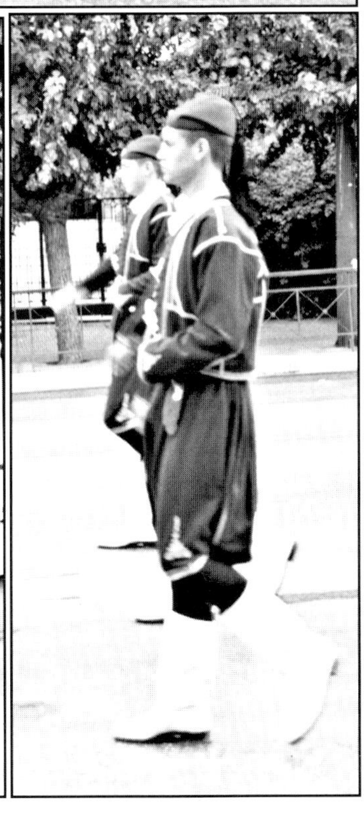

How the "Constitution" Got Into "Constitution Square"

When Greece became independent, the Great Powers insisted on appointing a monarch to rule over the new country. They chose the young Prince Otho of Bavaria, a Catholic. The Greeks fully expected that he would grant a constitution and rule according to law, and this was promised to them. But when he arrived, he came with a Bavarian military force and three regents who would rule as dctators until he came of age.

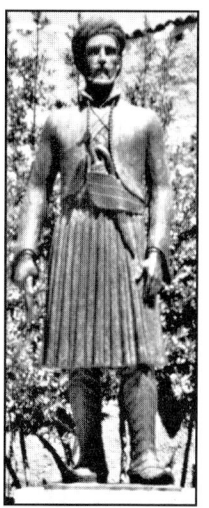

Makriyannis: statue opposite the site of his house

The regents immediately began to quarrel among themselves, ignored the claims of the fighters who had made sacrifices during the national uprising, imposed heavy taxes, failed to publish any accounts, and muzzled the press. It was not until 1837 that the Greeks were rid of the regents and the king appointed Greek ministers. But even then, Bavarians held key posts in the government and determined policy.

In the end, a revolution against the Bavarian tyranny was planned by a group of the leaders of the uprising against the Turks, with the support of British diplomats. Two military men headed the plot: Dimitrios Kallerges and Ioannes Makriyannis.

On 3rd September 1843 Kallerges went to the theatre to allay suspicion, but afterwards went to the house of Makriyannis at the foot of the Acropolis. To his surprise he found Makriyannis talking with a group of civilians, so he decided to begin the revolt alone.

Entering the infantry barracks, he drew his sword and shouted "Long live the constitution!" The soldiers decided to follow him. Then hearing that Makriyannis' house was besieged by police, who had been sent to arrest him, he sent a detatchment to rescue him, leading the rest to the square outside the palace.

By that time it was one o'clock in the morning, but the king was still at his desk. He went to the window and ordered the troops back to their barracks, promising to consider their request; but they were not inclined to disperse. Then civilian leaders arrived, and artillery was brought up. So the king agreed to dismiss all foreigners from his service except for those who had assisted in the War of Independence, and to produce a constitution within thirty days.

The crowd insisted that the king personally thank Kallegoras and Makriyannis, which he did, no doubt reluctantly. Finally, at three o'clock in the afternoon, the troops marched past the palace shouting "Long live the constitutional king Otto I"

In this way, at last, centuries of foreign domination were finally over. The square outside the palace was renamed *Syntagma Plataia* (Constitution Square). Makriyannis praised "the blessed people of our capital, who were all involved, yet no one even had a nosebleed." This apparent social harmony was not to last.

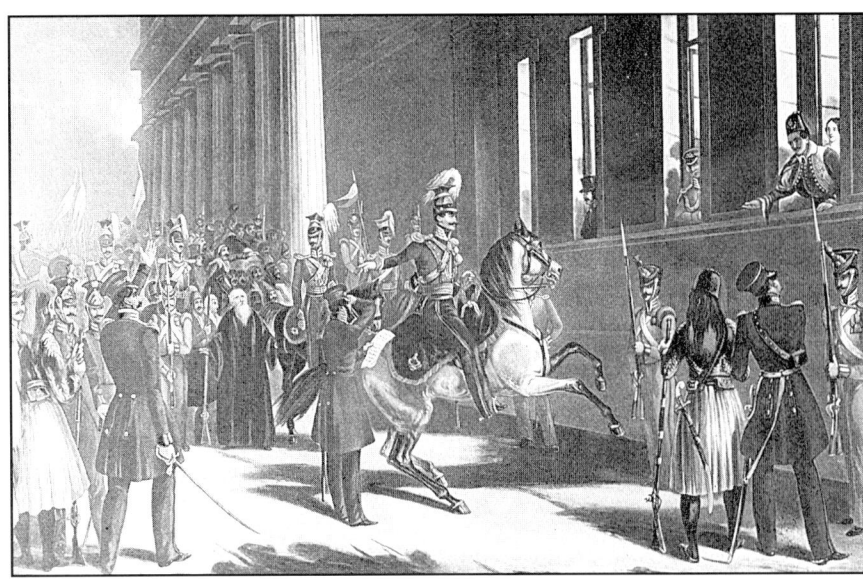

The rebels, led by Kallerges on horseback demand a constitution from King Otho

(Popular lithograph)

"Just a Tiny Palace"

In 1890, King George summoned the architect Ernest Ziller and told him that he wanted him to design a small palace for Prince Constantine and his bride Sophia. He had already decided that it should be built in what was then the royal vegetable garden, which was used to supply fresh produce to the palace.

Princess Sofia, the Kaiser's daughter, told him that she wanted "a small cosy home – something informal." She was very firm about this: "something small and comfortable...This is not Germany. We can hardly expect Greece to provide the kind of palace my father has." Ziller protested, but she continued: "A nice palace with a private air about it – *rustique*." The architect took her at her word, and obliged with the building which is now the presidential mansion. Despite its modesty, it took six years to build, because public funds were so low.

When it was presented to her, Princess Sofia was furious. "Idiot" she shouted, "You've built a cottage." The main problem, it appeared, was that there was no room to hold "even the tiniest ball." She insisted on adding an extra wing, despite the protests of the architect, who said that it would spoil his design. Ziller was promptly replaced, and the an architect who had done much to beautify the young capital, had to sell his own house to pay off his debts, and died a pauper on Solonos Street.

When the royal couple moved in, the king insisted that the vegetable garden, which still surrounded the mansion, remain undisturbed. It was not until he was assassinated in 1913 that English style gardens were laid out around the palace. The problem of the ballroom evidently persisted, since Queen Frederika later found it necessary to enlarge it for the wedding of Princess Sophia to Juan Carlos of Spain.

A Bull's Head and a Cairn of Stones

The Zappeion Building, erected and given to the nation by the two Zappas cousins of Northern Epirus (southern Albania) as a national exhibition hall in 1878, has frequently been the scene of displays of national achievement and pride. But during December 1916 and January 1917, it was the site of a double national humiliation.

A Bitter Rivalry

The outbreak of the First World War in 1914 found Greece deeply divided. King Constantine was a fervent admirer of everything German, especially its army, and his wife was a sister of the Kaiser. By contrast the popular Cretan prime minister, Eleftherios Venizelos, was by temperament and conviction, a supporter of the democracies, and saw the interests of Greece as lying with the Allies. There was deadlock between them as Greece observed an uneasy neutrality. When Venizelos tried to persuade the king to allow Greek participation in the Gallipoli Campaign, the king dismissed him, despite

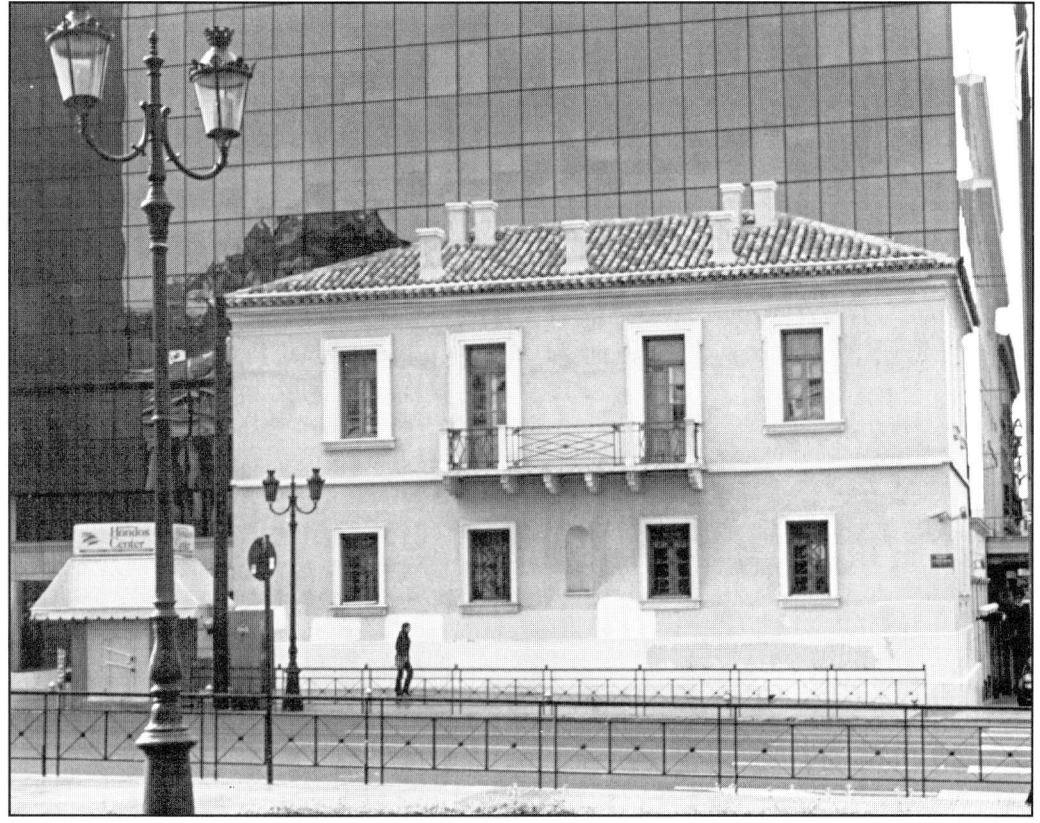

The house of Eleutherios Venizeolos in Athens, on Panepistemiou Street

129

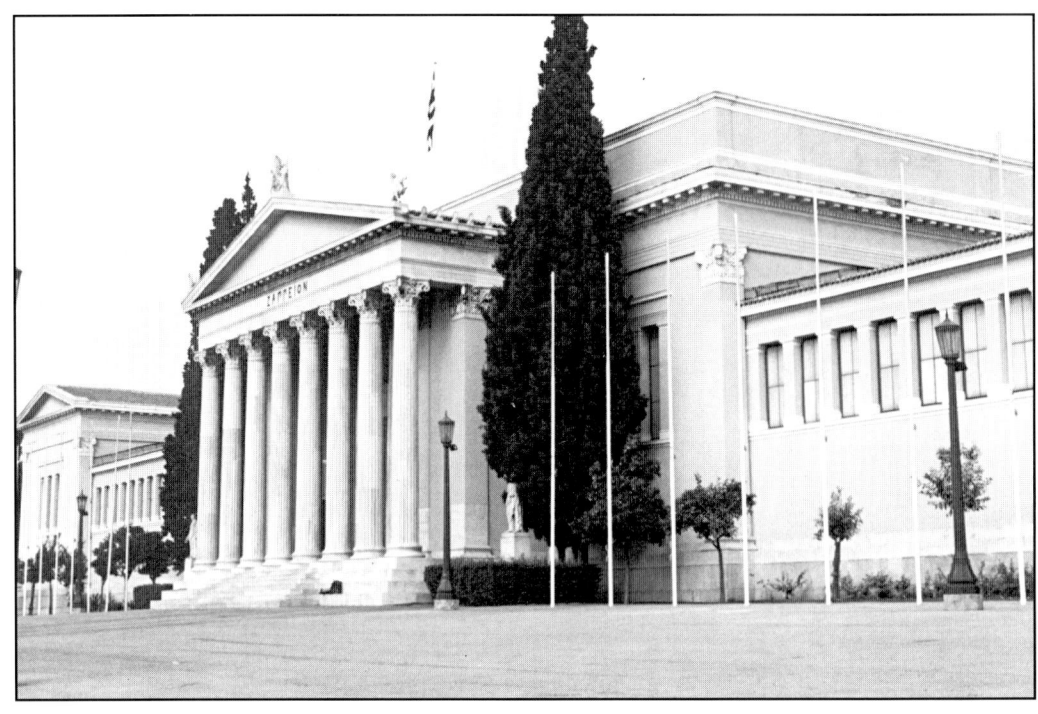

The Zappeion Exhibition Hall

his large majority in Parliament. He was promptly re-elected to office with large majority in the parliament, but when Venizelos invited Allied forces to Thessaloniki, the king dismissed him once again.

There was much more to this quarrel than personal antipathy or even rival war aims. Under Venizelos leadership, new territories had been brought under Greek sovereignty, effectively doubling the size of the country. The influx of this new population, represented by Venizelos, threatened the comfortable enjoyment of their privileges by the existing elite.

During the summer of 1916, Eastern Macedonia was overrun by German and Bulgarian forces, with virtually no opposition from the official Greek army. Royal treachery was suspected, and the Allies, increasingly afraid that Constantine might join forces with Germany and its allies, demanded the demobilization of the Greek army. The king complied, but then immediately re-formed it as a "League of Reservists", and chiefly used it to intimidate the pro-Venizelist opposition. In response, Venizelos set up his own "provisional government" in Thessaloniki, which declared for the Allies. The country was then effectively divided into two parts: Allied Greece, governed from Thessaloniki by Venizelos and his government, mostly comprising the newly acquired territories, and royalist neutral Greece, consisting of the territories of the former kingdom. The Allies then tried to put pressure on the king by making other demands.

The French admiral Dartige arrived at Piraeus with an Allied fleet, and demanded the surrender of a number of artillery guns as a pledge of royal neutrality. On December 1st, a French force of 2,500 landed in Piraeus to confiscate the weapons. His soldiers marched to Athens and took up headquarters in the Zappeion Building, from where they fanned out to occupy surrounding high points. Meanwhile, Dartige had also ordered four warships to lie off Faliron, threatening the capital with their artillery.

This was a humiliation which the forces loyal to the king could not accept without making a response. Soon shooting broke out between the King's soldiers and the invaders. It died down at lunchtime, but began again afterwards. Admiral Dartige ordered the ships in the bay to bombard the city in the vicinity of the royal palace. The queen took refuge in the cellars. At one point a shell struck a wall outside the king's study. When he offered to hand over six batteries, the bombardment ceased. Prisoners were exchanged, and the French forces withdrew to their ships during the night. The Allies had lost fifty-seven killed, while one hundred and fifty four had been injured. The Allied injured were treated in Greek hospitals. The Greeks lost thirty-five killed and suffered fifty-six injured.

Pogrom and Anathema

Their "victory" over the Allies emboldened the supporters of the king to initiate a violent pogrom against Venizelists throughout Athens. The houses of supporters of the prime mnister were attacked by armed gangs, and the householders forced to flee to the Allies for protection. Many hundreds were arbitrarily arrested by the League of Reservists. A few, less fortunate, were executed in cold blood, some on the banks of the Ilissos, and others in the military bases at Goudi and *Pedeion tou Areos*. The names of thirty-six victims are known, but there were probably more.

In order to force Constantine to abdicate, the Allies imposed a blockade. No foodships were allowed to enter any royalist-controlled port. Even fishing boats were not allowed to operate. This blockade turned many people in royalist controlled Greece against the Allies.

On Christmas Day 1916, the archbishop of Athens, together with a company of bishops and priests, solemnly excommunicated and anathematized Venizelos, using a ritual from the Dark Ages to expel him from the church and curse him. Since he was not present at the ceremony, the condemned prime minister was represented by a severed bull's head.

Afterwards, the bishops, priests and people processed to the *Parade Ground of Ares (Pedeion tou Areos)*, then on the city boundaries, where the archbishop led the way in stoning "the man who plotted against the King". Well-dressed society ladies joined in, leaving the bull's head on a stake buried under a cairn of rubble. During the following night, the cairn was covered with flowers, and someone left a placard on top which read: "From the Venizelists of Athens." The effect of these events was to make the Venizelists implacable enemies of the royal dynasty.

The "National Schism"

In consequence of these events, Allied troops occupied the city. On 29th January 1917, at a ceremony held at the Zappeion Building, the royalist army had to atone for its offence by marching past the flags of the Allies and saluting them. Meanwhile, the blockade continued and conditions close to famine began to develop. Infant deaths due to lack of mothers' milk became common.

At last giving in to the unremitting pressure, Constantine left the country on 17th June, and his son, Alexander, took the throne. Venizelos returned to Athens, and the country, outwardly united, took its place in the war beside the Allies. However, all royalist army and naval officers and civil servants were replaced with Venizelists, and Greece found itself left with a profound rift, which was not finally resolved until the formal abolition of the monarchy in 1974. Moreover, these events had made it clear that the "elite" of this small nation was not prepared to compromise or share the privileges they enjoyed, and were prepared to kill their fellow-citizens to defend them. This added a deadly edge to internal Greek politics for most of the twentieth century.

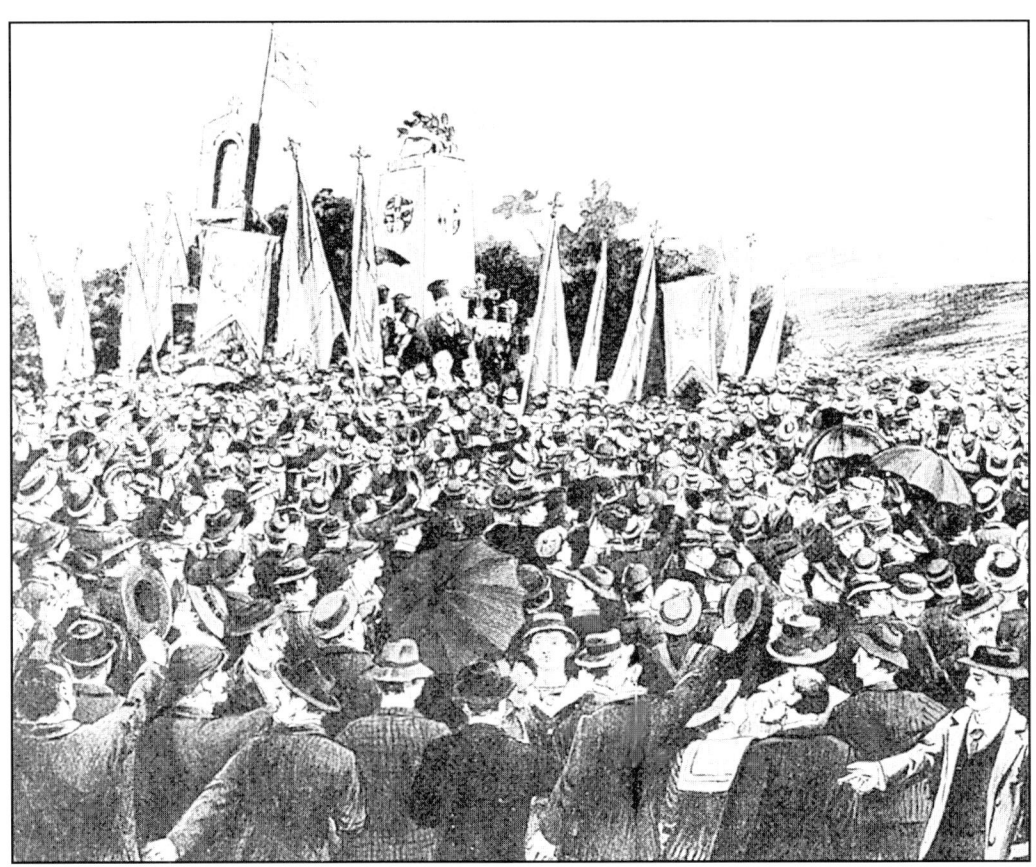

The solemn cursing of prime minister Venizelos at Pedion tou Areos
(Popular Lithograph)

A Great Betrayal

In 1940 when Western Europe groaned under the Nazi jackboot, only in Britain and Greece was the flame of freedom kept alive. At that time Greece was also engaged in a bitter struggle against the Axis powers. Italian invaders had been thrown back and driven from their Albanian bases by the small Greek army, but the country was forced to bow before the might of the Axis as German, Italian and Bulgarian troops converged on this small country. A British Imperial force, consisting mostly of Australian and New Zealand troops, briefly assisted in the defence of Greece before pulling out, and leaving it to the mercies of the conquerors.

One day in the early days of the Occupation, on 10th May 1941, two truckloads of British prisoners of war who had failed to escape in the evacuation were being transported through Athens under German guard. As they entered Syntagma Square the Athenians, who crowded the pavements, broke into spontaneous applause. For some reason, the German guards thought that the applause was intended for them, and they graciously acknowledged it, until the laughter which this provoked made them realise their mistake. Their embarrassment turned to anger as the crowds feted their prisoners with flowers, sweets and cigarettes.

This first spontaneous public demonstration against the occupying forces marked an end to a brief "honeymoon period", when the Germans had kept up the pretence that they had somehow arrived to "liberate" Greece from the British. There followed a long and bitter occupation of the country, marked by famine, oppression, acts of barbaric cruelty, and fierce guerrilla resistance.

Yet in December 1944, when V2 rockets were still landing in London, and when the Ardennes Offensive was still in progress, there occurred a remarkable betrayal. British forces which had landed in Greece supposedly to liberate that country, although German forces had already pulled out of their own accord, attacked the very partisans they had supplied with arms to fight the Nazis, and sided with those who had collaborated with the common enemy. Events which took place on Sunday 3rd December in Syntagma Square precipitated this bizarre and tragic twist of events.

The main force of for self-help and opposition to the Axis occupation forces had been an organisation known by the acronym EAM, with its military wing ELAS. As in many countries, such as France, Italy and Yugoslavia, the well-organised and highly motivated communists proved the most effective opponents of the fascists, and it was chiefly, but not exclusively, the communists who organised and led both EAM and ELAS. In retrospect, it is clear that the leaders of the West, already anticipating the end of the war, had their eyes set upon a new confrontation between the capitalist and communist powers, and were engaged, even at this date, in manoeuvring for advantage. Churchill, on a visit to Moscow, had proposed a share out of the Balkan states: with Rumania, Bulgaria and Hungary to fall within the Soviet sphere of influence, while Britain would control Greece. Stalin had accepted what became known as the "Percentages Agreement".

Churchill had no doubt that King George, when restored to his throne, would prove a reliable friend, i.e. act as an obedient British puppet. But the communists, and the other patriots in EAM and ELAS, together with the vast majority of the Greek people, did not want the restoration of a monarchy which before the war had connived in the establishment of an oppressive authoritarian dictatorship under General Metaxas which had imitated the fascists. Only the right wing, many of whom had actively collaborated with the Nazis during the Occupation, were royalist.

On the evening of Saturday, 2nd there was a meeting of the Greek cabinet in the building of the Foreign Ministry. The chief of the Athens police, Colonel Evert, informed the government that EAM-ELAS was planning a demonstration on Sunday and a general strike for the Monday. Prime Minister George Papandreu asked Evert's advice, which was to let the demonstration go ahead. Papandreu then asked what time it had been planned for. Evert replied: "Eleven o'clock." The Press Minister insisted that the demonstration could not possibly go ahead at that time, since General Scobie, head of British forces in Athens, together with the British Ambassador, would be attending a reception at the Parnassos Club. He insisted that the demonstration must be postponed. Police chief Evert doubted whether EAM-ELAS would agree to postpone their demonstration for such a reason, so Papandreu decided to forbid it altogether, sending an order to that effect to the headquarters of EAM-ELAS.

The intention of the popular movement to defy the ban soon became apparent. Church bells rang out across the city throughout the night. At daybreak loudspeakers in the suburbs called the people to gather in Central Athens. Buses were commandeered to ferry in workers from the outlying areas.

Large crowds gathered and marched to Syntagma Square. When they reached the Square at 10.50, the demonstrators were fired upon from the police station. It is not known whether the police panicked or whether they fired deliberately, but after the shooting had died down, when the dead and wounded were being attended to, a second fusillade occurred.

Eyewitness Mary Henderson observed: "...each reporter saw and reported the scene through eyes that matched his or her political beliefs. One US press man saw British tanks moving in on the crowd - no British tanks were involved. One British reporter said he heard the police give the order in Greek to shoot - he knew no Greek. Some said the "Fascist" police fired, while others said the "nervous" police, who had come under attack, fired. And others said the crowd was armed and had fired first...." There was no agreement about how long the firing lasted and certainly none about the number of casualties. The attentive observer will be aware that this "fuzziness" of facts is usual when they clearly condemn those who control the media.

By 11.25 the square was quiet once more, but the damage had been done. Prime Minister Papandreu tried to calm things down with a broadcast to the nation, but it was too late. He could not be heard, since the power had already been cut to most of the city. Extremists on both sides began to seek out their enemies and settle old scores incurred during the Occupation.

At first the partisans did not fire on British soldiers. But incredibly, Churchill ordered General Scobie to treat Athens "as a captured city where a local rebellion is in progress." Thus while Hitler was still alive, and while the war was still being fought, British forces were ordered to side with those who had collaborated with the Germans against the very partisans they had themselves armed. Artillery shelled, and Spitfires strafed, the working class suburbs of Athens. After suffering the horrors of the Nazi occupation, the Athenians found themselves under fire from the very "Allies" who had supposedly come to liberate them. Ironically, a city which had not been bombed during the war because of its historic associations came under attack from its own "allies" following its "liberation".

Significantly, and against those who chose to see the fighting as a Soviet inspired attempted coup, the Soviet Military Mission took refuge in the *Grande Bretagne*, the British military Headquarters. Equally significantly, the defence perimeter established by the British was extended to include the wealthy area of Kolonaki. The British chose to participate in a class struggle against the mass of the people.

In the bitter cold of that winter of "liberation", there was little food, fuel or medicine in the city. Its inhabitants were forced to hide in cellars from the bombardment launched by their "allies", while the dead lay rotting in the streets. Fighting was fiercest in the suburbs of Ampelokipoi and Kaisariani, but there was considerable destruction throughout the city before a cease-fire was negotiated.

The Greek poet Seferis wrote: "Blood brings blood and more blood."

A Hotel at the Heart of a Nation

The *Grande Bretagne* Hotel, standing at the heart of the capital as it does, at the corner of Syntagma Square with Panepistemiou Street, reflects closely the history of the nation in all its twists and turns.

Two Remarkable Entrepreneurs

The building started life as a luxurious private mansion in 1842, built by Antonis Dimitris, a wealthy expatriate Greek from Trieste. For many years after 1852 it was rented to the French School of Archaeology.

Its career as a hotel is due to another Greek expatriate, a poor one this time. In 1863, eleven year-old Stathis Lampsas was brought to Athens with his family, when they walked from Odessa. After getting a job in the kitchens of the Royal Palace, he was spotted as a talented chef and was sent by King George I to the famous *Maison Doree* in Paris for training in *haute cuisine*, before being employed in the palace as a master chef. By the age of twenty-two, Lampsas had repaid the King's investment in him before becoming *chef de cuisine* to millionaire banker Armand Oppenheimer. But Lampsas became homesick and decided to return to Athens to open a hotel.

Athens could boast no first-rate hotel at that time. The *Hotel d'Europe* in Monastiraki had the distinction of being run by two proprietors, an Italian and his

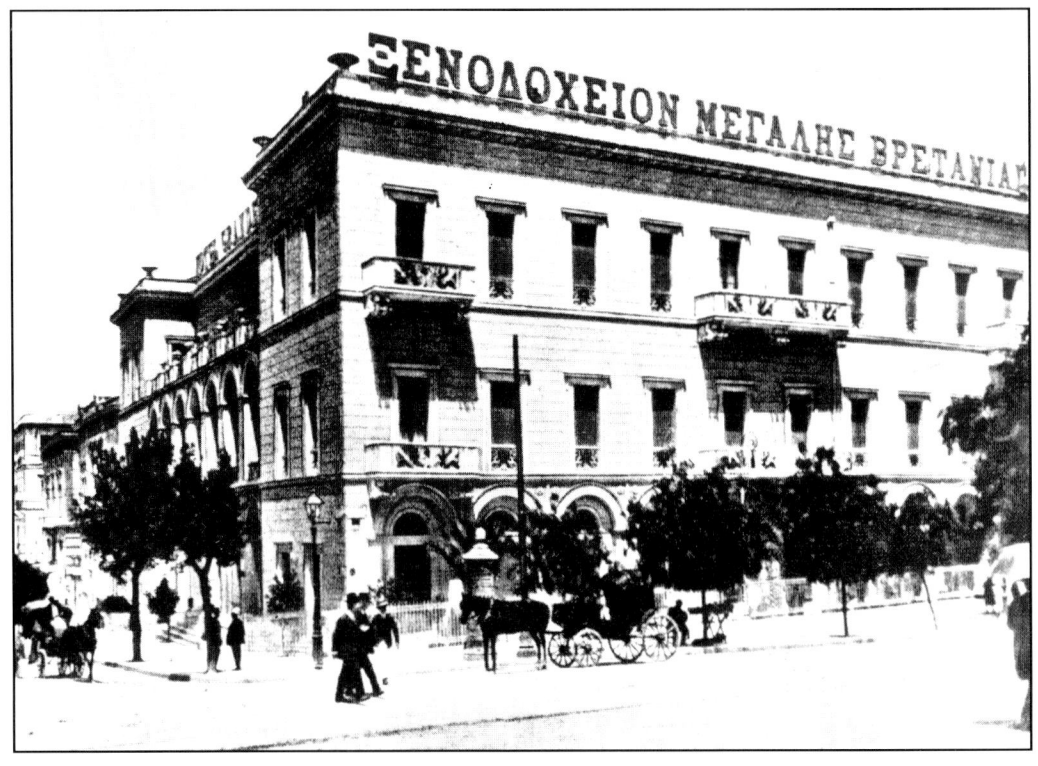

*The "Grande Bretagne" Hotel
at the end of the nineteenth century*

Viennese wife, who were both one-eyed: he had an eye on the right she on the left. There were several other hotels; all undistinguished.

Lampsas made friends with Savas Kendos, owner of the *Megali Bretannia* at the corner of Stadiou Street and Karageorgis Servas on Syntagma Square. The two bought the Dimitriou Mansion and opened it in 1874 as the *Grande Bretagne*. The interior design reflected the taste of the *Belle Epoque,* and it was luxuriously furnished throughout. When Kendros died in 1888, Lampsos bought his shares in the business.

Maintaining a hotel of the highest calibre was not easy. Most houses drew their water from public fountains or bought from water-sellers, while the flow of running water was always unpredictable. Staff frequently had to purchase water from water sellers in the streets and carry it into the building in tins. At that time, the hotel had eighty beds but could boast only two bathrooms. Despite the difficulties, it was quickly successful, and was the first hotel to install electricity in Greece. In 1896 Baron de Courbetin and the other distinguished visitors who attended the first modern Olympic Games all stayed there.

When Theodore Petrokopoulos, a young lawyer and journalist wrote a striking article on the Italian tourist trade, Lampsas not only interviewed the young man, he gave him the job of hotel manager. Soon afterwards, he followed that up by offering him the hand in marriage of his adopted daughter, Margarita. Petrokopoulos was an ardent supporter of the politician Eleftherios Venizelos, and during the years of the First World War, the *Grande Bretagne* became the centre of the political discussion and plotting of the Venizelist faction. In addition to managing the hotel, Petrokopoulos was sometimes used by Venizelos on special political missions.

Military Headquarters

The advent of war in 1940 did not pass the hotel by. The Government requisitioned it as the General Staff HQ. Guests were given one hour to evacuate the hotel. Only the German Military Attachι objected, but he was finally expelled. Unfortunately, the Germans were soon back, the hotel being requisitioned by the *Wehrmacht* for use as the HQ of their occupation forces. Initially, they objected to the name of the hotel, until Rudolf Schmidt, the Swiss manager, pointed out that one of Hitler's favourite hotels in Germany was named the *Hotel Bristol*. Hitler, Goering, Himmler and Rommel all stayed at the *Grande Bretagne* during the Occupation.

The British Expeditionary Force under General Scobie also set up their HQ in the hotel following their return after the German evacuation. When fighting broke out in Athens in December 1944, the hotel became home to one and a half thousand guests. British paratroops manned machine guns in the lobby. Even so, General Scobie was nearly killed when a mortar shell landed two feet away from him as he was sitting in the room he had adopted as his office.

A Plot to Kill Churchill

During the same month Winston Churchill arrived with Field-Marshall Alexander and Foreign Secretary Anthony Eden to hold talks with EAS-ELAM. He landed at Kalamaki airport, and was taken to the *Ajax*, moored out of range of shellfire at Faliron.

The sewers of Panepistemiou Street lie eight feet below road level, and inside are six feet high. The British were aware that this posed a security threat, and had barricaded the entrances. After hearing of rumours of an attempt to blow up the hotel during Churchill's visit, the access points were regularly patrolled. At midnight on Monday nothing was amiss, but by 6.00 am on Tuesday morning, a three-man patrol of British soldiers noticed that the wire had been cut. Investigating further they came across about one ton of dynamite, together with German detonators lying directly beneath the door of the *Grande Bretagne*. Significantly, later that morning, rumours began to circulate throughout the city that the hotel had actually been blown up. ELAS dynamiters had entered the tunnels at the Profitis Daniel church, over four kilometres away, on the far side of the front line at Omonia Square, and had waded through water to get to the *Grande Bretagne*.

The talks between the British and EAM-ELAS were held on the *Ajax* in Faliron Harbour, under the chairmanship of Archbishop Damaskinos. Before meeting him,

Churchill is alleged to have asked: "Is he a cunning, scheming medieval prelate, more interested in temporal power than celestial glory?" Told that he was, Churchill replied: "Good, then we can use him." This ex-wrestler boarded the ship during a Christmas fancy-dress party held by the sailors. Amid the various pirates, gypsies and men in drag, the burly black-robed figure was initially confused with one of themselves and the partying sailors danced around him. He initially assumed that this was a calculated insult.

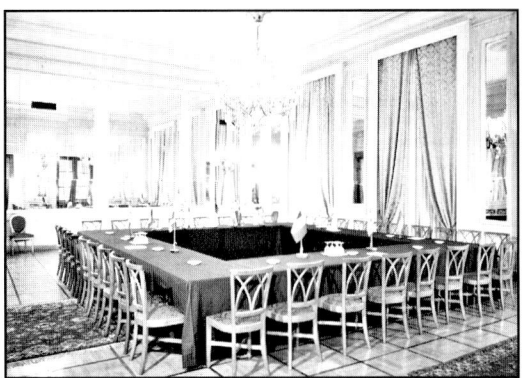

The Mirror Room

On Boxing Day, Churchill attended a meeting at the British Embassy. It had to be held in a back room, warmed only by an old and inefficient evil-smelling paraffin stove, since that was the only place secure from snipers. The leaders sat with their coats on and blankets around their knees. As Churchill left the embassy, a sniper's bullet ricocheted off the wall nearby.

Churchill returned to Athens on his way back from Yalta, and laid a wreath at the Tomb of the Unknown warrior. He was to return to the *Grande Bretagne* as a guest of Aristotle Onassis some years later.

The "Snake Pit"

One evening in 1949, CBS reporter George Polk mentioned at the hotel bar that he was going north to visit the secret mountain HQ of the Communist partisans. The next day he flew to Thessaloniki. A few days later, his body was discovered floating in the harbour. The communists were blamed, but most Athenians thought that right wing extremists had killed him to smear the communists. The bar of the *Grande Bretagne* became known as "the Snake Pit".

Constantine Karamanlis returned from Paris in 1974 to restore democracy, a Government of National Unity, and formed it in the hotel. From a balcony on the second floor, archbishop Makarios addressed the Greek people before returning to Cyprus after narrowly escaping an attempt to assassinate him.

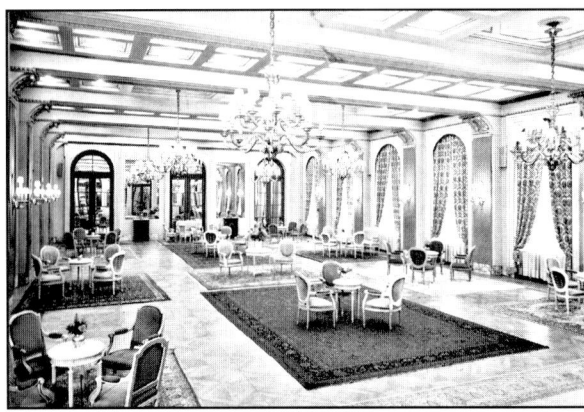

The Ballroom

Quirks of the Rich and Famous

Almost everyone of fame or importance who has visited Athens has stayed at this hotel. Its guests have included forty crowned heads and other heads of state, and many of the most famous names in the worlds of politics, culture and entertainment.

The *Grande Bretagne* has had to tolerate the quirks of its rich and famous guests. Mary Pickford, wife of Douglas Fairbanks, required an entire spare room for her shoes. Aristotle Onassis, faced with a wine list which offered anything the sophisticated palate could desire, always chose a cheap red table wine which could be found in any shop in the working-class areas of the city.

Two guests were especially noteworthy. One day during the First World War a wealthy American woman, who always insisted upon anonymity, stormed out of her suite to complain that a valuable pearl necklace had been stolen from her room. Obviously, this was very bad for business, and the management felt that determined action had to be taken to minimise the threat to the good name of the hotel. The scandal was hushed up, a huge sum of money paid to the irate guest in compensation, and the valet who serviced her room arrested. Some years later, when new wash basins were being installed, plumbers found the missing necklace lodged in a pipe.

Another noteworthy guest was US businessman Samuel Insull. Originally an assistant to Thomas Edison, he made a fortune in electricity, and increased it by setting up worthless stock-holding companies. When these collapsed, during the Wall Street Crash of 1929, Insull fled to Greece to avoid federal indictments, and lived openly in the hotel in considerable style. Although Greece had no extradition treaty with the USA, the US Government exerted pressure, and in 1933 Insull was ordered to leave the country. He boarded the *Maiotis* for Egypt, but as no country would admit him, he had to stay on board until being arrested when the ship put into Istanbul. Although found not guilty three times of various offences, he died in poverty on the Paris metro in 1938.

This hotel, which combines traditional elegance with the most modern facilities and conveniences, has justifiably been listed among the fifty best hotels in the world.

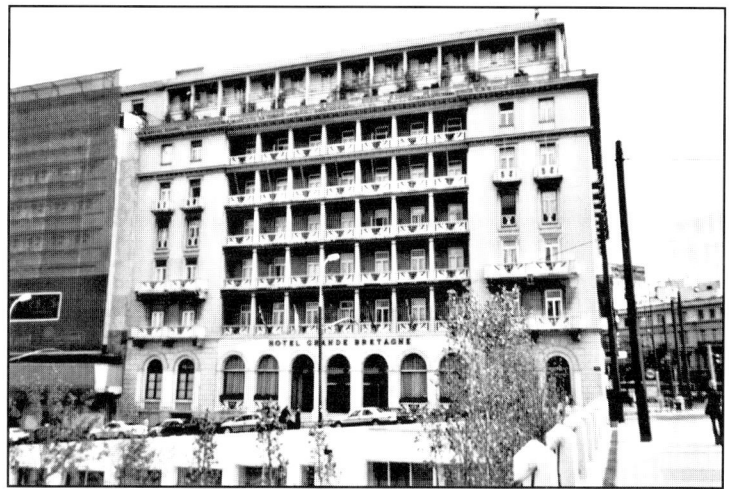

*The "G-B"
at the end of the
twentieth century*

THE COMMERCIAL QUARTER

"Weeping Square"

When King Otto and Queen Amalia arrived in Greece, they rented three houses on Klafthmonos Square, until they moved into the palace in 1843. The present name of this square means "lamentation"and was acquired in the following way: During the nineteenth century, a cafe on the square became a regular meeting place for civil servants, all of whom, in those days, held their jobs only as long as the government which had appointed them enjoyed office. As one party lost power and was replaced by another, so the civil servants appointed by the previous government would lose their jobs. One day, the historian Dimitris Kambouroglou was sitting in this cafe when he noticed the agitation of those civil servants who had just lost their jobs for this reason, and who were facing the prospect of a future without their salaries. He went home and wrote an article for a satirical newspaper entitled "Weeping (*Klafthmonos*) Square". This name was quickly taken up by the public, and the square soon became known by this name. In time the authorities were forced to accept this *fait accompli*, and make the name official.

"Rififi" Athenian-Style

The term "Rififi", which comes from the French film, *Du Rififi chez les hommes* (1955), in which a team of thieves broke into a store through its ceiling, is now used to describe all robberies which are committed by gaining access to a building when it is locked up, by breaking through the fabric of the building itself. In 1867, Klafthmnos Square was the scene of a rififi-style robbery of the Central State Treasury.

The line of what is now Stadiou Street was originally a deep, and usually dried up water-course. Difficult to cross and a great inconvenience, in 1858 it was covered over, leaving a large sewer tunnel underneath. Four men decided to rob the Treasury, which stood on the square, by means of this tunnel. Its entrance at Omonia Square was at that time still a comparatively unfrequented spot, and the plotters expected that their comings and goings would be safe from observation.

Having penetrated the tunnel as far as the Treasury, the robbers intended to enter the building through its wooden floor. Their main problem was that they needed to know where to aim for in breaking through. Then they heard of a Piraeus merchant who had a warrant for a sum of money on which the Treasury was delaying payment. The merchant needed his money quickly, so the gang paid him in cash, saying that they would themselves collect on his warrant. One of their number then took it along to the Treasury and tried to cash it. When the cashier insisted upon a delay, he pretended to get very angry, and repeatedly struck the floor with his heavy iron stick. The others were waiting in the tunnel for this signal, and it gave them the location to aim for. That night they broke into the strong room and emptied the deposit boxes.

Next morning, the police entered the hole in the floor and followed the sewer to its entrance. When they emerged into the light of day, they were lucky in almost immediately finding someone who had seen the four men emerge from the tunnel. He was able to identify one of them by sight, and the others were arrested shortly afterwards. Most of the money was recovered.

In a copycat crime, in 1992, thieves used the course of the Illisos under Kalirhoes Street to enter a bank. The strongroom alarms repeatedly went off, but since no sign of entry could be detected by the guard above, he was advised by telephone that the alarm must be "playing up", and that he should either ignore it or switch it off.

The Mansion of Ilion

One of the most remarkable buildings in Athens, a renaissance mansion with a painted frieze inscribed "Iliou melathron" or "the hall of Ilion (Troy)", was built for the renowned German pioneering archaeologist Heinrich Schliemann.

Adventurer ... or Liar

Johann Ludwig Heinrich Julius Schliemann, was born in the small town of Neu-Bukow, in Mecklenburg-Schwerin, Germany, in 1822. Fascinated from childhood by the stories and legends told by Homer and Vergil, he always retained a fervent belief that these epics were based on historical records.

When he was eleven he was sent to a prestigious school, but his dream of becoming a classical scholar was shattered when his father, a pastor, was discovered to be

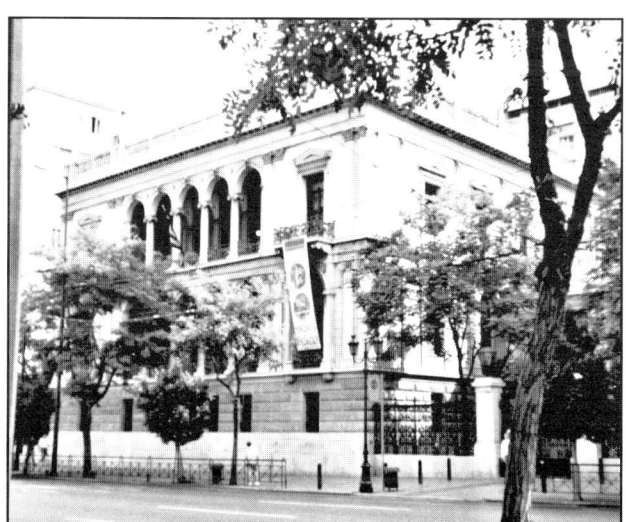

having an affair with their maid and embezzling church funds. Unable any longer to pay his fees at the private school, Heinrich found himself obliged to attend the local school, and had to leave that when he was fourteen because his father had already squandered the compensation he had received for his dismissal.

*The mansion of
Heinrich Schliemann
in Panepistemiou
(Venizelou) Street*

141

Initially, he was apprenticed to a grocer. Then he decided to go to Venezuela, but was shipwrecked off Holland, and ended up as an office boy for a firm in Amsterdam, a job which gave him time to study. Schliemann had a flair for languages. He is said to have taught himself eighteen in all, including Dutch, English, French, Spanish, Italian, Portuguese, Russian and both ancient and modern Greek. He had a phenomenal photographic memory. He once learned Scott's novel *Ivanhoe* by heart, and could recite it years later. His company sent him to St. Petersburg, Russia, where in time he founded his own business importing indigo and tea. To build up his wealth, he travelled to America for the California gold rush, and was a witness of the Great Fire of San Francisco. At thirty-six he had himself circumcised so that he could visit Mecca during the Hadj pilgrimage. He kept this adventure secret for many years for fear of reprisals from Muslim fanatics. During the Crimean War he made a fortune as a military contractor, enabling him to retire at the age of forty-one.

Today, while it is accepted that he did travel widely and certainly did build up a fortune, considerable doubt has been cast upon the veracity of many of his more picturesque adventures, since it is clear that he was also an inveterate liar who routinely exaggerated, and sometimes simply fabricated, his "adventures" in the cause of what would today be called "public relations".

Despite his financial success, and travelling the world, he was unhappy. His marriage was a failure. With his divorce from his first wife still in progress, Schliemann sent a letter to the archbishop of Athens, whom he had known before he became archbishop, asking him to find him a poor, beautiful, dark-haired, well-educated Greek woman who was interested in Homer. The search turned up Sophia Engastromenos from Kolonos. They were married in September 1869.

Treasure Hunter

From that point onwards, Schliemann devoted himself to archaeology. First he went to Ithaca, where, according to the *Oddyssey*, Odysseus had lived. Then in 1870, with Homer's *Iliad* as his guide, he began to excavate the site of what he thought was ancient at Troy. At that time, Bunarbashi was believed to be the site of Troy, but Schliemann thought that the nearby hill of Hissarlik was a much more likely area for investigation. Frank Calvert, an Englishman who owned the eastern half of the hill, agreed with this, and said that he had already discovered the ruins of a palace or temple there.

After some time excavating, Schliemann had found little and became depressed and discouraged. Then during 1872-3 he came upon a variety of finds which convinced him he had indeed discovered Troy. Shortly after that he found a hoard of treasure. To keep it secret, let the diggers have the rest of the day off while he and Sophie quietly excavated themselves, certain that they had found the treasure of King Priam. Among the objects they uncovered were a copper shield and cauldron, copper daggers and lance-heads, silver vases, a silver goblet, silver knife blades, a gold bottle, cups, diadems, earrings and a fillet, and thousands of gold rings and buttons.

Schliemann smuggled these artefacts out of Turkey in a caique in 1873. He split the find up, and hid the various objects with friends all over Greece. The Turkish government eventually discovered what he had done, and demanded the return of the hoard. Schliemann refused, and offered them to the Greek government, if only they would let him excavate at Mycenae and Mount Olympus, but they refused the bribe.

Schliemann has been criticised for using methods that seem crude by comparison with the highly developed techniques of today. At Hissarlik his workers had dug through the ruins of the Troy of Homer's time and located older cities. It was later established that there had been nine cities on this site. He had claimed that gold jewellery from the Troy II layers was part of "King Priam's Treasure."

He later presented the treasures to a museum in Berlin, but they disappeared from thee at the end of the Second World War. Only in 1993, did the authorities in Russia admit to being in possession of them. In October 1994, a team of western researchers was able to view the Schliemann Treasure in the Pushkin Museum. Turkey, Germany, and Russia all claim ownership.

There is some question about whether the find is a genuine hoard, or whether he put many finds together to make it more newsworthy and valuable. Schliemann may have taken some of the treasure from the eastern half of the Hisarlik mound, which belong to Frank Calvert, a British field archaeologist and diplomat. Calvert was not kept informed of all of the finds and their locations.

Donald F. Easton British archaeologist who has studied Schliemann's diaries is convinced the collection of treasure was found on Calvert's land in 1890. For this reason, Calvert's descendants also claim that they are entitled to a share.

In August 1876, using ancient texts and local legends, Schliemann began excavations at Mycenae, the home of Agamemnon, leader of the Greeks in the Trojan War. He immediately started digging near the Lion Gate, an imposing structure with a large lintel topped by a relief of two Lionesses facing each other. In a great circular space south of the Lion Gate, perhaps an ancient open-air meeting place, his workers found two tombstones. They excavated these graves, as well as several others within the circle, and found an abundance of gold funerary goods. Schliemann was convinced that he had found the bodies of Agamemnon Clytemnestra, and other famous figures. David Traill, in his book, *Schliemann of Troy*, charges him with bringing together artefacts from different finds, and also suggests that the so-called Mask of Agamemnon is a fake.

In July of 1878, Schliemann left Mycenae and excavated at Ithaca. He identified a site he thought was the palace of Odysseus and uncovered the ruins of nearly two hundred houses. He also excavated at Marathon, Nauplion, Cythera and Pylos. Since he found no gold, these sites disappointed him.

The more he pondered his discoveries, the more he became plagued with doubt that what he had discovered at Hissarlik was really Troy. In May 1881 he returned to the site. When found a slab of marble on the top of nearby Mount Ida, he claimed it was the ruins of Zeus' throne.

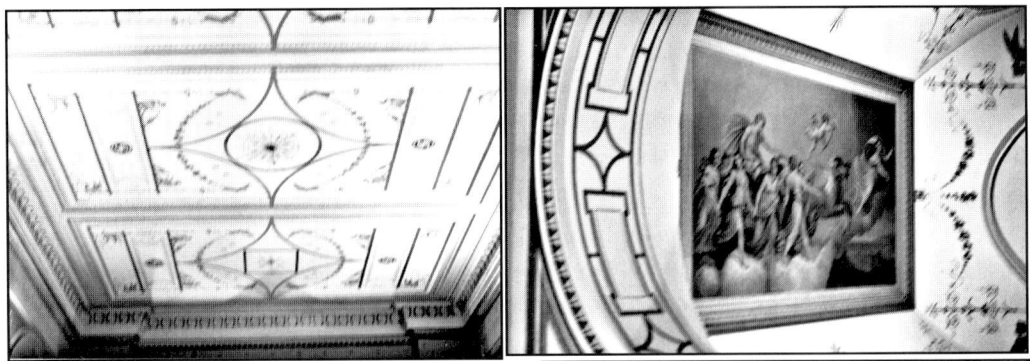

The interior of Schliemann's Mansion

An Indecent House

Schliemann had the mansion built on Panepistemiou Street in 1879. It is considered by many to be the finest example of the work of Schiller. The interior has been lavishly decorated by wall paintings in the "Pompeian" style. He filled the house with examples of early Greek art, and presided there like a Homeric king.

He began by throwing a housewarming party, the guests including cabinet ministers. Next morning he received a demand from the State Council that the nude statues on the roof either be taken down or covered up. Instead of removing them, Schliemann had a ballerina's tutus made in violently clashing colours and clothed the statues with them. Then he

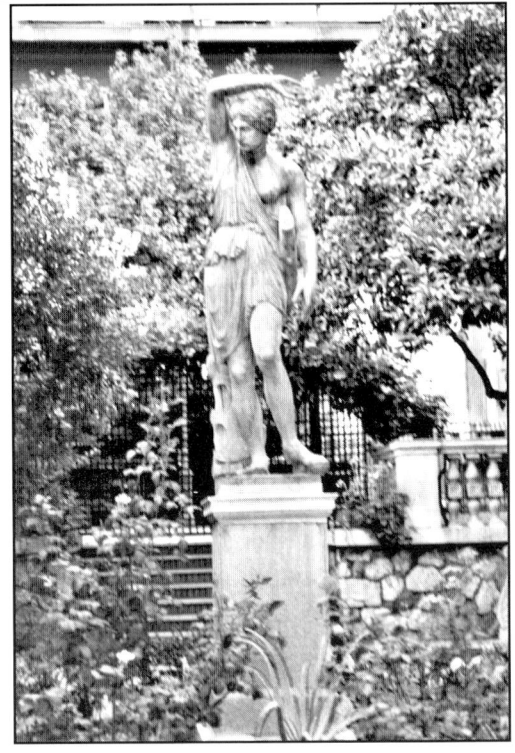

circulated among the amused crowd which gathered to stare in the street below, telling everyone that the Council of State had required it. After another hastily convened meeting the Council ordered the dresses removed. Schliemann took them off himself, one by one, each time waving the discarded tutu to the delighted crowd below. The statues had to be taken down in 1935 when they were found to be crumbling and in danger of falling into the street below.

Growing increasingly eccentric, Schliemann named his children and renamed all his servants after characters in Greek mythology and history, insisted that ancient Greek be spoken at the dinner table, and that messages be sent to him in that language. Although a rich man who sent his shirts to be laundered in London, he frequently engaged in acrimonious disputes with tradesman over a few drachmas.

Schliemann died on December 26th 1890, in a Naples hotel room. He had contracted a severe ear infection, but the doctor who attended him turned out to be an amateur archaeologist, so instead of attending to his ear, they both set out to see the new excavations at Pompei. In severe pain on the next day, he presented himself at the hospital, but was turned away because he had no papers. Although police eventually identified him, he died within twenty-four hours. He was buried in the First Cemetery in the a mausoleum he had built for himself. The inscription above the entrance reads, with characteristic lack of modesty: "For the hero Schliemann."

Controversy about the significance of Schlieman's work continues to this day. He bulldozed his way through valuable historical evidence in search of gold and other spectacular finds which would serve his agenda of self-publicity, effectively ruining sites for later, more careful and more scientific, archaelogists. He was naive to the point of childishness in identifying every significant find he made with some character from Greek mythology or history, frequently on the basis of no ascertainable evidence whatsoever. He may even have engaged in theft and deliberate fraud. But he cannot be justly criticised for failing to use techniques which had not been developed in his day. His work popularised the subject, and led to continuing investigations that in time revealed the civilisation of pre-classical Greece, which, before Schliemann, had been indistinguishable from myth.

In 1929 the state bought the mansion from Sophia and used it as the high court. Today it houses the Numismatic Museum, although this fine building is worth a visit on its own account.

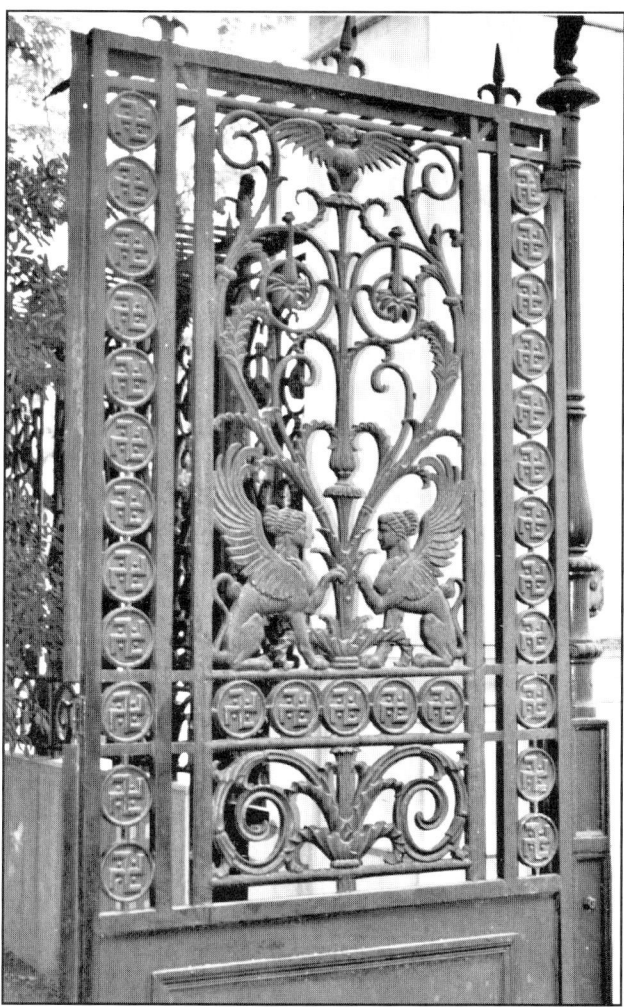

The gates of the mansion, decorated with the symbol of the crooked cross, later to become better known as the infamous swastika

Gamblers' Revenge

During the late nineteenth century, gambling had become a major social evil. Many people lost all their property to professional card-thieves. The government of Prime Minister Deliyiannis decided to close the casinos. This policy was strictly enforced by the legendary police chief, Dimitrios Baoraktaris, causing turmoil in the underworld, and depriving many professional card players of their livelihoods. Some determined to get revenge.

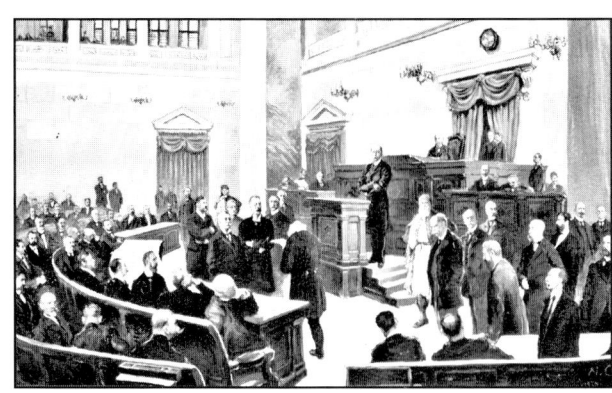

The interior of the Old Parliament Building (National Ethhnological Museum, Athens)

On 31ˢᵗ May 1905, when the Prime Minister got out of his carriage and prepared to walk up the steps to the old Parliament building in Stadiou Street, a man rushed up to him and stabbed him in the stomach with a long knife. The officer on guard outside the Parliament caught hold of him and said, "Hey! Why did you do that?"

"Because he stopped the card games and killed the hungry," the assassin replied.

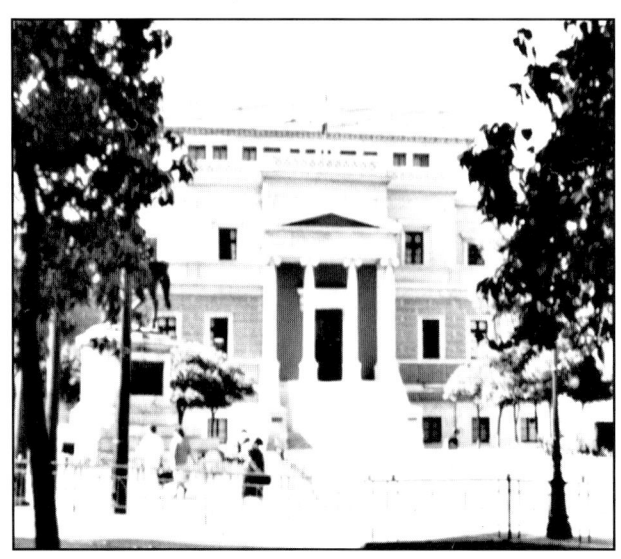

The Old parliament Building, Stadiou Street. Today it houses the National Ethnographical Museum

Although the seriously injured Prime Minister was rushed to hospital, it was too late to save his life.

The subsequent police investigations revealed that the killer, thirty-five year-old Antonios Yerakaris, was an immigrant into the capital from Mani, living in a hovel at Areo Pagou 44, where his five children were found in conditions of extreme poverty. After being found guilty, Yerakaris was beheaded by guillotine at the Palamidi Fortress in Nauplion. Police investigations also revealed an accomplice at his casino who may have put him up to it, who was given eight years.

Massacre at the Polytchnic

Following a period of political instability, in the early hours of the morning of 21st April 1967, a cabal of middle-ranking army officers led by Colonel George Papadopoulos, siezed control of the state. Although the CIA probably did not actually organise and direct the overthrow of democracy, the plotters used American weapons and a plan which had been devised by NATO to ensure Western control of Greece, and the coup leader was in receipt of CIA pay.

"The Colonels", as they came to be known, regarded themselves as the guardians of the traditional values of Greek Christianity. They condemned long hair and short skirts, cutting the hair of male tourists whose locks were deemed long enough to offend Christian sensibility. Historian C. M. Woodhouse records that "It was almost impossible to name any Greek of international reputation ... who did not regard them with contempt." yet although the dictatorship of the Colonels had an absurd aspect, it was a genuine tyranny. The press was censored, many books, songs and public meetings of over five persons were banned. A powerful secret police under military control spied on citizens and thousands were arrested as "Communists"; many being tortured, and many imprisoned in concentration camps on islands.

While a mild show of disapproval was made by foreign governments, the US Government soon resumed arms sales, and the vice-president visited Greece. Only the Scandinavian governments resolutely refused to countenance the overthrow of democracy in its original home.

In the autumn of 1973, large-scale student demonstrations, provoked by repression in the universities and a drastic increase in inflation, openly defied the regime's ban on public meetings. In November, students began a "sit-in" in the Polytechnic University, and transmitted clandestine radio broadcasts calling upon the people to rise up against the tyranny. On the night of 16-17th army tanks bulldozed the locked gates and, covered by sniper fire from buildings opposite, armed police swarmed into the grounds. The students' radio station broadcast appeals for doctors and priests, but none turned up. At least twenty students were killed.

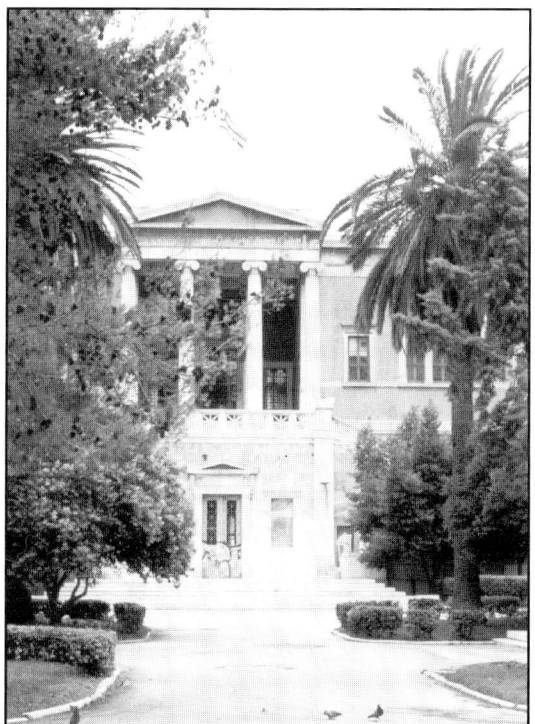

The Athens Polytechnic Univesity

Ironically, these events led immediately to a worse state than before. Senior officers decided that Papadopoulos was incompetent, and the blame for the Polytechnic massacre was laid on him, and he was removed from power. He was, however, replaced by the sinister Brigadier Ionnides, head of the military security police, who arrested Papadopoulos and installed a puppet of his own in his place. Repression increased. Ionnidis decided to assassinate Archbishop Makarios and replace him with journalist Nikos Sampson, who would proclaim the union of Cyprus with Greece. Makarios escaped, but the Turks siezed the opportunity to invade the island and carve out the north for themselves. When the Greek government ordered mobilization, the result was a shambles. It was clear that the army commanders could not even organise their own forces efficiently. Senior officers invited Constantine Karamanlis to return to restore the rule of law and democracy.

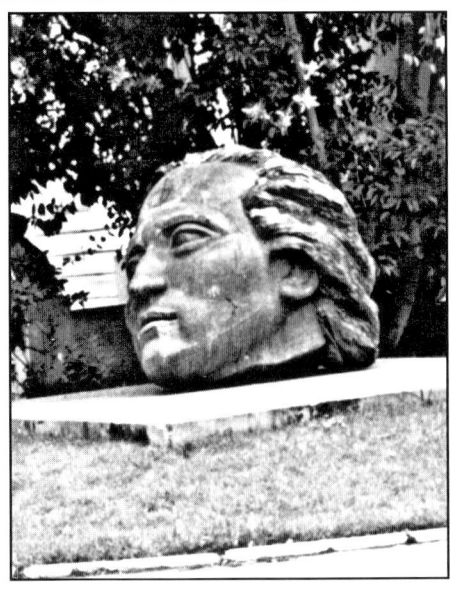

Monument to the martyred students of the Athens Polytechnic on the grounds of the campus of the university

Some of the students who took part in the events of 1973 remained political activists, and have since held high office, both in political parties and in the government of the country. A commemoration of the 1973 events at the Polytechnic takes place in Athens each year on November 17th. Wreath laying at a memorial to the deceased in the grounds of the Polytechnic is followed by a large and well -attended march through central Athens to the United States Embassy, headed by a group of women dressed in black - the mothers of the martyred students.

The monument to the students covered with wreaths and individual flowers during the commemoration of the uprising in November 2000

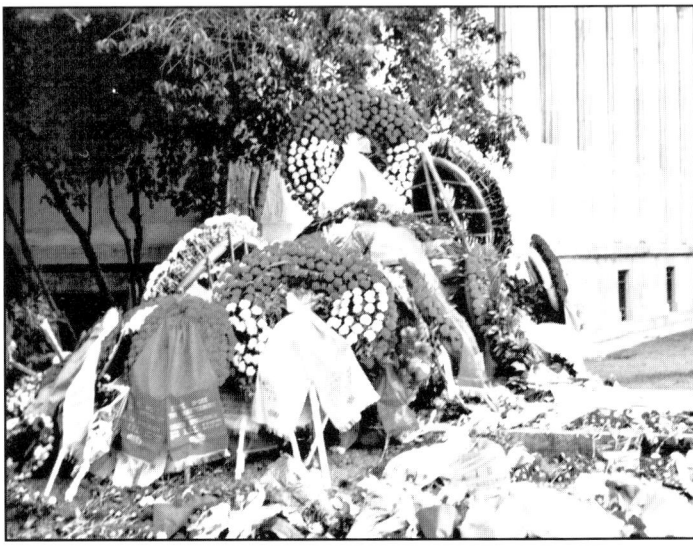

Lycabettos

Bibliophile or Bibliomaniac?

Ioannis Gennadios spent most of his life, from eighteen to eighty-eight, in London. He worked in the City with the merchants Rallis Brothers, and later became a diplomat, and Greek Ambassador to the United Kingdom. But the real love of his life was books. He spent much of his life in sale rooms and second-hand bookshops, in search of anything in Greek and anything related to Hellenism.

He managed to acquire the first edition of Homer ever printed in Greek for £425 at Sotheby's. He did not usually pay so much. He managed to obtain a series of watercolour drawings of scenes in Greece made between 1848 and 1864 by the famous writer of comic verse Edward Lear, for only £25.

Despite his eye for a bargain, his mania for collecting in time led him into debt, and in 1895 he had to sell off three thousand lots of books at Sotheby's, including a copy of Aesop's *Fables* owned by Queen Elizabeth I. Luckily, in 1902 he married a Scottish woman who not only shared his passion, but also enjoyed a substantial income. Between them, they added a further 13,000 volumes to their collection.

In 1905 they donated three thousand etchings and lithographs of Greece to the National Library, but discovered several years later that they had all been "mislaid." This led them to seek alternative and more secure means of leaving their collection to the nation. In 1921, when Gennadios was the Greek representative at a Naval Disarmament Conference in Washington, he met Mitchell Carroll, who had attended the American School of Archaeology in Kolonaki. Carroll suggested that he leave his

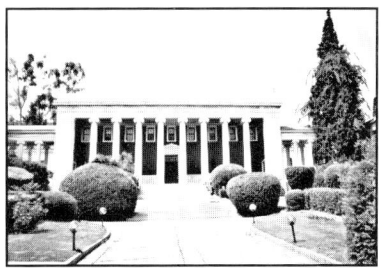

The Gennadeion Library

collection to the School. Gennadios agreed, on condition that suitable premises be built to house it, and that no item ever leave those premises. A site across the road from the School of Archaeology was provided by the Greek Government, and money to build the library supplied by the Carnegie Foundation.

Today the Gennadion houses the best collection of rare books on Hellenism in the world, including the only surviving copy of the first book to be printed in Athens: the *Lyrical and Bacchic Verses* of Athanasios Christopoulos, of 1825. Of sixty-seven known Greek books printed before 1500, the Gennadion possesses thirty-nine. The Library also functions as an archive and contains, among other collections, the diaries, notebooks and letters of Heinrich Schliemann; the records of Ali Pasha of Epirus, and the papers of the Nobel-prizewinning poets Seferis and Elyetis.

Gennadeios died bankrupt, and his wife paid off debts of £1,500 to book dealers.

Ampelokipoi

Watergate: A Greek Dimension?

The Watergate affair, which led to the resignation of President Richard M. Nixon, one of the greatest political scandals in US history, arose as a consequence of the illegal covert operations of the President and members of his staff.

Discontent with the Vietnam War was rife, and an increasingly paranoid Nixon had become convinced that there was a conspiracy to "get him". In June 1971, he verbally endorsed a scheme for a series of illegal espionage activities, which included burglaries, surveillance, and an array of "dirty tricks" designed to undermine the effectiveness of his political opponents. This policy was derailed when the five Watergate burglars were arrested by police on June 17th 1972 in the act of breaking into the Democratic National Committee Headquarters. Their immediate objective had been to repair a bug they had installed during an earlier break-in.

Nixon endorsed a cover-up designed to lead the FBI to believe that sensitive CIA assets were involved, and that they should not push too hard on the investigation; by this means implicating himself in the obstruction of justice. When it was learned that conversations in the Oval Office were routinely taped, the Chairman of the Senate Watergate Committee and the Special Prosecutor sought to investigate the tapes. Nixon refused to hand them over until the Supreme Court ruled that he had to release them. Then on October 20th, Nixon ordered the firing the Special Prosecutor. The Attorney General refused to comply, and resigned in protest. When the Watergate burglars were indicted for breaking into the office of Daniel Ellsberg's psychiatrist, in order to find something to use to destroy his reputation in retaliation for releasing the *Pentagon Papers*, which revealed how the U.S. became involved in the Vietnam War, the last tatters of Nixon's credibility were finally destroyed.

The House voted articles of impeachment, charging the President with abuse of power, obstruction of justice, and sabotage of the democratic process in a manner that warranted his removal from office. Warned that the Senate would convict him if he did not resign, Nixon recognised the inevitable and left office on August 8th 1974.

New information about these events was released in 1997, when Stanley Kutler's *Abuse of Power* was published. Kutler had gained access to previously unreleased White House tapes through a Freedom of Information Act lawsuit. His transcripts revealed an intriguing Greek dimension to the affair.

John Dean, Counsel to the President, revealed that Nixon had approved a request from the burglars for hush money on June 23, 1972. John Mitchell, then Attorney General, arranged to obtain the funds from a wealthy Greek businessman, Tom Pappas, in exchange for promising a further term of office as ambassador to Greece for Pappas' friend, Henry Tasca. On March 2nd, Haldeman told Nixon that White House counsel

John Dean and Attorney General John Mitchell were getting money for the burglars from Pappas, that Pappas had the great advantage that he dealt in cash, and that in return Pappas wanted the retention of U.S. Ambassador Henry Tasca in Athens.

On March 7th, the president thanked Pappas in person in the Oval Office. A little later, he became alarmed at the indiscreet way he had expressed his appreciation. A May 23rd tape has him reminding his secretary, Rose Mary Woods, of Pappas visit, and telling her: "Good old Tom Pappas ... came to see me about the ambassador to Greece, that he wanted to - he wanted to keep Henry Tasca there. We did not discuss Watergate at that point. It's very important that he remember that." On June 6th he said to Rose Mary again: "But I just want to be damned sure that Pappas, Jesus, doesn't get implicated in this damn thing, see. And of course I don't want to have anything indicating that I was thanking him for raising money for the Watergate defendants."

In 1975, Ambassador Tasca told a congressional investigator that some of the hush money had come not from Pappas himself, but from the Greek military junta. This was not the first time that Greek money had benefited Nixon politically. In 1968, Pappas had contributed $549,000 in cash to the Nixon election campaign. That money is thought by many investigators to have come from the KYP, the Greek intelligence service. Since the KYP was

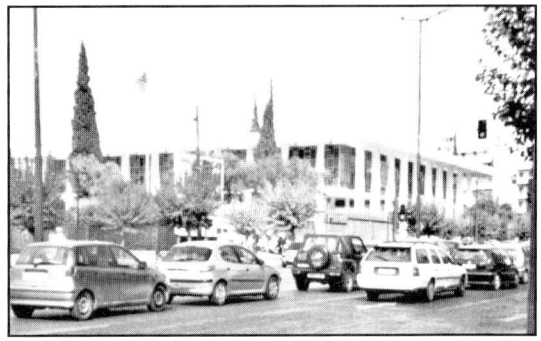

"Fortress America"
US Embassy, Ampelokipoi

at that time being directed and funded by the CIA, United States law was being broken in two ways: Republican campaign funds were being supplied, indirectly, by a foreign dictatorship, and US intelligence money, ultimately derived from US taxpayers, was being employed to influence the outcome of the US electoral process.

Elias Demetracopoulos, a Greek journalist, had informed Larry O'Brien, chairman of the Democratic National Convention, of this, and O'Brien had publicly demanded an explanation of the connection of Pappas with the Nixon-Agnew election campaign. Christopher Hitchens points out that this may have been the real reason for the Watergate break-in. "How much the DNC knew of the Pappas connection might well have been a question on the minds of the Watergate burglars, whose boss, Charles Colson, had been bugging the Demetracopoulos telephone as well."

We still do not know what the Watergate burglars had been told to look for during their break-in, except that it was "financial stuff." And we still do not know what was on a deliberately erased section of the tape of June 20th 1972. Haldeman's memoirs hint that it had to do with the corruption or politicization of the CIA. Hitchens argues persuasively that it may have concerned the "Greek connection", since the mere mention of this "was enough to make Richard Nixon ... babble with nerves."

The Subterranean Museums of Athens

The excavations for the new Athens Metro, which began in 1992, have brought to light much of the city's ancient history. Fifty archaeologists followed the progress of the work, sifting through debris and frequently stopping the machinery to inspect the newly uncovered earth. More than 30,000 items of archaeological interest were brought to light, and experts' knowledge of the history of the city considerably enlarged.

Despite the care of the workers and specialists, there were some surprises. The digging of a trial tunnel near the Acropolis broke into an ancient well, spilling out thousands of clay jars and potsherds. Payments to Charon to ferry the dead over the River Styx, they had been dropped into the well as offerings at funerals.

Work for the central underground station at Syntagma Square revealed much about the Roman city of Hadrianopoulis. Great baths were found a few feet under the pavement of Syntagma Square, dating from the third and fourth centuries AD. They included two great halls and many smaller rooms. Heating was by underfloor ceramic piping. The establishment was periodically repaired and renovated for over three centuries. Below that level a cemetery dating from the classical and Hellenistic periods was uncovered. The road to Marathon and the Messoyeia, the central plain, ran through it.

Among the more interesting items uncovered was a large stone slab listing those fallen in battle during the Peloponnesian war, the tomb of a dog, complete with its collar and offerings in glass, and the bronze head of a young man embedded in the wall of a building dating from the first quarter of the fifth century BC.

Finds from the Metro excavations are on display on the sites on which they were found in the concourses of some of the new stations, making these stations museums in their own right.

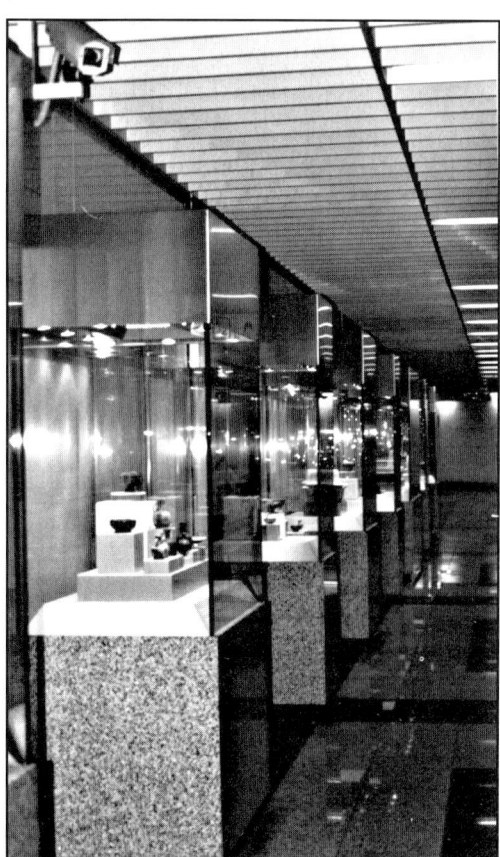

Exhibition cases at Panepistemiou Station

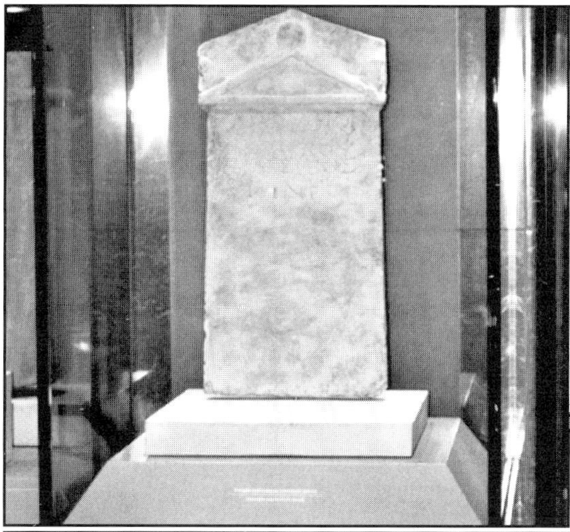

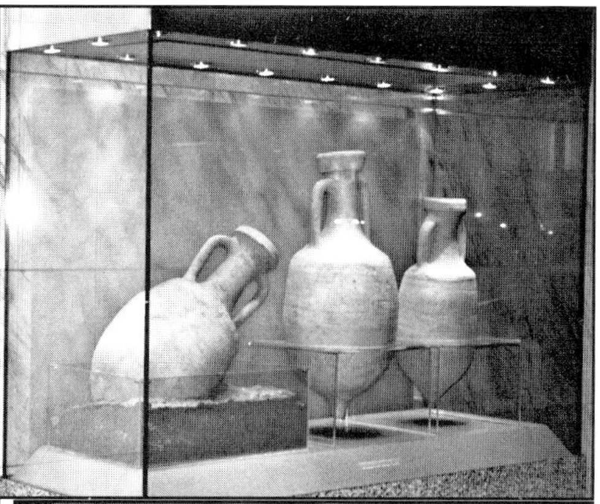

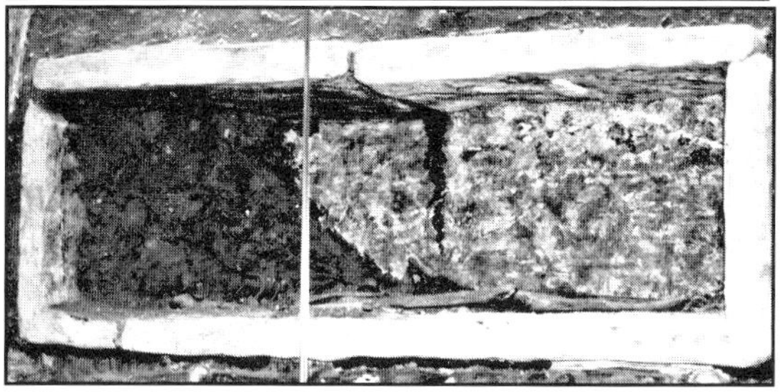

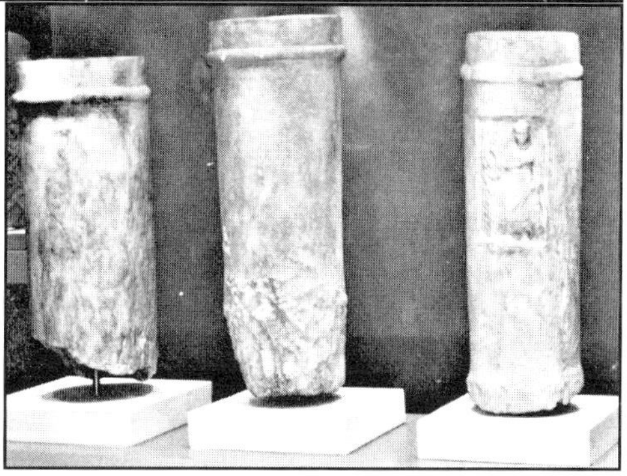

Top, above right and below left:
Exhibits at Panepistemiou and Syntagma Stations
Above left: Close up of a tomb containing a skeleton at Syntagma Station
Successive layers of settlement and subterranean traces of roads,
sewage pipes and burial places may be seen preserved under glass .
The metro stations also function as galleries of contemporary art.
Below right: "Dying Warrior" by Dimitris Kalamaras,
exhibited on the platform of the "National Defence" Station

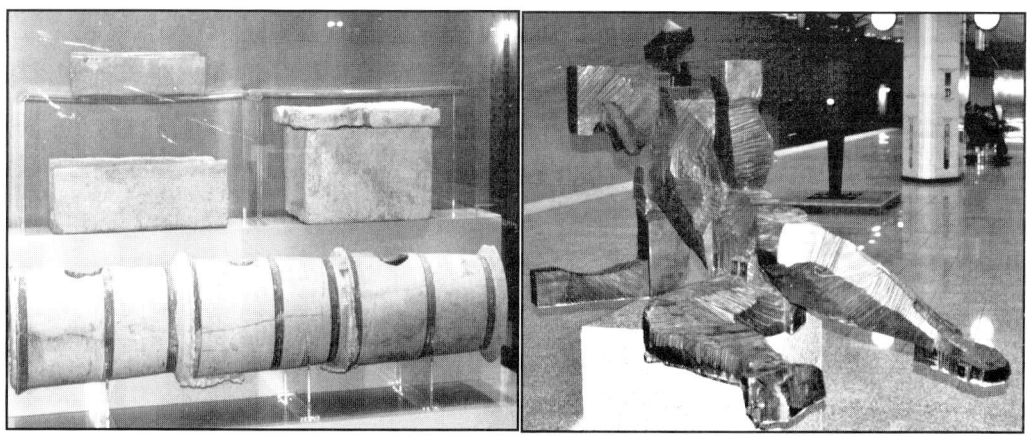

ATHENS TIMELINE

40000-3000 BC	**Stone Age: earliest period of human settlement**
3000-1500	**Minoan Age:earliest European civilisation centred upon Crete**
1500-1200	**Mycenaean Age: earliest civilisation based on mainland Greece**
1200-750	**Dark Age: civilisation retreated in an age of folk movement**
750-478	**Archaic Age: Greeks colonise the shores of the Mediterranean**
508	First beginnings of democracy in Athens
490	Seaborne invasion of Greece by the Persians; Battle of Marathon
480-79	Invasion of Greece by the Persians under Xerxes
478-339	**Classical Age: Greek states centre of civilised world**
447	Construction of Parthenon begun
432-404	The Great Peloponnesian War - a Greek "world war"
399	Death of Socrates
339-168	**Hellenistic Age: Greek empires of the Macedonian kings**
168-330	**Roman Age: Greece under Roman rule**
146	Athens under Roman rule
86	Sulla sacks Athens
54	Saint Paul visits Athens
267	Heruli plunder Athens
396	Visigoths plunder Athens
330-1204	**Byzantine Age: Greek empire of Constantinople**
435	Emperor Theodosius II closes the pagan temples
529	Emperor Justinian orders the closure of the philosophical schools
c. 590	Slavs plunder Athens
1204-1453	**Frankish Period: Greece under rule of Western Crusaders**
1205	French Crusaders take control of Athens
1260	Duchy of Athens created
1311-1388	The Catalan Company takes control of Athens
1388-1456	The Florentine Acciajuoli rule Athens
1456-1821	**Turkish Period: Greece under the Ottoman Empire**
1645	Explosion of gunpowder on the Acropolis
1687	Venetian admiral Morosini attempts to capture Athens
1821-27	War of Independence
1827-present	**Modern Period: Independent state of Greece**
1830	Kindom of Greece set up
1836	Athens becomes capital of Greece
1843	King Otho forced to grant a constitution
1863	William of Denmark becomes KingGeorge I of Greece
1896	First modern Olympic Games held in Athens
1922-3	Asia Minor Catastrophe; arrival of refugees
1940	War with Italy
1941-44	Axis Invasion and Occupation
1944	Civil strife in Athens
1946-49	Civil War
1967-74	Dictatorship of the Colonels
1973	Massacre at the Polytechnic University
1981	Greece becomes a member state of the European Community

SELECT BIBLIOGRAPHY

ABOUT, Edmund, *Greece and the Greeks of the Present Day*, (Edinburgh, 1855)

ANDREWS, Kevin, *Athens*, (London, 1967)

ANDREWS, Kevin, *Greece in the Dark*, (Amsterdam, 1980)

ARCHER, Laird, *Balkan Journal*, (New York, 1944)

BECK, Charles, *The Olympic Games, 776 BC - 1896*, (London, 1896)

BIDDISS, Michael, "Faster, Higher, Stronger: The Birth of the Modern Olympics," *The Historian, 50* (Spring 1996) pp. 2-7.

BOSANQUET, *Days in Attica*, (London, 1914)

BRITISH MUSEUM, *An Historical Guide to the Sculptures of the Parthenon*, (London, 1969)

BURMAN, Julia, "The Athenian Empress Eudocia," *Post-Herulian Athens, Papers and Monographs of the Finnish Institute at Athens*, (Helsinki, 1994)

BURY, J.B., *History of the Eastern Roman Empire*, (London, 1912).

CAMPBELL, John & SHERRARD, Philip, *Modern Greece*, (London, 1968)

CAPEL, Richard, *Simiomata: A Greek Note Book 1944-45*, (London, n.d.)

CAREY, Jane Perry & CAREY, Andrew Galbraith, *The Web of Modern Greek Politcs*, (London, 1968)

CURTIS, Thomas P., "High Hurdles and White Gloves," *The Atlantic Monthly; 198*, (December 1956)

DAVIS-KIMBALL, Jeannine, "Warrior Woman of the Eurasian Steppes," *Archaeology, 50*, 1, (Jan/Feb 1997)

DODWELL, Edward, *Classical and Topographical Tour Through Greece*, 2v, (London, 1819)

EDWRDS, Anne, *Maria Callas: an Intimate Biography*, (New York, 2001)

ELDER, Anne, "A Pasion to Collect: a Treasure to Preserve", *Athenian* (Jan. 1994)

FERGUSON, W. S., *Hellenistic Athens*, (London, 1911)

FINLAY, George, *A History of Greece*, 7v (Oxford, 1877)

FRASER, Sir James George, *The Golden Bough*, abridged ed. (London, 1922)

FREELY, John, *Strolling Through Athens*, (London, 1991)

GALT, John, *Voyages and Travels in the Years 1809, 1810 and 1811* (London, 1812)

GEORGIOU, Lolita, *Asty, The City of Athens...*, Tr. Judy Ayer-Giannakopoulou, (Athens, 1993).

HENDERSON, Mary, *Xenia – A Memoir: Greece 1919-49*, (London, 1988)

HICHENS, Robert, "Skirting the Balkan Peninsula, Part 2: In and Near Athens" *Century Illustrated MonthlyMagazine, LXXXVI*, 1, (May 1913)

HICHENS, Robert, "Skirting the Balkan Peninsula, Part Three: The Environs of Athens" *Century Illustrated Monthly Magazine, LXXXVII* 1, (June 1913)

HIGNETT, C., *History of the Athenian Constitution*, (London, 1969)

HOBHOUSE, John Cam, *A Journey through Albania...*, (London, 1813)

HOUSE, Michael, "The Plunder of the Past," *Athenian*, (July 1989)

HOWARTH, David, *The Greek Adventure*, (London, 1976)

JAY, W. (ed.) *The Anglican Church of Saint Paul's Athens: A Short History*, rev. ed., (Athens, 1998)

KAROUZOU, Semni, *National Museum, Illustrated Guide to the National Museum*, (Athens, 1999)

KNIGGE; Ursula, *The Athenian Kerameikos*, (Athens, 1991)

KUTLER, Stanley, *Abuse of Power: The New Nixon Tapes*, (New York, 1998)

NEILS, Jennifer, *Goddess and Polis*, (Princeton, 1992)

LAWSON, John Cuthbert, *Modern Greek Folklore and Ancient Greek Religion*, (Cambridge, 1910)

LEAKE, William M., *The Topography of Athens...*, 2nd ed., 2v, (London, 1841)

MARCHAND, Leslie, *Byron, A Portrait*, (London, 1971)

MAZOWER, Mark, *Inside Hitler's Greece: The Experience of Occupation 1941-44*, (London, 1993)

MELAS, Evi, *Temples and Sanctuaries of Ancient Greece: A Companion Guide*, (London, 1973)

MICHELI, Liza, *Monastiraki, Athens' Old Market*, Tr. Kevin Andrews, (Athens, 1985)

MICHELI, Liza, *Unknown Athens*, (Athens, 1990)

MILLER, William, *The Latins in the Levant*, (London, 1900)

MILLER, William, *The Ottoman Empire and Its Successors 1801-1927*, (Cambridge, 1927)

MURTAGH, Peter, *The Rape of Greece*, (London, 1994)

NEILS, Jennifer, *Goddess and Polis*, (Princeton, NJ, 1992)

PETERS, Ann, "A Very Grand Hotel," *Athenian*, (May 1991)

PETSALIS-DIOMIDIS, Ncholas, *The Unknown Callas: the Greek Years*, (London, 2001)

PHOKION, Demetriades, *Shadow Over Athens*, (New York, 1946)

POOLE, Lynn and Gray, *One Passion, Two Loves*, (London, 1966)

PSICHARI, J.N., *The Language Question in Greece*, (Calcutta, 1902)

RAPHAEL, Frederick, *Byron*, (London, 1982)

RODD, James Rennell, *The Customs and Lore of Modern Greece*, (London, 1892)

ST. CLAIR, William, *Lord Elgin and His Marbles,* (London, 1967)

ST. CLAIR, William, *That Greece Might Still Be Free...,* (Oxford, 1972)

SETTON, Kenneth M., *Athens in the Middle Ages*, (London, 1975)

SETTON, Kenneth M., "On the Raids of the Moslems in the Aegean in the ninth and tenth centuries and their alleged occupation of Athens," *American Journal of Archaeology, 58*:4, (Oct. 1954)

STAVROPOULOU, Joanna, "Inside the Presidential Palace," *Athenian* (May 1996)

STAVROPOULOU, Joanna, "Psyrri: Tales of Old Athens," *Athenian* (June 1995)

STONEMAN, Richard, *Land of Lost Gods,* (London, 1987)

The City of Athens and the Grande Bretagne: One Hundred and Fifty Years Duet in History, 6th ed. (Athens, 1997)

THURSBY, J.M., "Four Days of Christmas: Churchill in Athens, December 1944" *Athenian*, (Dec. 1994)

TOBIN, Jennifer, *Herodes Atticus and the City of Athens*, (Amsterdam, 1997)

TRAILL, David A., *Schliemann of Troy: Treasure and Deceit*. (New York, 1995)

TUCKERMAN, Charles K., *The Greeks of Today*, New York, 1872

VAN DER KISTE, John, *Kings of the Hellenes: the Greek Kings 1863-1974*, (Stroud, 1994)

VRANOPOULOS, Epaminondas, *The Parthenon and the Elgin Marbles*, (Athens, 1985)

WHELER, George, *Journey Into Greece*, (London, 1672)

WOODFORD, Susan, *The Parthenon*, (Cambridge, 1981)

WOODHOUSE, C.M., *Modern Greece: a Short History*, 5th ed. (London, 1998)

WODEHOUSE, C.M., *The Philhellenes*, (London, 1969)

WORDSWORTH, Christopher, *Athens and Attica: Notes of a Tour*, (London, 1836)

WYSE, Thomas, *Impressions of Greece*, (London, 1871)

HERODOTUS, *Histories*, Tr. Aubrey de Selincourt, Rev. John Marincola, (London, 1997)

PAUSANIAS, *Attica*, in *Guide to Greece*, Tr. Peter Levi, (London, 1971).

PLUTARCH, *Lives*, in *The Rise and Fall of Athens*, Tr. Ian Scott-Kilvert, (London, 1960)

PSEUDO-APOLLODORUS, *The Library*, Tr. J.G.Fraser, (London, 1921)

THUCYDIDES, *The Peloponnesian War*, Tr. R. Warner, (London, 1954)

ΑΝΤΩΝΑΚΟΣ, Σ. Π., Αλή Χασεκής, ο Τύραννος των Αθηνών, *Ιστορία* (Φεβ. 1986)

ΓΙΑΝΝΟΠΟΥΛΑΚΗΣ, Π., *Μυστική Αθήνα*, (Αθήνα, 1999).

ΘΕΟΔΟΣΙΑΔΗΣ, Ν., Ταξίδι Στην Κρύφη Αττική, Γιαννοπουλάκης, Π., *Μυστική Ελλάδα*, (Θεσσαλονίκη, 1999)

ΗΛΙΟΠΟΥΛΟΣ, Διον. Β., Εν Αθήναις, Κάποτε… (Αθήνα, 2000)

Κ. Ψ. Η "Κόρη των Αθηνών" και Λόρδος Βύρων, *Ιστορία* (Δεκ. 1987)

ΚΑΛΛΙΤΣΑΣ, Θ., Οι Πρώτοι πανελλήνοι αθλητικοί αγώνες, *Ιστορία* (Μαϊ. 1988)

ΚΑΜΠΟΥΡΟΓΛΟΥ, Δ. Γρ., *Αι Παλαίαι Αθήναι*, (Αθήνα, 1922)

KERENYΪ, Κ., *Η Μυθολογία των Ελλήνών*, 6 εκ (Αθήνα , 1998)

ΚΩΝΣΤΑΝΤΑΡΑ, Βύρωνος, Μοίρες καί Νεράϊδες, καί οι Παλλαιοί Αθηναίοι, *Ελληνική Δημιουργία, 52*, (1950) 537-540.

ΚΟΡΟΜΥΛΑΣ, Γ. και ΚΟΡΟΜΥΛΑΣ, Λ., *Η Αθηναίκη Περίπέτεια*, (Αθήνα, 1981).

ΛΑΖΟΣ, Χρηστός Δ., Αμαζόνες: θρύλος και Ιστορία, *Ιστορία* (Φεβ. 1990)

ΛΕΟΥΣΗ, Αντ. Χρ., Ριφίφι του 1867, *Τα Αθηναϊκα*, (Αθήνα, 1997)

ΜΑΡΚΕΤΟΣ, Σπυρος, Τα Νοεμβριανά, *Ιστορικά* (Νοε., 2000)

ΜΑΤΖΑΡ, Ε., Αρμενικό Ζήτημα και Τουρκία, *Ιστορία* (Απρ. 2000)

ΟΙΚΟΝΟΜΙΔΗ, Φοιβου, Οι 33 ματωμένες μέρες, *Ιστορικά* (Δεκ., 1999)

ΠΑΝΟΥ, Ευας, Αθηναίοι Αγίοι πού μαρτύρησαν μακρυά από τήν Αθήνα, *Τα Αθηναϊκα*, (Αθήνα, 1984)

ΠΟΛΙΤΗΣ, Νικόλαος, *Παραδόσεις*, 2τ, (Αθήνα, 1994)

ΣΙΣΙΛΙΑΝΟΥ, Δημητριου, *Παλαίαι και Νέαι Αθήναι*, (Αθήνα , 1955).

ΣΤΟΦΟΡΟΠΟΥΛΟΥ, Θ., Η Τουρκική πρακτική και το διεθνές δίκαιο, *Ιστορία* (Απρ. 2000)

ΤΖΙΚΛΙΔΗΣ, Μ. Γ., *Αττική, Η Μαγική Γη*, τ.1 (Αθήνα, 1998).

ΤΣΕΛΕΜΠΙ, Εβλιά, *Ταξίδι στην Ελλάδα*, Μετ. Ν. Χειλαδάκης, (Αθήνα, 1991)

ΨΑΡΟΜΗΛΙΓΚΟΥ, Αρτεμη, Ενας Ελληνικός πεσσός στη διεθνή σκακιέρα, *Ιστορικά* (Δεκ., 1999)

ANAGNOSIS

www.anagnosis.gr

Greece beyond the Guidebooks

Also in this series:

2. Athens: The Suburbs

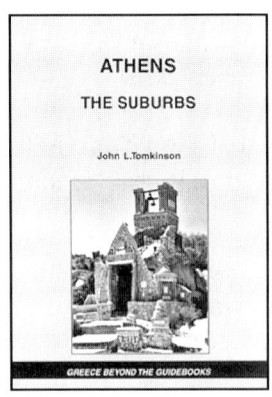

ISBN 960-87186-1-9

24 X 17 cm

160 pages

224 illustrations (b&w)

- A Monastery Born of a Romance • The "Bastille" of Greece
- Self-Castration and the Bloody Rites of the Great Goddess
- An Unspoken "No!" which Altered the Course of a World War
- The Iron Bedstead of Death • When Greeks were Hunted for Sport
- A Girl who Went to Join the Neraides • A School for a Prince
- The Oldest Family Name in the World • A City Built Over a Lake
- The Royal Air Force Besieged • The "Beast" of Kifissia
- The First Ever "Marathon Man" • A Vision over Mount Hymettos
- When the Allies Helped Cause a Famine • A Quarrelsome Saint
- When Politicians were Really Held Accountable for their Actions
- The Billionaire who Created a Philosophers' Paradise
- A Cannibal Island off the Coast of Attica ... and much, much more.

3. Attica

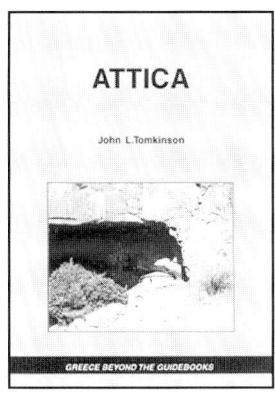

ISBN 960-87186-2-7

24 X 17 cm

160 pages

137 illustrations (b&w)

• The SS and a Hill of Horrors in Pallene • Nymph-Descended Families
• A Fatal Monkey-Bite that Led to Disaster • The Devil's Cave
• A Wagnerian Death • Rough Justice Peasant-Style • Jesus Christ in Attica?
• The Best Kept Secret of the Ancient World • A Fatal Hair Shampoo
• Strangled Monks • A Tailor, His Wife and Two Lightouses • A Dream Oracle
• A Road which Seems to Defy Gravity • The Virgin's Pulley
• A Close Encounter of the Third Kind that Predates the UFO Mania
• A Graveyard Wager that Went Wrong • A Haunted Mansion
• The Vanished Villagers • A Secret Concentration Camp in the "Free" West
• The Dark Foundations of Athenian Greatness • The Laws of the Brigands
... and much, much more.

In Preparation...

4. The Saronic Gulf
The area covered will include the islands of **Salamis
(Salamina), Aigina, Angistri, Hydra, Poros and Spetses,**
together with the area of Attica on the coast of the Saronic Gulf in the
Peloponnese, including **Troizen (Damala)** and **Methana.**

5. The Isthmus
The area covered will include **Korinthia** and the **Megarid:
Corinth, Acrocorinth, Loutraki, Nemea, Stymphalos,
Sikyon, Phlious, Dervenakia, Sofikon, Megara,** etc.

6. The Northern Cyclades
The area covered will include
Mykonos, Delos, Tinos and **Andros.**

ORDER FORM
(for convenience of photocopying)

Number of copies ordered at €15 each

    ATHENS: THE CITY ....copy(ies)
    ATHENS: THE SUBURBS ....copy(ies)
    ATTICA ....copy(ies)

Postage:
For regular mail, please add for postage and packing:

	One book	Two books	Three books
Greece and Cyprus	€1.50	€2.00	€2.50
Rest of the world	€2.00	€2.50	€3.00

For registered mail, add a further €2 to the appropriate postage for regular mail.

Payment enclosed: Books   ....
                              Postage ....
                              Total   ....

Please make bank and postal cheques payable to **Anagnosis.**
Orders will be dispatched promptly upon clearance of cheques

Parcel to be sent to: Name ....
                         Number and Street..
                         City/Town ....
                         State...
                         Postal (Zip) Code ....
                         Country ....

Please send your order to: Anagnosis
                                Harilaou Trikoupi 130
                                145 63 Kifissia
                                Athens, Greece

Please add your email address if you would like to be placed on our emailing list to receive notification of the publication of further books in this series, together with similar publications by *Anagnosis* on Greek culture.

....

(Our list is strictly confidential. Brief text messages are sent out once only on the publication of new books. Customers' names will be removed immediately upon request.)

For up-to-date details of all our publications and prices, visit our website at:

www.anagnosis.gr

Enquiries (including trade enquiries) are welcome at **info@anagnosis.gr**